THE FAR WEST AND THE ROCKIES
HISTORICAL SERIES
1820-1875

VOLUME IX

MAJOR JOHN SEDGWICK
From a portrait made about the time of the Mexican War.
Courtesy of The State Historical Society of Colorado, from
The Correspondence of John Sedgwick, Major General, (1902).

Relations with the Indians of the Plains, 1857-1861

A Documentary Account of the Military Campaigns, and Negotiations of Indian Agents—with Reports and Journals of P. G. Lowe, R. M. Peck, J. E. B. Stuart S. D. Sturgis, and Other Official Papers

Edited, with Introductions and Notes by

LeRoy R. Hafen

Professor of History, Brigham Young University

and

Ann W. Hafen

THE ARTHUR H. CLARK COMPANY

Glendale, California, U.S.A.

1959

To our friend

MAURICE FRINK

Executive Director of the
State Historical Society of Colorado

Contents

Illustrations

Preface

The conquest and occupancy of the high plains east of the central Rockies were not accomplished without a struggle between the red claimants and the white intruders. The climax of this contest occurred in the Indian wars of the middle 1860s. For the Sand Creek Massacre and other soldiers' campaigns, the Indians retaliated with the burning of Julesburg, attacks on the Platte River routes, and Platte Bridge fight of 1865.

These significant conflicts are well known to students of Western history; not so the preliminary clashes. The United States military campaigns of 1857, 1858, and 1860 against the Indians of the central plains have received meager attention. The present volume is intended to correct this deficiency. It presents accounts of these expeditions and of the peace negotiations and the treaty. Many of these reports come from official documents in the War and the Indian departments of the National Archives; some are from diaries and other personal accounts preserved in private and institutional libraries. All are duly acknowledged as they appear in the volume. The great help of the cooperating persons and institutions is sincerely appreciated by the editors.

I
The Campaign against the Cheyennes
1857

The Campaigns against the Cheyennes
1857

INTRODUCTION

The first collision between the Cheyenne Indians and United States troops occurred in 1856. The initial incident, a minor, unfortunate affair, took place on the North Platte in April. Some Cheyennes had come in to trade at Upper Platte Bridge (near the site of present Casper, Wyoming), where United States troops were stationed. It having been reported that the Indians had four stray horses, the commander of the troops ordered that these animals be given up, but he gave assurance that the Indians would be paid for finding and herding the strays.

Though the Indians agreed to the terms, they brought in only three horses. Little Wolf, owner of the fourth, refused to give it up, insisting that this horse had not been found at the time and place described by the claimant. The commanding officer ordered the arrest of three of the Indians. While they were being put in irons, two made a break for freedom; one of these was shot down, the other escaped. The third, Wolf Fire, was held a prisoner, and ultimately was to die in the guardhouse. Following the arrest and break, Wolf Fire's relatives fled toward the Black Hills, leaving their lodges behind. The troops confiscated the abandoned Indian property.

The next night these fleeing Cheyennes came upon an old trapper, Ganier, and killed him in retaliation for the loss of the Indian brave. The rest of the Cheyennes fled southward and joined the Southern Cheyennes on the Arkansas River.[1]

Near the end of August a war party of Cheyennes, moving against the Pawnees, camped on Grand Island in the Platte River a few miles below Fort Kearny. While resting they saw a mail coach coming up the road near the river. A young half-breed among the Cheyennes was urged to go over and meet the mail and ask the driver for some tobacco. With a companion he complied, signaling the coach to stop. But the driver, frightened at the approach of the two Indians, whipped up his horses and fired his pistol at the Cheyennes. The Indians then shot arrows at the driver, wounding him in the arm.

The main Cheyenne party, hearing the shot, mounted their horses and hurried out to see what had happened. Learning that the young men had shot at the driver, the Indian leaders rode after the two young men and quirted them severely for what they had done. The day being rainy, the Indians remained encamped. Next morning troops from Fort Kearny charged the Indian camp. The Indians, upon seeing the hostile intent, fled on foot, leaving behind their bows, arrows and horses. Several Indians were killed.[2]

---

[1] Account by Indian Agent Thomas S. Twiss, in his official report September 12, 1856, printed in *Annual Report of the Commissioner of Indian Affairs, 1856* (Washington, 1857), 87. George B. Grinnell's account in his *The Fighting Cheyennes* (New York, Charles Scribner's Sons, 1915), 107-108, agrees with that of Twiss.

[2] Grinnell says six, taking his information from William Rowland, who was in the Cheyenne camp. Capt. G. H. Stewart, commander of the troops, reported ten Indians killed and about ten others wounded; while the soldiers sustained no losses. Grinnell, *op. cit.*, p. 109; and Secretary of War's report in *House Ex. Doc. 2, 35* Cong., 1 sess., p. 53.

The fleeing Indians, coming upon a small wagon train, killed two men and a child, and took a woman captive. A few days later some of the Cheyennes attacked another party, killing a woman and taking a child captive. Another war party went to the emigrant road near O'Fallon's Bluffs, attacked and killed Almon Babbitt (Delegate to Congress from Utah Territory) and two companions. The next night the Indians attacked another party, killed two men, one woman, and a child, and took a woman captive.[3]

During the summer other Cheyenne war parties, searching in vain for Pawnees, went to Fort Kearny. The commanding officer told them nothing about the killing of the six Cheyennes, but said there had been fighting to the west. He brought out two arrows; the Cheyennes identified them as Sioux arrows, and pointed to one Sioux brave among their party. Seeing some soldiers riding up to the post, most of the Cheyennes went outside and mounted their horses. The soldiers arrested the Sioux, and the three Cheyennes with him ran away. The Sioux picked up the ball and chain and ran. Helped onto a horse, he escaped. Shots were fired at the fleeing Indians, but all escaped. The soldiers saddled up and pursued the Indians, came upon their camp and captured thirteen horses. Later a Cheyenne party recaptured these horses from the Fort Kearny herd.[4]

In response to the call of William Bent, the Southern Cheyennes came in to Bent's Fort on the Arkansas in the fall of 1856 and received their regular annuities. The Northern Cheyennes came in to Agent Twiss and

---

[3] These are the results of the Cheyenne raids as these Indians reported them to their Agent Twiss. – Twiss's Report of Sept. 25, 1856, in *Annual Report of the Commissioner of Indian Affairs, 1856,* pp. 99-100.

[4] Grinnell, *op. cit.,* pp. 110-11.

expressed regret to him for what had happened, but said "they could not control the war party when they saw their friends killed by the soldiers after they had thrown down their bows and arrows and begged for life."[5] Twiss got the Northern Cheyennes to pledge themselves to cease further depredations, and on October 13th he reported: "The Cheyennes are perfectly quiet and peaceable and entirely within my control and obedient to my authority."[6]

Most of the Cheyennes, both Northern and Southern bands, gathered on the upper waters of the Solomon, in western Kansas. During the winter they discussed their experiences of the preceding summer, and their grievances grew with the telling. The Cheyennes became convinced that their injuries justified further war. Two medicine men worked up the fervor, assuring the warriors that with the power of their medicine the balls from white man guns would fall powerless, and the Indians would win an easy victory.

With spring grass and improved horseflesh, the enthusiasm for battle mounted. Necessary ceremonies were performed, and other preparations made for war. Tim Goodale, well-known Mountain Man and trader, who spent the winter of 1856-57 on Green River, came down to Missouri in the early spring. On the way he met at Ash Hollow the Sioux Chief Long Chin, who told him of Cheyenne efforts to get the Sioux to join them against the whites; but the Sioux declined.[7]

---

[5] Twiss's report of Sept. 25th, *op. cit.*, p. 100.

[6] *Ibid.*, p. 101.

[7] Goodale is reported (in the *Kansas City Enterprise,* May 2, 1857, and copied in the *Kansas Chief,* June 11, 1857) as saying:

"Long Chin told him that the Cheyennes had sent word to the Sioux that if they would meet them at the forks of the Platte, and take their old men,

Reports of the Cheyenne raids upon travelers on the great emigrant road along the Platte, convinced the military leaders and the government that stern punishment must be given the attackers. Accordingly, a campaign against the Cheyennes was launched in the spring of 1857. Colonel Edwin V. Sumner set out from Fort Leavenworth on May 20th. Accounts of the campaign are given in the documents that follow.

A brief outline only need be given here. Sumner divided his command, sending Major John Sedgwick with four companies of cavalry up the Arkansas River, while he led the rest of the troops up the Platte. They found no Indians and joined forces on the South Platte, July 4th. Now leaving behind the wagon train and cutting supplies to what could be carried on pack animals, Sumner and Sedgwick pushed into the Indian country between the Platte and Arkansas rivers. On July 29th they contacted the Cheyennes drawn up for

women, and children to the lodges of the Sioux, north of the Platte, they would give them sixty or seventy horses and mules, and then the young men of the Sioux to join them in their excursions against the emigrant trains on the plains.

"But Long Chin said he had been down among the whites, on their big boats, and seen so many men, that he knew it was no use to fight, and that the Sioux would have nothing to do with the matter.

"On his way in, Mr. Goodell saw a few lodges of Cheyennes. They told him that they had killed more Indians than the whites had killed of them, and if the government wanted to make peace they were willing; but if more fight was wanted, they were ready. He also learned at Ash Hollow, through a Cheyenne squaw, the wife of a white man named Sailor Jack, that she had just returned from a visit to the village – that the Cheyennes were mostly collected on the Republican Fork of the Kansas, and that they were expecting a visit from the United States troops the coming summer. They did not expect or intend to fight the troops a great deal, but were going to put the women and children out of the way, and then scatter in small bands from the Platte to the Arkansas, and they say that they can, in this way, 'kill all they want, and get plenty of white women for prisoners.' This is their exact language."

battle. A surprise cavalry charge with drawn bayonets demoralized the Indians and put them to flight. In the running battle that ensued, most of the Indians escaped. Sumner followed, found their hastily deserted village, and burned the abandoned tepees and accoutrements.

Let us now follow the documentary accounts of the Sumner campaign against the Cheyennes in 1857.

A: OFFICIAL REPORTS

1. COLONEL SUMNER'S GENERAL REPORT OF HIS CAMPAIGN AGAINST THE CHEYENNES, 1857 [1]

HEADQUARTERS FIRST CAVALRY,
Fort Leavenworth, K.T., September 20, 1857

SIR: I have the honor to submit a report of my operations during the past summer, or rather a brief recapitulation of the reports already forwarded. I detached Major Sedgwick,[2] with four companies of cavalry, from this post on the 18th of May, to move by the Arkansas River, and to meet me on the south fork of the Platte on the 4th of July. I marched, with two companies of cavalry, on the 20th of May for Fort Kearney, where, in compliance with orders, I took up two companies of the 2d dragoons stationed at that post, and moved on towards Fort Laramie. When about eighty miles from the latter post, I received an order

---

1 "Report of the Secretary of War," in *House Ex. Doc. 2*, 35 Cong., 1 sess., vol. II (ser. 943), pp. 98-99. Also found at the National Archives in A.G.O., Letters Received, 1857, S. 589.

Edwin Vose Sumner was born in Boston, Massachusetts, on Jan. 30, 1797. Commissioned in 1819 a second lieutenant in the 2nd Infantry, he served in that regiment until appointed, on March 14, 1833, a captain in the newly organized 1st Dragoons (later, 1st Cavalry). He served in the Mexican War and won General Scott's approbation. He became colonel of the 1st Cavalry in 1855. After his campaign of 1857 he became commander of the Department of the West, with headquarters in St. Louis. In the Civil War he won the rank of major general of volunteers. He died March 21, 1863. Two of his sons became generals in the regular army.– F. B. Heitman, *Historical Register and Dictionary of the United States Army,* etc. (Washington, Government Printing Office, 1903), I, p. 936; and *Dictionary of American Biography* (New York, 1936), XVIII, pp. 214-15.

2 See the sketch of his career below, in I, c, fn. 2.

to leave the two companies of dragoons at Fort Kearney for General Harney's expedition to Utah.[3] As they were then so near Fort Laramie, insteading of sending them back to Fort Kearney, to march over the same ground three times, I took them to Fort Laramie, and left them there; which, I trust, was approved by the general commanding the army. On the 27th of June I moved south from Fort Laramie with two companies of cavalry and three companies of the sixth infantry.

On the 4th of July I reached the south fork of the Platte, and should have formed a junction with Major Sedgwick on that day, but the river was entirely impassable. On the next day I attempted to establish a ferry with the metallic wagon beds, but found them entirely useless, and was obliged to abandon it. The two commands then moved down the river until I found a ford, and I then brought Major Sedgwick's command over to my camp.

It was my intention to establish a larger camp somewhere in that vicinity, and form two columns for the pursuit of the Indians; but hearing they would be in force, and would resist, I determined to abandon my wagons, train, tents, and all other incumbrances, and proceed with my whole command in pursuit of the Indians. The train was sent back to Fort Laramie, with orders to meet me at the lower crossing of the south fork of the Platte in twenty days; but in pursuing the Indians, I was drawn across the country to the Arkansas River, and we had nothing but fresh beef to subsist upon for some time. I found the trail of the Indians on the 24th of July, and on the 29th came upon them, as

---

[3] For an account of the Utah Expedition see *Far West and the Rockies Series,* VIII.

already reported; which report narrates the battle, the destruction of the town, and the pursuit through to the Arkansas.[4] On arriving there, I found the agent for the Cheyennes had taken to Bent's Fort the annual presents for that tribe, including arms and ammunition. I knew the government could never intend to send an expedition against a tribe of Indians, and at the same time give them arms and ammunition. I therefore determined to proceed at once to Bent's Fort to prevent the Indians from getting this property, especially as they had threatened that it would not be taken out of the country.

I had also a hope of finding the Indians collected again in that vicinity. I trust my reports in relation to this matter were satisfactory to the commanding general, and that he endorsed them to that effect, for without his approval the measures that I felt bound to take may involve me in difficulty with the Department of the Interior. On my arrival at Walnut Creek, I received the order to break up the expedition, and to detach four companies of cavalry and three of infantry for the expedition to Utah. I immediately put the detachment in as good order as possible, by stripping the two companies which were to return to this post, and directed Major Sedgwick to proceed across the country to Fort Kearney, on his route to Utah. We had then marched sixteen hundred miles, and, although this order was entirely unexpected, and the men and horses were much worn down, not a man deserted, when they could easily have made their escape by taking the best of the horses. The conduct of my command throughout the summer has been all I could wish; the officers and

---

[4] Report of Aug. 9th, printed below as doc. 4.

men have not only shown bravery in action, but they have shown the higher quality of a manly and cheerful endurance of privations.

Six days after I detached Major Sedgwick, as I was returning to this post with the two remaining companies, I was very happy to receive the countermand of the order for Utah. I arrived at this post on the 16th instant, after marching over eighteen hundred and fifty miles.

I am, sir, very respectfully, your obedient servant,

E. V. SUMNER,
Colonel 1st Cavalry, Commanding
Cheyenne Expedition [5]

ASSISTANT ADJUTANT GENERAL,
Headquarters of the Army, New York City.

----

2. COMMUNICATION EN ROUTE [6]

HDQTRS 1ST CAVALRY   CAMP ON "LITTLE BLUE"
80 miles from Fort Kearny   May 31st, 1857
SIR: I wish to inform the General-in-chief, that the emigration to California this year, by this route,[7] is much larger than anyone anticipated. They are driving across an immense number of cattle, and I feel obliged to time my movements in some measure, so as to cover

----

[5] Alfred Cumming, Superintendent of Indian Affairs, Central Superintendency, St. Louis, and presently to become Governor of Utah, wrote from St. Louis his report of Aug. 20, 1857:

"The growing spirit of insubordination is everywhere manifested among the wild tribes of the prairies. To subdue and control this spirit a cordial co-operation among the various civil and military agents of the government is indispensable, and this can only be effected by restoring to the War Department the control of the Indian service." *Annual Report of the Commissioner of Indian Affairs, 1857*, p. 118.

[6] Found in the National Archives, Washington, D.C., A.G.O., Letters Received, 1857, Book 33, 399 S, and S 85.

[7] The route of the Oregon-California Trail, up the Platte River.

the road up the Platte, until the most of these Emigrants have passed.

The revival of this route of travel to California, which will no doubt increase on the completion of the road, (for which the appropriations have been made) [8] would seem to make the continuance of Forts Kearny and Laramie highly important. It is not too much to say, that if these posts are withdrawn, this whole road – from the "Big Blue" to the Rocky mountains – will be thrown open to Indian depredations.

Very Respectfully, Yr. Obt. Svt.

E. V. SUMNER

ASST. ADJT. GEN'L   Col 1 Cavly Comdg.

Hd Qtrs Army.

---

3. REPORT FROM THE NORTH PLATTE [9]

HDQRS

Camp near Fort Laramie   June 26, 57

SIR: I have the honor to report that I shall march tomorrow morning for the Cheyenne country, with two companies of cavalry, and three of infantry, and I expect to meet my other column, under Major Sedgwick, on the south fork of the Platte, on the 4th of July — I leave the squadron of the 2d dragoons at this Post to await the orders of Gen. Harney — I intend to establish a large camp in the heart of the Cheyenne country, and have two columns, without baggage, constantly in motion after the Indians — I hope to accomplish the object of the expedition, but the country is

---

[8] The Wagon Road appropriation voted by Congress was being expended under the direction of W. M. F. Magraw and F. W. Lander. See W. Turrentine Jackson, *Wagon Roads West* (Berkeley and Los Angeles, Univ. of Calif. Press, 1952), 190-217.

[9] A.G.O., Letters Received, *op. cit.*, 466 S, S 102.

very extensive, and some of it very difficult of access, owing to the want of water and grass.

Very respectfully, Your obt. Servt.

E. V. SUMNER

To THE ACT G   Col. 1 Cavly Comdg.

Head Qrs Army

---

4. COLONEL SUMNER REPORTS THE BATTLE OF JULY 29 [10]

HEADQUARTERS CHEYENNE EXPEDITION
Arkansas River, near the site of Fort Atkinson [11]
August 9, 1857

SIR: I have the honor to report that, on the 29th ultimo, while pursuing the Cheyennes down Solomon's Fork of the Kansas, we suddenly came upon a large body of them, drawn up in battle array, with their left resting upon the stream and their right covered by a bluff. Their number has been variously estimated from two hundred and fifty to five hundred; I think there were about three hundred. The cavalry were about three miles in advance of the infantry, and the six companies were marching in three columns. I immediately brought them into line, and, without halting, detached the two flank companies at a gallop to turn their flanks, (a movement they were evidently prepar-

---

[10] "Report of the Secretary of War," *op. cit.* (ser. 943), 96-97. Also in A.G.O., Letters Received, 1857, S 514.

[11] Fort Atkinson had been established by Col. E. V. Sumner, Aug. 8, 1850, and was sometimes called Fort Sumner. It was located at a crossing of the Arkansas in Ford County, six or eight miles from present Dodge City. Being built of sod, the soldiers often called it Fort Sod, or Sodom. It was called Camp Mackay (for Col. A. Mackay) until June 25, 1851, when the name was changed to Fort Atkinson. It was abandoned September 22, 1853; was temporarily re-occupied in June, 1854, and abandoned October 2, 1854. See George A. Root (ed.), in the *Kansas Historical Quarterly*, I, p. 199.

ing to make against our right,) and we continued to march steadily upon them. The Indians were all mounted and well armed, many of them had rifles and revolvers, and they stood, with remarkable boldness, until we charged and were nearly upon them, when they broke in all directions, and we pursued them seven miles. Their horses were fresh and very fleet, and it was impossible to overtake many of them. There were but nine men killed in the pursuit, but there must have been a great number wounded. I had two men killed, and Lieutenant J. E. B. Stuart,[12] and eight men wounded; but it is believed they will all recover. All my officers and men behaved admirably. The next day I established a small fort near the battleground, and left my wounded there, in charge of a company of infantry with two pieces of artillery, with orders to proceed to the wagon train, at the lower crossing of the south fork of the Platte, on the 20th instant, if I did not return before that time.

On the 31st ultimo I started again in pursuit, and at fourteen miles I came upon their principal town. The people had all fled; there were one hundred and seventy-one lodges standing, and about as many more that had been hastily taken down, and there was a large amount of Indian property of all kinds of great value to them. I had everything destroyed, and continued the pursuit. I trailed them to within forty miles of this place, when they scattered in all directions. Believing they would reassemble on this river, (for there are no buffalo in their country this summer on which they can subsist,) I have come here hoping to intercept them and to protect this road. I was obliged to send my wagon

---

[12] A sketch of Stuart will be given below, in connection with his Journal.

train back to Laramie from near Fort St. Vrain, and to take pack-mules.

My supplies have been exhausted for some time, except fresh beef, and I have beef only for twenty-four days. I shall send an express to Fort Leavenworth to have supplies pushed out to me as soon as possible, for I do not think these Indians have been sufficiently punished for the barbarous outrages they have recently committed. The battalion of the 6th infantry, under Captain Ketchum, belonging to my command, has had a long and arduous march. It is matter of deep regret to them, as it is to myself, that I could not wait to bring them into the action.[13] As I have no supplies with which I can send these troops back to Laramie, I must take them to Fort Leavenworth; and if they are to return to Laramie this fall, I would respectfully ask for authority to send them up in a light train.

I have the pleasure to report, what I know will give the lieutenant general commanding the army the highest satisfaction, that in these operations not a woman nor a child has been hurt.[14]

I am, sir, very respectfully, your obedient servant.

E. V. SUMNER

Colonel 1st Cavalry, Commanding Expedition

TO ASSISTANT ADJUTANT GENERAL,

Headquarters of the Army, New York, N.Y.

---

[13] The companies of the 6th Infantry had joined Sumner's force at Fort Laramie. Being in the rear of the cavalry they did not participate in the battle on July 29.

Capt. William Scott Ketchum, a native of Connecticut, graduated from the U.S. Military Academy in 1830. He became a captain in the 6th Infantry in 1842. He was to serve in the Civil War and die June 28, 1871 – Heitman, *op. cit.,* I, p. 595.

[14] In contrast to Harney's fight with the Indians on Blue Water, not far from Ash Hollow and near the North Platte, in 1855.

5. REPORT OF THE KILLED AND THE WOUNDED [15]

HEAD QUARTERS CHEYENNE EXPEDITION
Arkansas river (near the site of Ft. Atkinson)
August 9, 1857

SIR I have the honor to inclose herewith a return of the killed and wounded, in an action with the Cheyennes on the 29th of July 1857. A detailed report of the operations against the Cheyennes has been forwarded to the Commanding General.

I Am Sir Very Respectfully Your Obt Servt,

E. V. SUMNER

Col 1 Cavlry Comdg Expedition

ADJUTANT GENERAL, U.S.A.

Washington D.C.

[Enclosure, with above]

RETURN OF KILLED AND WOUNDED IN AN ACTION WITH THE CHEYENNES ON SOLOMONS CREEK JULY 29TH 1857

KILLED

Martin Lynch.— Arrow wound in head & Pistol wound through chest.

George Cade.— Arrow wound entering at one side & passing out at the other.

WOUNDED

J. E. B. Stewart, 1st Lt.— Pistol wound in the chest, from present symptoms thought not dangerous.

George C. McEawen.— Rifle wound through arm and chest (Dangerous).

Henry B. Robinson.— Sabre wound of hand.

Franz Piot.— Arrow wound entirely through Chest (Dangerous).

Francis T. Freer.— Arrow wound deep in hip.

Alexander Wilkey.— Arrow wound in face, slight.

---

[15] A.G.O., Letters Received, 1857, 506 S. A summary is also given in "Report of the Secretary of War," *op. cit.* (ser. 943), 57.

James M. Cooke.— Arrow wound in Abdomen (Dangerous).
Rollin Taylor.— Arrow wound in head. Pvt. Taylor killed
the Indian who wounded him, with his sabre.
Thomas Wilson.— Arrow wound through arm.

E. V. Sumner

A. V. Colburn   Col. 1 Cavlry   Comdg
2d Lt Ast Adjt.

---

6. SUMNER GOES UP TO BENT'S FORT [16]

Headquarters Cheyenne Expedition,
Arkansas River, one march below Fort Atkinson

Aug. 11, 1857

Sir: I have received authentic information from
the mail party today that the agent for the Cheyennes
has gone up to Bent's Fort with the yearly presents for
that tribe, and that he has been informed by them that
they would not come to receive their presents in the
usual way, but that he should never carry the goods out
of the country. Under these circumstances, I consider
the agent and the public property in his charge in
jeopardy. I have therefore decided to proceed at once
to Bent's Fort with the elite of my cavalry, in the hope
that I may find the Cheyennes collected in that vicinity,
and, by another blow, force them to sue for peace; at all
events, this movement will secure this agent and the
public property. Another motive is, that by this march
up the river I shall more effectually cover this road
from Indian depredations this summer.

I have directed Captain Ketchum, with his battalion
and a part of the cavalry, to proceed, by easy marches,
to Walnut Creek,[17] and there await my return.

---

[16] *Ibid.,* pp. 97-98; and A.G.O., Letters Received, 1857, S 515.
[17] Farther east, on the Santa Fe Trail.

I am, sir, very respectfully, your obedient servant,
E. V. SUMNER
Colonel 1st Cavalry, Commanding
ASSISTANT ADJUTANT GENERAL,
Headquarters of the Army, New York City.

---

7. COLONEL SUMNER'S ORDERS TO
INDIAN AGENT MILLER [18]

HEAD QUARTERS CHEYENNE EXPDN
Bents Fort   August 19th   1857

SIR   The object of the Cheyenne Expedition was to demand from that tribe the perpetrators of their late crimes against the whites and ample security for their future good conduct – failing in this, those Indians were to be chastized. As they showed no disposition to yield to the demands upon them, but on the contrary, met the troops in battle array, they have been whipped, and their principal town burnt to the ground. Under these circumstances I know it would not be the wish of the Govt that the *Arms Ammunition* and other goods sent into the country for those Indians should be left here a prey for them to seize, (which they would certainly do) as some indemnity for the chastisement they have received. I therefore feel it to be my duty to direct, that all the goods for the Cheyennes now at this place be disposed of as follows. As you have no means of transportation you will please turn over to Lieut. Wheaton, Act. Asst Comg, all the subsistence stores, to be paid for at cost and charges, or replaced at this point whenever required by your dept. The ammunition will be destroyed. The guns and as many of the goods as the

---

[18] A.G.O., Letters Received, 1857, 550 s. Robert C. Miller had been appointed Indian Agent for the Indians of the Upper Arkansas Agency.

Quartermaster can transport will be taken out of the
country, the residue of the goods, you will please distribute as you may think proper to the friendly Indians
as an advance on their next years annuity – This however, will of course be subject to the approval of your
dept. As I am not authorized to leave troops here for
your personal protection, and as you cannot of course,
remain here without it, you will please accompany the
Command when it leaves the Indian Country.

    I Am Sir   Very Respectfully   Your obt servt
                (Signed)   E. V. SUMNER
       Col. 1st Cavalry   Comdg Cheyenne Expn
            Official   A. V. COLBURN
                2d Lieut.   Ast Ajt
MAJOR ROB. C. MILLER   Agent for the Cheyennes
Walnut Creek   September 3d 1857

8.   AGENT R. C. MILLER'S REPORT [19]

LEAVENWORTH CITY, October 14, 1857

    SIR: I present the following as my annual report
for the year 1857:

    The train containing the annunity goods for the
Comanches, Kiowas, Apaches, Cheyennes, and Arapahoes, which I accompanied, left Westport, Missouri,
June 20, and proceeded without any interruption or
incident, save the usual reports against the Kiowas, as
far as Walnut Creek, where it arrived on the 3d of
July. From there I sent forward a "runner" to notify
the Comanches, Kiowas, and Apaches, of my approach,
and to gather them together, near Fort Atkinson, for
the purpose of receiving their presents.   .   .

    After distributing to the Comanches and Kiowas, I

19 *Annual Report of the Commissioner of Indian Affairs, 1857*, pp. 141-48.

proceeded with the train towards Bent's Fort. On the evening of the 13th I came upon the camp of the Arapahoe Indians upon the Arkansas River, some ten miles above Fort Atkinson. They were driven to seek the buffalo country for want of food, and they were thus far on their way when I met them. They seemed very glad to meet me, stating that their people were in a starving condition, and expressed the hope that I would not compel them to return to Bent's Fort in order to receive their presents, but that I would give them to them there so they might proceed on their way without further interruption; to which I unhesitatingly consented.

They were assembled in much larger numbers than last year, numbering about three hundred lodges; consequently they got a large portion of presents. My interview with the chiefs of this tribe was very agreeable and pleasant. They expressed an earnest desire to maintain peace and friendship with the whites. The distribution was made without the least interruption or complaint on their part, they appearing to be perfectly satisfied.

In council the chiefs spoke of the conduct of their young men at Bent's Fort on the occasion of my previous visit among them, at which time they had demanded their goods immediately, declaring "they would not wait the coming of the Cheyennes," for I had sent over to the "Smoky Hill Fork" of the Kansas River, excusing themselves by saying "they had been waiting many days for their goods, and their women and children had become very faint and hungry," and "their young men would not be controlled," "but now their hearts were very glad, their Great Father had sent them many presents, and they would never be seen making war upon the whites like the Cheyennes, nor murdering and stealing like the Kiowas." Little Raven,[20] the principal chief, expressed a wish for his people to learn to cultivate the soil and become farmers, as he felt the buffalo and other game were rapidly disappearing from the prairie, and in a few years would be entirely gone, when, unless they had some other resource, they must starve. He desired I would ask the Great Chief to send them hereafter farming instruments and white men to teach them their use.

It was my intention, if the state of affairs had permitted me to remain in the country, to have examined the district embraced within my agency, with a view of reporting to the department the points adapted to cultivation and susceptible of producing sufficient to sustain the several tribes, should it hereafter be deemed expedient to colonize them.

From Walnut Creek, along the Arkansas River, to within a short distance of Bent's Fort, there is not a foot of country fit for the plough; but immediately around the fort, and for a distance of one hundred miles above, about the regions of the "Boiling Springs,"[21] the bottoms are extensive, with deep, rich soil, susceptible of the highest degree of cultivation, and the uplands afford the finest grazing.

Arriving at Bent's Fort on the 19th of July, I applied to Captain Bent[22] for permission to store the goods within the fort until I could communicate with Colonel

---

[20] Little Raven was a notable, friendly chief, frequently mentioned in the literature of the period. He signed the Fort Wise Treaty of Feb. 18, 1861, the Little Ark. Treaty of Oct. 14, 1865, and the Medicine Lodge Treaty of Oct. 28, 1867.

[21] Manitou Springs, near present Colorado Springs, Colorado.

[22] William W. Bent, owner of the fort — Bent's New Fort — located on the north bank of the Arkansas, about eight miles west of Lamar, Colorado.

Sumner, commanding the Cheyenne expedition, but he, without hestiation, refused; giving as the reason, that as soon as the Cheyennes learned that the goods were within the fort and would not be distributed until the soldiers came, an attack would be made which would result not only in the loss of the government property, but also of everything he possessed, and the massacre of every one within. I then turned to Mr. Childs, the contractor for the land transportation, and remarked that I would be compelled to detain his wagons until an express could go and return from Colonel Sumner's camp, which was said to be near old Fort St. Vrain,[23] on the South Platte, but he utterly refused to remain. I then replied, I would not receive the goods of him, as I claimed the right to detain the wagons until I was prepared to make the distribution, and went immediately in search of some one to ride the express. After great difficulty, as the country was very dangerous to cross, there being small bands of Indians (very hostile) roving to and fro, I succeeded in inducing a Frenchman by the name of Dubray[24] to undertake the trip, provided he could pursuade two Mexicans to accompany him, in which he was successful. He was to start on the following morning at daybreak. That night, about nine o'clock, Bent, fearful that if the goods remained even in the vicinity of the fort any length of time without being distributed he would suffer thereby, came to me, proposing to abandon the fort and deliver it up to me, for which rent and storage was to be paid;

[23] On the South Platte, about 35 miles north of the site of Denver. For a history of the fort see L. R. Hafen, "Fort. St. Vrain," in the *Colorado Magazine,* XXIX (1952), 241-55.

[24] Antoine, or Chet, Dubray, a French trapper, had spent several years among the Arapahoes and spoke their language. He was in and near Denver in 1858-59. He has descendants at Pine Ridge Reservation today.

I accepted of his proposition, and entered into a written agreement with him, for the terms of which I refer you to the paper accompanying my letter to Colonel Cumming, then superintendent, of the 20th July.[25] He accordingly, having packed up all his goods and transported them to his wagons, left on the morning of the 21st, with his family, cattle, and horses, for the States, leaving behind, however, according to agreement, wagons and teams sufficient to remove the government goods to the States, in case Colonel Sumner should deem it improper that they should fall into the hands of the Cheyennes.

After riding all night and day, the messenger I had despatched to Colonel Sumner returned on the 27th without finding him, or learning anything of his whereabouts. Having no further control over the wagons which Captain Bent had left behind, they left on the following morning for the States, leaving me with but four white men and one negro, I having control only over one man and the negro.

Notwithstanding my weak force, I believed the goods were safer behind stone walls than in the wagons on the road, as it was said to be infested with hostile Indians as far as the crossing of the Arkansas. It was well I did remain at the fort, as I have since learned that the day after the wagons left Fort Atkinson the whole of the Cheyennes, flying from Colonel Sumner after his battle with them, crossed the Arkansas forty miles above. If the wagons had been loaded they would have travelled slower, and would have been just in time to have met the Indians in their full flight, who, smarting from their recent defeat, would have wiped the train entirely out.

---

25 For the subsequent purchase of the fort by the Government, see below.

A few days after the departure of Bent's wagons, learning from two Apaches who came from the Cheyenne village, on the Smokey Hill fork, that a few of the principal chiefs and a number of young men of influence were anxious for peace, and were using their influence to bring it about, and believing that good might be the result of an interview, I procured the services of a Mexican and an Arapahoe Indian, and despatched them to their village to invite all the head men who were so disposed to come to the fort. They had proceeded several days on their way, when they were met by a party of straggling Cheyennes, who informed them that a great battle had been fought, in which six of their principal chiefs had been killed, and their village of near two hundred lodges had been destroyed – burnt to the ground. They said though their people had been defeated by the loss of many horses and their entire village, they were not subdued, "but had only gone over to Crooked Creek for the purpose of joining the Kiowas, who had promised to unite with them against the whites, and that so soon as they could recruit, they were coming to the fort to help themselves to the goods, and take the scalp of the agent and every one with him."

The report was repeated to me by every Indian who came to the fort. Various reports came to my ears of the treatment of the prisoners they had taken during the summer, the details of which are too disgusting and horrible for repetition here. Suffice it to say, that they were the most terrible that can be possible for even Indian iniquity in inventing modes of cruelty to conceive.

On the 5th of August, I despatched an express man to the crossing of the Arkansas, to meet the mail, with some official papers, who, after being absent a sufficient length of time, returned with a story trumped up, as it turned out afterwards, that he had arrived at the proper point on the morning of the 9th, and remained there until the evening of the 12th, without meeting the mail, which should have passed on the 10th. He said that on his arrival at the spot he noticed the fresh tracks of seven animals, five mules and two horses, which indicated that they might have been moving in a very rapid manner, as if they were flying from danger; from the fact of the animals being shod, they must have belonged to the mail party, which doubtless had been attacked by Indians, and were able to make their escape with only that small number of animals, leaving their wagons behind to the mercy of the Indians. The state of the country and the hostilities of several tribes of Indians rendered his story very plausible. On the same day of his return to the fort, (the 15th of August), an expressman arrived bearing me a letter from Colonel Sumner, stating that he was marching to my relief and would be with me by the 18th, having learned from a gentleman, by Santa Fe mail, that I was at Bent's Fort, unable to get away. He arrived accordingly on the 18th, and on the 19th addressed me the accompanying communication.[26] Having no alternative but to comply with his directions, I proceeded to turn over to his quartermaster the sugar, rice, coffee, hard bread and flour. The powder and lead and flints were thrown into the Arkansas River. To the few Arapahoes who were present I distributed all the goods, excepting what could be transported in two wagons, which I intended for distribution to the Arapahoes I might meet on the road. Colonel Sumner

---

26 The preceding document, no. 7.

with his command, which I accompanied, took up his line of march for the States on the morning of the 20th. On the third day after leaving the fort, the cattle, being very poor, and only seven yoke in number, gave out completely. The wagons having mired down to the axle-trees, there seemed to be no alternative but to abandon them on the prairie. Fortunately, a village of the Apaches was discovered on the opposite side of the river; I sent for the chiefs and delivered to them all the goods, (excepting the guns, which had been brought to Fort Leavenworth, and where they are now in store,) giving them to understand that these presents were given to them as a reward for their good behavior, and, as they were the goods designed for the Cheyennes, also, we show them that it was the determination of their Great Father to punish that tribe for the violation of the treaty with the government.

Colonel Sumner informed me that while at Bent's Fort, that he had learned from passengers by the inward-bound Santa Fe mail, which he had met at the "crossing," that a party of four or five Kiowa Indians came up with Colonel Johnson's command on the Cemmerone, and for several days followed it in an apparently very friendly manner, but on the first opportunity shot the driver of his private ambulance and cut his mules loose from the harness, with which they fled.[27] The driver had fallen behind the command. I have been subsequently informed that they were Comanches

27 Lt. Col. Joseph E. Johnston, later famous in the Confederate Army, was directing the survey of the southern boundary of Kansas. He had a force of 400 men. The incident referred to here, occurred on July 30, 1857. See Eugene Bandel, *Frontier Life in the Army, 1854-1861,* (ed.) R. P. Bieber *Southwest Historical Series,* II, pp. 41-45; and N. H. Miller (ed.), "Surveying the Southern Boundary Line of Kansas," in *Kansas Historical Quarterly,* I, pp. 104-39.

and not Kiowas, but am not inclined to believe the
Comanches would be guilty of such an outrage.

The Cheyennes, before they went into battle with the
troops, under the direction of their "Great Medicine
Man," had selected a spot on the Smoky Hill, near a
small and beautiful lake, in which they had but to dip
their hands, when the victory over the troops would be
an easy one, so their medicine man told them, and that
they had but to hold up their hands and the balls would
roll from the muzzles of the soldiers' guns harmless to
their feet. Acting under this delusion, when Colonel
Sumner came upon them with his command, he found
them drawn up in regular line of battle, well mounted,
and moving forward to the music of their war song
with as firm a tread as well disciplined troops, expecting no doubt to receive the harmless fire of the soldiers
and achieve an easy victory. But the charm was broken
when the command was given by Colonel Sumner to
charge with sabres, for they broke and fled in the
wildest confusion, being completely routed. They lost,
killed upon the field, nine of their principal men, and
many more must have died from the effects of their
wounds, as the bodies of several were found on the
route of their flight. Their village, which was about
fourteen miles distant, was found to have been deserted
in a most hasty manner, everything having been left
behind, even their winter supply of buffalo meat,
amounting to between fifteen and twenty thousand
pounds. Colonel Sumner ordered everything to be
destroyed either by fire or otherwise.

The loss of their winter supplies, and the destruction
of their lodges, is a blow that they will not soon recover
from; still they are not yet subdued, have not yet been
brought to respect the government, and I trust the government will not be content with the punishment in-

GENERAL EDWIN V. SUMNER
From a photograph made during the Civil War.
Courtesy of The National Archives, Washington.

flicted upon them by Colonel Sumner, but will continue to follow them up until they shall have been brought to subjection, and been taught that they cannot commit their depredations with impunity. This is necessary for the protection of the immense amount of travel passing over the various roads through their country.

Before closing, I would call the attention of the department to the immense number of small Mexican traders that are continually roving over the country, and to whom many of the difficulties with the Indians may be traced. They come into the country ostensably to trade provisions to the Indians, but in reality to introduce among them their miserable Mexican whiskey, using their influence, which is in many instances very great, to keep up the hostile feeling against the whites. There were several of these miscreants about Bent's Fort during my stay there, going in and out whenever they chose, they having been in the employ of Bent for some time. I had no reason to apprehend any harm from them; but I was informed by an Arapahoe Indian, on the day I left, that they were in league with the Cheyennes, and had determined to massacre every one within the fort, but the coming of Colonel Sumner prevented the carrying out of their plans.

I would, therefore, urge that some decisive measures be adopted to rid the country of these people. The agent can do nothing – he is utterly powerless, and only the presence of a strong military force will be able to keep them back.

ROBERT C. MILLER
Indian Agent

JOHN HAVERTY, ESQ.,
Superintendent of Indian Affairs, St. Louis.

9. REPORT OF AGENT T. S. TWISS [28]

INDIAN AGENCY OF THE UPPER PLATTE
September 1, 1857

SIR: In submitting my annual report on the state of Indian affairs within the Upper Platte agency, I would state that all of the tribes, with the exception of the band of the Cheyennes, are peaceable and quiet, and manifest on all occasions a desire to remain at peace with the United States.

With the Cheyenne band I have held no intercourse since last October, except to send messages by Indian runners that I expected the chiefs would fulfil the conditions that I had imposed upon the Cheyennes in the councils held in September and October, and which I am able to state were strictly observed.

I directed the Cheyennes to remain in the southern and southeastern parts of the agency, their usual hunting grounds, and not to mix with the Sioux.

I permitted some few lodges of Cheyennes to winter with the Minneconjoux on the Cheyenne River, and with the Crow tribe on Powder River. The circumstances and the reasons for granting this permission were reported to the department in November last. The Arapahoes, who are usually found hunting on the tributaries of the South Fork of the Platte, were directed to remove to the Parks,[29] or to the western part of their agency, early in April, in order that they might not become involved in the Cheyenne difficulties, and I

[28] *Annual Report of the Commissioner of Indian Affairs, 1857,* pp. 140-41. Thomas S. Twiss was appointed Indian Agent for the Upper Platte Agency in 1855. For his career as an Agent see A. W. Hoopes, "T. S. Twiss, Indian Agent on the Upper Platte, 1855-61," in the *Mississippi Valley Historical Review,* XX, 353-64.

[29] North Park, Middle Park, and South Park, in the mountains of Colorado.

proceeded to the North Platte bridge [30] to see that this order was observed.

I am satisfied that both the Sioux and the Arapahoe bands have not sympathized with the Cheyennes, and that the young warriors and braves have not listened to the appeals to join with the Cheyennes.

I would again take occasion to call the attention of the department to the condition of these wild tribes within this agency. I would again repeat the suggestions contained in former reports, as to the steps that, in my opinion, should be adopted in order to ameliorate the condition and domesticate these tribes.

The expense to the government would be inconsiderable, compared to the advantages that would result to the Indians, by relieving them from this constant necessity of roaming the whole length and breadth of this agency in pursuit of game to supply them with a precarious subsistence, even in the most favorable seasons. If one-half of the toil and labor which are employed in the chase was devoted to agriculture these tribes would have abundance of food, and would entertain better feelings towards the whites.

I would earnestly and urgently press the consideration of this matter upon the attention of the honorable the Commissioner of Indian Affairs, and respectfully solicit that he will be pleased to ask for an appropriation, at the next session of Congress, for the purposes of agricultural and manual labor schools within the Upper Platte agency.

Very respectfully, your obedient servant,

THOMAS S. TWISS
Indian Agent, Upper Platte

COLONEL CUMMING,
Superintendent of Indian Affairs

---

[30] Near present Casper, Wyoming.

10. BREAK-UP OF CHEYENNE EXPEDITION [31]

HEAD QUARTERS ARMY FOR UTAH
Fort Leavenworth, July 28th 1857
COL. E. V. SUMNER
1st Cav. Commanding Cheyenne Expd.

COLONEL.   The following telegraphic communications have been received by General Harney from the Adjutant General, viz. –

(First Telegraph)

ADJUTANT GENERAL'S OFFICE
Washington, July 22nd, 1857

Send the following by Express to Col. E. V. Sumner, First Cavalry, Commanding Cheyenne Expedition; — The Secretary of War directs that you break up the Cheyenne Expedition and out of the Six Companies of the First Cavalry subject to your orders make up four full companies send them with Major Sedgwick and the two companies of the 2nd Dragoons and the three companies of the Sixth Infantry belonging to the Cheyenne Expedition to Fort Laramie, there to receive the orders of General Harney.[32] With the two remaining companies of your regiment you will return to Fort Leavenworth.

By order of the Secretary of War
(Signed)   S. COOPER   Adjutant General.

---

[31] Department of Utah, Letters Sent, 1857-61, vol. 1, pp. 8-9, National Archives.

[32] On pp. 24-28, *ibid.,* are orders to Maj. Sedgwick, directing his activities. Then on p. 33 is the following order:

"HEAD QUARTERS, ARMY FOR UTAH
Fort Leavenworth, September 8, 1857

"MAJOR JOHN SEDGWICK
1st Cav. Comd 4 Companies   En route for Utah, Fort Laramie
SIR: You are instructed by the General Commanding to repair with your Command to this Post.
I am, Sir, very respectfully,   Your Obt. Servt
A PLEASANTON   Captain 2nd Dragoons   A.A.A.G."

11. SUMNER'S REACTION TO BREAK-UP
OF CHEYENNE EXPEDITION [33]

HEAD QUARTERS CHEYENNE EXPEDITION
Walnut Creek, September 3d 1857

SIR I reached this yesterday on my return from Bents Fort, and found the order breaking up the Cheyenne Expedition. I regret extremely after my success against these Indians, to leave this matter unfinished. They are now more hostile than they were before they were punished, and it will require another severe blow to bring them to sue for peace. I inclose my order to the Indian Agent disposing of the Cheyenne goods.

It certainly seems very strange that *Arms* and *Ammunition* should have been sent to these Indians at the same time that I was directed to punish them. I hope the Com. General will approve of my measures with regard to the Cheyenne presents, and if he does, I would respectfully ask him to put an indorsement to that effect upon my order to the Indian Agent.

I Am Sir Very Respectfully

E. V. SUMNER
Col 1 Cavalry Commanding
Cheyenne Expedition

ASST ADJT GENERAL
Head Quarters Army New York City, N.Y.

[On back of Document:] INDIAN AFFAIRS. Colonel Sumner orders seem to have been judiciously adapted to the existing circumstances of the moment. Respectfully submitted to the Secretary of War

WINFIELD SCOTT

---

[33] A.G.O., Letters Received, 1857, 550 s.

B: P. G. LOWE'S JOURNAL
OF THE SUMNER WAGON TRAIN [1]

The 1st of May, 1857, I was placed in charge of transportation for the Cheyenne expedition, to be commanded by Colonel E. V. Sumner, First Cavalry, with Lieutenant J. E. B. Stuart, quartermaster and commissary of the expedition.[2] It was at Lieutenant Stuart's request that I was detailed for this duty.

After the necessary preparations for the long campaign, Major Sedgwick, with four troops of the First Cavalry (now Fourth), five Delaware Indian scouts and forty six-mule teams, Mr. "Nick" Berry as chief wagonmaster, was to go up the Arkansas by the Sante Fe route to about where now stands Pueblo, then strike across to where is now Denver, and down the South

---

[1] Taken from Percival G. Lowe, *Five Years a Dragoon ('49 to '54) and other Adventures on the Great Plains* (Kansas City, The Franklin Hudson Pub. Co., 1906), 246-98. In writing his book Mr. Lowe relied upon the "accurate daily journal" (p. 3) which he had kept. From the above book we extract the following biographical data. Mr. Lowe, born Sept. 29, 1828, was reared on a farm, and then served three years as a sailor. From extensive reading of travels and explorations he became enthused about adventure, and at the age of 21 enlisted in the Second Dragoons. His five years with the cavalry took him to various parts of the far West and gave him many experiences. After release from the Dragoons, he took employment in the Quartermaster's Department and as a wagonmaster. For the Cheyenne Expedition of 1857 he had charge of transportation.

In 1859 Lowe went to Denver, where he engaged in freighting and other business. Later he did freighting and contracting in New Mexico and Arkansas, and engaged in the cattle business in Wyoming. His last years were spent at his home in Kansas, where he served as sheriff and then as state senator. He married Margaret E. Gartin, who bore him two sons and two daughters.

[2] Lt. Stuart resigned as quartermaster and commissary on June 1.

Platte to Fort St. Vrain, where it was expected he
would arrive on or about the 4th of July. Colonel
Sumner, with two troops of his regiment (First
Cavalry) would proceed to Fort Kearney, where he
would be joined by two troops of the Second Dragoons
(now Second Cavalry), and thence to Fort Laramie,
where three companies of the Sixth Infantry would
join him. At Laramie he would take provisions for his
whole command, including Major Sedgwick's up to
the end of July. Major Sedgwick's column started on
the 17th of May; on the 18th and 19th we loaded
Colonel Sumner's train, and at 8:00 a.m. on the 20th
the column moved out, cavalry in advance.

The transportation consisted of the Colonel's four-
mule ambulance, fifty wagons (six-mule teams) and
twenty extra mules. Traveled eighteen miles and
camped on Stranger Creek.[3]

Without incident worthy of note, the command
camped near Fort Kearney June 4th, Captain Wharton,
Sixth Infantry, commanding;[4] drew forage and provisions to last to Fort Laramie. Two troops of the
Second Dragoons joined here, Lieutenant Smith[5] in
command of Troop E and Lieutenant Vilipigue[6] of
Troop H. Lieutenant Higgins,[7] Sixth Infantry, also

[3] It flows into the Kansas River at present Linwood. The common places
on their general route, which was along the Oregon Trail, up the Platte
River to Fort Laramie, are too well known to need identification here.

[4] Henry W. Wharton, became a 2nd lieutenant in 1837, and a captain in
the 6th Infantry in 1847. He retired from military service in 1863 and died
March 23, 1868.– Heitman, p. 1022.

[5] W. D. Smith, of Georgia, graduated from West Point in 1846, and
became a 1st Lt. 2nd Dragoons in 1851. He fought for the South in the Civil
War, and died Oct. 4, 1862.– Heitman, p. 904.

[6] John B. Villepigue of South Carolina, graduated from West Point in
1850. He became a 1st Lt. of the 2nd Dragoons in May, 1857. He fought for
the South in the Civil War.– Heitman, p. 987.

[7] Silas P. Higgins, of Alabama, graduated from the U.S. Military Academy
in 1849. He became a 1st Lt. in the 6th Infantry in 1856, and died July 18,
1860.– Heitman, p. 529.

joined with 100 recruits for Companies B, C, D, and G, Sixth Infantry, at Laramie. Colonel Sumner employed five Pawnee scouts, "Speck-in-the-Eye" chief of the band, and ten wagons were added to the train.

June 6th. Command left Kearney, and without incident of importance camped four miles below Beauvais' Crossing [8] of South Platte, June 13th.

June 14th. Command lying by; thankful for this. It gives men a chance to clean up, and men and animals a rest. Threw covers off every wagon and let in the sun to dry out dampness sure to accumulate.

Lieutenant Stuart resigned as Acting Quartermaster and Commissary June 1st, and Lieutenant R. H. Riddick [9] succeeded him.

June 15. Leaving trains in charge of one wagon-master, I took the others and assistants with me at 5 o'clock and rode to the crossing. The river was very high, banks full, and just half a mile by measurement from bank to bank; current three to four miles an hour; usually half the width was bare sand-bars, but now all was covered with water; it is the "June rise." Large numbers of emigrants waiting for river to get lower. On account of the melting snow in the mountains, they may have to wait a long time. I pointed out the landing on the north side; told Eskridge, who had quick perception and a clear head, to remain on the south bank and direct me step by step in case I got to drifting down. The others followed a short distance apart. The bottom was very uneven, sometimes a foot deep, suddenly becoming two, three, and in a few places, four feet deep. The changes were sudden, as often three feet as one, but mostly two or three. On a small island just

---

[8] Beauvais' Crossing, generally known as the Lower Crossing.

[9] R. H. Riddick, a native of North Carolina, became a 2nd Lt. in the 1st Cavalry in 1855. He resigned in 1861 to serve the Confederacy, and was killed June 27, 1862.

above the crossing on the north side grew many tall, slim willows; we each cut several, ten or twelve feet long, and trimmed them so as to leave a few leaves on the top. Each took several of these long switches. Standing on the north bank, I directed them straight to Eskridge. In the shallowest water, where the current would have little force, a switch was stuck deep in the quicksand. By a tedious struggle we got a straight line from bank to bank.

Along came the cavalry, and I explained to Colonel Sumner and the Quartermaster that if they would keep close up to the line of willows, they would beat down and level the quicksand bottom so as to improve the crossing for the wagons.[10] The Colonel knew this very well, as he had been here in 1850, though, he said, the water was not then high. I volunteered to show the way and rode in ahead. The head of the column kept up fairly well but some men a few files back had trouble, drifted, and before the north bank was reached the column was a rainbow – the center 300 yards below the direct line – many horses floundering in the quicksand and several men nearly drowned. For a wonder all got out, but my road-bed was not benefited. However, experience had shown me that there could be no helter-skelter hurrying, and the chance of losing some mules, wagons, and possibly men was very good. That tumbling, boiling cauldron of sand and water was dangerous for the strongest and most experienced men with teams. Be it remembered that the man, horse or wagon standing still will soon sink in the sand; one must keep moving constantly or sink; a blockade of

---

[10] Quicksand in the streams was always a treacherous hazard. Lowe, an experienced traveler, knew that only by tamping down the quicksand by repeated crossings could wagons be safely taken across the stream. We have here a good account of how this could be done.

wagons meant the loss of some. I asked the Colonel and Quartermaster if they had any instructions or directions to give me. The Colonel said, "Be very careful," and left me to work it out my own way. The company teams were looked after well under the instructions of officers and non-commissioned officers interested, and there was no friction, each team following in turn, all cheerfully helping. In addition to the wagon-masters I had a dozen teamsters on their saddle-mules strung along the crossing ready to help. A strap or rope tied to the bridle of the lead mule was held by a mounted man starting in ahead of the team, while one or two more mounted men rode at the lower (off) side to whip up the mules and keep them from drifting down, and the teamster on his saddle-mule did the best he could to keep moving. In this way the first wagon got safely over.

Each wagon-master and mounted teamster understanding his part of the programme, the wagons were started in about fifty yards apart, care being taken to have no more than half a dozen in the river at the same time. Most of the teams had more or less trouble, causing outriders to get off into the water to help out, so that all clothing was soon wet through. The day was dark and cloudy, the water cold from snow-clad mountains and the north wind cold, and all suffered much. As soon as a team was over, the teamster unhitched his saddle-mule and came back to help. Half the teams were safely over when the oldest wagonmaster started in with a wagon for the first time. It was the lightest loaded, and it seems that he thought it would go over casily, and it would, with good management. It was the hospital wagon, containing all medicines for the command. In the middle of the stream, the team tangled up, the leaders swung round and the saddle-mule sank in the sand and got under the tongue, the lower (off) wheels sank, and the wagon rolled over in the deepest water. The boy who drove the team, eighteen years old, was trying to extricate himself from his saddle-mule and crying for help. The man on the lower side could not reach him and the wagonmaster sat on his horse like a wooden man. I was fifty yards away, but put spurs to my horse and reached the boy in time to keep him from going under the tongue with the saddle-mule, which drowned. The men cut the harness from the other mules, and they found their way out. I took the boy on behind me, rode to the north shore, and he was soon made comfortable by his comrades.

At last all but one of the wagons were over – one mule, wagon and medical stores lost. And now, with plenty of mounted men we crossed the beef herd with little difficulty. I did not hear a complaint then or ever afterwards about the management. No one interfered with me from first to last. For my part, with some others, I had been in the cold river, mounted and dismounted, more than six hours; others had been in three, four or five hours; all at least one or two hours. About two infantry recruits climbed into each wagon and were the only ones who got over dry, except a few of the cavalry. Fortunately none were in the hospital wagon.

As soon as the last wagon was over, the cavalry column moved out. Lieutenant Stuart's servant came with the Lieutenant's compliments and presented me with a fine hat; Stuart had gotten it out of his trunk when he saw me lose mine in saving the boy. My ever present bandana was tied on my head.

Lieutenant Riddick said we were going six miles to some water hole; we found the holes but no water. Water kegs contained enough for cooking purposes and to drink, and there were buffalo chips enough to make

coffee and heat water for whiskey toddies, but no fire
for the benumbed, worn-out men to warm themselves
and dry their clothes by, that dreary, miserable day. I
had a few bottles of fine whiskey which had not been
touched since I left Fort Leavenworth, and now I gave
it all out in small doses to the men. I insisted on every
man changing his clothing, and with coffee and plenty
to eat, it was surprising how cheerful all were. My
drowned boy had been well cared for, laid away in
blankets, and was all right.

That boy's name was Hayes, a German of Leavenworth, and when he returned home with one arm, at
the close of the Civil War, he came to see me. He
became a prosperous farmer in Jefferson County,
Kansas – a good soldier and citizen. The Colonel sent
for me and seemed well pleased at the manner in which
the crossing was effected, and when I expressed im-
patience at the loss of the wagon and medical stores, he
said he thought I should be well satisfied. He made me
feel a little more reconciled to the unnecessary loss.

June 22d.   We reached Fort Laramie,[11] and camped
one and one-half miles above on the south side of
Laramie River. Orders were received by Colonel Sumner for E and H Troops, Second Dragoons, to be ready
to go with General Harney to Utah,[12] so that they are
no longer a part of the Cheyenne expedition.

23d.   Everybody getting ready for the Cheyenne
campaign. This is the last chance for any sort of outfit

[11] Founded as a fur trade post in 1834, Fort Laramie had become a military
fort in 1849. For its history see L. R. Hafen and F. M. Young, *Fort Laramie
and the Pageant of the West* (Glendale, Arthur H. Clark Co., 1938). The
fort was located on the Laramie River, about a mile and a half above its
junction with the North Platte. The site and the remaining buildings are
now a National Monument.

[12] Gen. Harney was replaced by Col. A. S. Johnston in the leadership of
the Utah Expedition. See vol. VIII in this *Series*.

until it is over. Mr. Seth E. Ward,[13] the sutler here, has a good stock of campaign goods. Fitting out more teams, having mules' shoes fitted, drawing provision, forage, etc. Laramie probably presents a busier scene than ever before in its history. We left Fort Leavenworth with about 300 fat oxen, had been killing some from day to day for beef, and to-day we drew 150 more from the Commissary. We have not seen a buffalo since leaving Fremont's Spring. The Colonel employed two guides – one a mountaineer white man, the other a Mexican.

27th.   Three companies of the Sixth Infantry, under Captain Ketchum – his G, Lieutenant Carlin's [14] D, and Captain Foote's [15] C, marched from Laramie at 8 o'clock, passed our camp with the guides and Pawnees – trains following. Gradual rise eight miles south to top of steep, rocky hill; an hour going down 500 yards; crossed and camped on Cherry Creek at north side of "Goshen's Hole." [16] This "Goshen's Hole" is a level plain thirty miles across from north to south, and is said to be the hottest place this side of the home of Dives, and, except at the extreme south and north ends, about as dry.

28th.   Infantry and Pawnees marched at 6:00, cav-

---

[13] Seth E. Ward, born March 4, 1820, in Virginia, had come into the far West as a fur trader in the employ of L. P. Lupton in 1838. After seven years as a trapper and fur trader, he engaged in freighting and merchandising. In 1856 he became sutler at Fort Laramie, and retained the position for fifteen years. From this position and later freighting and business activity he made a fortune, and became a leading citizen of Kansas City. He died Dec. 9, 1903. See *Encyclopedia of the History of Missouri,* VI, pp. 372-73.

[14] William P. Carlin, of Illinois, graduated from West Point in 1846. He became a 1st Lt. in the 6th Infantry in March, 1855. He served the Union in the Civil War and reached the rank of brigadier general.– Heitman, p. 282.

[15] R. W. Foote, native of New York, became a captain in the 6th Infantry in 1853. He served the North and was killed in action on June 27, 1862.– Heitman, p. 428.

[16] On a branch of Horse Creek, affluent of the North Platte. See this *Series,* IV, p. 217.

alry and train at 7:00, eighteen miles over flat plain, the sun shining on the light sandy ground, creating such intense light and heat that men and animals suffered much – blinding heat without a breath of air. Our camp on Box Elder looked like an old apple orchard minus the fruit. Scattering box-elders and good grass made as lovely a camp as one could expect without a drop of water. Water kegs were full and cooking went on all right, but the poor horses and mules were great sufferers. The white guide said that the water always sank in the sand during a hot day, but there would be a good running stream at 11:00 p.m. In sympathy with my part of the caravan, by permission of the Colonel and Quartermaster, I told the herders to turn the mules up the creek towards a high point of bluff a mile away. The horses occupied all the shade near camp except that monopolized by the men, and I saw nothing but hours of suffering with stifling heat for the mules before the broiling sun would go down. It was the hottest place I have ever seen without artificial heat. Horses stood at the lariats and chewed the grass they were unable to swallow, and spat it out.

Taking some pieces of "hard tack" to nibble on, I mounted my horse, and with "Billy" Lowe a Cincinnati youth, who, with his brother, was roughing it for adventure, I leisurely drifted off ahead of the herd. Arrived at the point of bluff I noticed under the north side, where the sun had not struck since early morning, a trickling stream which ran into the sand twenty feet away. Then I began to hunt up the creek, the water increasing as I went. Two miles from camp the bluffs were high and brush and trees shaded the creek-bed, and our animals drank comfortably. Half a mile further I found a long hole worn in the sandstone and a good stream running into it, but disappearing in the hot sand within two hundred yards. I wrote on a leaf of my memorandum book to Lieutenant Riddick, telling him that if the Colonel would permit the mules to be driven three miles from camp, they could get plenty of water, and could graze leisurely back before the sun set; also, that there would be plenty of water for the cavalry horses. I told "Billy" to deliver the note to Lieutenant Riddick as quickly as possible. It was now 2 o'clock. With my glass, from a high point, I could see the camp and the mules. In less than an hour I saw the mules moving towards me, and as they came towards the water and smelt it, they struck a trot and finally a stampede, and such braying from four hundred mules I never heard before or since. The bluffs resounded with their music until their noses were buried in the lovely stream.

And now a column of dust indicated that the cavalry were coming; I showed them some nice holes above the mules. There was great rejoicing over the water. Captain W. N. R. Beall [17] said to me, "Are you the guide of this command?" I replied that I was not, but, that if I were I should know what was in the country or try to find out; I had no use for guides who could only follow a trail and knew nothing of the surroundings; anybody could follow a trail without a guide.

When I reported to the Colonel at sunset, he seemed greatly pleased, and questioned me about how I thought of looking for water. I thought of it as a matter of course, but admitted that it was an accident.

29th.   Infantry off at 6:00, cavalry and trains at 7:00, ten miles and watered at Willow Creek; three

---

[17] W. N. R. Beall, native of Kentucky, graduated from West Point in 1844, and became a captain in the 1st Cavalry on March 27, 1855. He served the South in the Civil War and died July 26, 1883.– Heitman, p. 203.

PERCIVAL G. LOWE
Courtesy of The Kansas State Historical Society.

more to pass through high bluff, the outlet from "Goshen's Hole"; four hours getting train up the hill and through the pass, half a mile – steep quicksand hill; three more, and camped on Bear Creek [18] at 7:00 o'clock. Fine camp, but everybody and everything too tired to enjoy it.

30th.   Off as usual, one mile to a branch of Bear River. This small stream, ten feet across, had by recent rains been made a bog one hundred yards wide. The slough grass was as high as a man's head, and one could cut with a butcher-knife an armful a minute. All soldiers and teamsters had butcher-knives. Cavalry dismounted and all cut grass, and a causeway was soon made. It seemed a huge job to cut with butcher-knives sufficient grass to causeway one hundred yards of bog. All took hold in good shape and we crossed without accident, greatly to the surprise of officers and men, to whom this causewaying with grass was a new thing. Seventeen miles more, crossing five branches of Horse Creek, and camped at 4 p.m. on Mud Creek.

July 1st.   Off as usual. Looking from a hill at the course the guides were taking the infantry, I suggested another course for the wagons. I could see with my glass a smooth plain that would save trouble. The Colonel said, "Well go ahead," and I did, he following with his ambulance. Captain Beall said that we saved two miles. These guides have no idea of a wagon-road; they have been following Indian trails on ponies, and do not know very much about them. Eighteen miles over a hard gravel road and crossed Pole Creek.[19] This is called "Pole Creek" because the Indians get large

---

[18] A west branch of Horse Creek.

[19] Lodgepole Creek, which runs from Cheyenne Pass and enters the South Platte at the site of Ovid, Colorado.

numbers of lodge-poles near the head of it in the mountains. Four miles more and camped on big "Mud Creek"; heavy rain-storm in the night.

2d.   We have a butcher named Smith who has charge of the cattle herd. He never was on the plains before, and imagines that he can handle cattle here as he could on his father's farm in Rhode Island. I cautioned him to have his Mexican herders on the alert during the storm for fear of a stampede. This morning he came in greatly distressed and swore there "Wa'n't a critter in sight." And sure enough, with the exception of one cow owned by him and one lame beef, there was not a horned "critter in sight." Fortunately for our command, Quartermaster Sergeant Clark, who was commissary clerk, and my mess mate since leaving Leavenworth, overtook us about 10 o'clock with all the cattle, having found them ten miles from camp, nearly in the direction of our line of march. Off as usual, ten miles to main branch of Crow Creek;[20] road muddy and bad from last night's rains; ten miles more, and camped on south side of slough, which delayed us three hours in causewaying with grass. Good many mules gave out to-day.

3d.   Off as usual, one and one-half miles to slough that occupied two hours in crossing, with assistance of cavalry and plenty of slough-grass. Six miles, and struck spring branch of Crow Creek – four more to crossing. Much time spent in crossing nine wagons, and Captain Beall found a good crossing half a mile below. This shows the worthlessness of the guide. Here the Colonel called me, and said, that by the guide's estimate it was eight miles to where we will camp to-night, twelve more to crossing of South Platte below the

---

[20] Crow Creek runs by the site of Cheyenne and reaches the South Platte about ten miles east of present Greeley, Colorado.

mouth of Powder River,[21] and thirteen more to Fort St. Vrain, where he wanted to meet Major Sedgwick the next day; that is twenty-five miles by the usual trail from to-night's camp to St. Vrain, besides crossing the river. The guide also says, that if we could go direct from to-night's camp to St. Vrain, it would be only twenty miles, and crossing at St. Vrain much better than below the mouth of Powder River. Guide thinks the route practicable. So far I had not been impressed by anything the guide had done – if he had given any valuable information it had not come to my notice; so I told the Colonel that the guide's statement could be easily verified – that I would ride that twenty miles to St. Vrain, and back to his camp before starting-time in the morning, and then there would be no uncertainty about it. "All right," said the Colonel, "take both guides and any others that you want with you." I took with me Simeon Routh, a teamster in whom I had con- fidence, soon overtook the infantry, and got both guides, and struck out west towards the mountains at 3 o'clock. In referring to the guide, I mean the white man – the Mexican talked little English and kept quiet. The guide pointed out what he called "South Fork Peaks," and said that St. Vrain lay in a direct line between us and them, and we traveled straight as possible towards them.

We first came in sight of the Rocky Mountains at Scott's Bluffs,[22] then, forty-six miles east of Laramie, Laramie Peak being the only spur then in sight. Since leaving Laramie we have been traveling nearly south and about parallel with the main chain, which now we

---

[21] Cache la Poudre, which runs by Fort Collins, Colorado.

[22] This landmark was across the river southwest of the city of Scottsbluff, Nebraska. He is referring to their preceding trip up the North Platte River.

estimate to be about forty miles distant. Over nearly level plain we went – walk, trot, gallop – pushing along at an average of six miles or more an hour. We have been traveling a little up grade, and at 5 o'clock, as we reached high ground, we could see the timbers of Powder River in the distance. The afternoon was lovely and the scene before us beautiful beyond description – vivid lightning, clouds and rain – storms on various peaks along the snowcapped range could be seen far beyond the sound of thunder, the sun shining brightly on tempest, peak and plain, the scenes changing with the rapidity of a kaleidoscope. At last we are on the bank of the Powder River at 7 o'clock, certainly twenty-five miles from where we started, and I do not know how much farther to St. Vrain; and it makes little difference. The river is a raging torrent, overflowing its banks from ten to twenty feet deep, from the effects of rains at its source, which we have been viewing all along. This settles the question about going that way, and, as I concluded then and have since proved, not a mile could have been saved by going that way – another damper on the guide's knowledge of the country. Troops and trains would have traveled over an untrodden plain half covered with cactus – one mile worse than two over a partially beaten track. For half an hour, with my glass I watched the glittering rays of the setting sun upon clouds, storms and whitecapped peaks; I might never view such a sight again, and, though I have seen much of the magnificent range since, to me nothing has ever equaled that view.

I do not want to retrace the twenty-five miles to camp, and the guide says it is but twelve miles to the Platte below the mouth of the Cache le Poudre. So that, miserable as the prospect is, we will camp here. Our horses are tormented with mosquitoes that rise from the thick grass and cover them all over, so we fill canteens and betake ourselves to a hill half a mile from the river, but they follow. The animals are hobbled, fuel is brought, and in a few minutes we have a fire, pile on green grass and make a big smoke, to which all animals – biped and quadruped – come for protection. Each man puts his slice of meat on a stick and broils it while seated in the smoke. Armijo, the Mexican guide, has a coffee pot and some coffee – each one has a few pieces of "hard tack," and we feast. Having both guides, I determined to send one back to Colonel Sumner, and wrote the following note:

CAMP ON CACHE LE POUDRE
July 3, 1857, 10 p.m.

To COLONEL E. V. SUMNER, COMMANDING CHEYENNE EXPEDITION, CAMP ON CROW CREEK:

COLONEL: On leaving you I traveled due west about twenty-five miles over a fairly level country and arrived here at 7 o'clock. Found the water from ten to twenty feet deep and storms in the mountains indicate that it will continue so, rendering this route impracticable for the train. I will meet you on the South Fork of Platte to-morrow. I send Armijo with instructions to be in your camp by sunrise.

I am, Colonel, very respectfully,   P. G. LOWE

Armijo saddled his horse and with rifle across the pommel said "Adios, Señor," and was gone. Before he left camp we all agreed upon a star that he should follow, believing that that course would take him close to Colonel Sumner's camp. We kept up the smoke; the night was cool, and by midnight the mosquitoes had settled down into the grass and there was peace for man and beast.

4th.   Coffee, small piece of meat and "hard tack" made our breakfast, and at 5 o'clock we started down stream. Arrived at usual crossing of South Platte below

the mouth of Cache le Poudre at 8 :oo. Unsaddled and
let horses graze while we rested an hour. Then I proposed to try the crossing, but the guide said, "No, it is
impracticable." Routh was willing to try it, but I
would not permit it with his mule. Divesting myself of
everything except underclothes, and with nothing on
my horse but myself and a bridle, I felt my way into
the river cautiously, and was half way over without
much trouble. Then my horse had a hard struggle in
deep water and quicksand, being hard pressed for some
time to keep his head above water, but he took it quietly,
rested when he could, and finally landed safely. I took
the bit from his mouth and let him graze for half an
hour while I fought mosquitoes with switches, and
then we recrossed with the same difficulty. Our wagons
cannot cross here at this time. The guide said: "You'll
take the advice of a guide next time." Feeling nettled
at what I conceived to be his utter uselessness, I admonished him that guides and other employees were
supposed to furnish information to the commanding
officer, and if not, I could see no use for them. The dust
of the command is visible four miles away. I selected
a camp a mile lower down and rode out to meet the
Colonel, who was in his ambulance in advance. He
said that Armijo reached him in time. He was anxious
to know about the crossing, and I was able to tell him,
and he went into the camp that I had selected. Our
battery was manned and salute fired just as we heard
Sedgwick's guns up the river on the other side.

Someone cried, "A horseman on the south side of the
river!" and all rushed for a sight of him. After long
exertion, everyone having given him up for lost half a
dozen times, the horseman emerged from the river,
and proved to be "Fall Leaf," one of the Delaware

Indian guides,[23] from Major Sedgwick. He brought a letter from the Major to the Colonel, who sent "Fall Leaf" back with an answer, requesting the Major to move down opposite to him tomorrow. Overcome by excitement and fatigue, and the effects of a good dinner, I retired to my tent and was soon fast asleep. But, alas! "there is no rest for the wicked." I was soon aroused by the alarming cry of "Stampede!" oft repeated. Twenty steps from my tent stood my horse (Ben). Always after coming into camp he was saddled and already to mount. (I always rode a mule during the day.) This time I had left the saddle off to give him a rest and had him picketed so that he could graze. I mounted without saddle or bridle, put the lariat in his mouth to guide him, dropped the picket pin, and was soon three miles back on the road with the horses and mules headed toward camp. Others came promptly, and every animal was safe. A few cavalry horses stampeded and ran among the mules, which were being herded. Two or three horses were hurt by picket pins,[24] but no other damage.

5th.   While at breakfast Lieutenant Riddick came and said we were to try to cross the river, therefore three metallic water-tight wagon beds, tools to work with, etc., were needed at the river. These, with six coils of rope, wheelwright, blacksmith, etc., were soon there. The Colonel and his adjutant, Lieutenant Colburn, and Lieutenant Riddick were the only officers who participated in the work. A strong detail of men was made from each troop and company. I was not supposed to work any of my men unless asked to, and I

23 Fall Leaf was a notable guide. At some time on this trip he obtained some gold dust, which he took back to Kansas. Displayed there it led to the organization of the Lawrence Party of gold prospectors the next spring. This party became prominent in the early history of Colorado

24 A picket pin at the end of a tethering rope became a serious hazard.

was glad not to be called upon. The first thing was to stretch a rope from the north shore to an island in mid-river. The water was over a man's head in some places and current strong. The three metallic wagon beds were to be lashed together and the raft so made attached by two pulleys to a rope at each end and pulled over by men on the raft. After a long, hard struggle, wading, swimming and pulling, exposed to the hot sun when not under water, they succeeded by noon in getting a rope stretched to the island and two wagon-beds in position to use, but the other one got away and floated down the river.

While three men were working with the rope in mid-river, they lost their hold, and, being exhausted, one of them drowned, while the other two barely escaped. One of them caught overhanging willows at the island with his left hand, and reached back with his right and caught the hand of his comrade, and held on until the men on shore pulled them out. They were cavalrymen of the best type. Fifty men saw this fine young soldier, Daugherty by name, go down to death, with no power to assist him, in that stream of yellow sand and water, and his loss caused deep regret.

Major Sedgwick's command camped opposite to us. At 5 o'clock the Colonel gave orders to take tools to camp, including ropes, indicating that the effort to cross here was abandoned.

6th.   Two commands moved down the river on opposite sides, eighteen miles, and camped on river. Lieutenants Lomax [25] and Bayard [26] crossed over from

[25] Lunsford L. Lomax, of Rhode Island, graduated from West Point in 1852. He became a 2nd Lt. in the 1st Cavalry in 1856. He became a major general in the Confederate Army.– Heitman, p. 639.

[26] George D. Bayard, native of New York, graduated from the U.S. Military Academy in 1852. He became a 2nd Lt. in the 1st Cavalry in 1856. He served the Union and died of wounds received at the Battle of Fredericksburg.– Heitman, p. 200.

Major Sedgwick's to Colonel Sumner's camp. The river is wider and shallower here, and current not so swift. Major Sedgwick having exhausted most of his forage and provisions, his wagons are nearly empty, and he will cross to our camp.

7th.   Major Sedgwick's four troops crossed with little difficulty. With my wagonmasters and a number of good teamsters mounted on saddle mules, we helped Beery's trains over without serious accident. Mr. Beery brought my metallic wagon-bed, lost yesterday, which he found on a sand-bar. Colonel Sumner calls this "Camp Buchanan," in honor of the President. This evening orders are out, dated "Camp Buchanan, July 7, 1857," in which we are informed that pack and riding mules must be made ready to accompany the six troops of cavalry and three companies of infantry in pursuit of the hostile Cheyennes. Pending the campaign, the train is to return to Fort Laramie, be refitted and loaded with provisions and forage, to meet the command at some time and place not named in the order.

8th.   Centrally located is the blacksmith shop, under awnings of wagon covers, supported by poles, with portable anvil, bellows, etc., soon in full blast. Small coal pit burned during the night, and another being made ready; saddler shop near by under similar awnings, trying to make pack-saddles of all sorts of old wagon saddletrees found at Laramie. We found but few real pack-saddles there, and brought none from Leavenworth. Carpenter and helpers are fitting panniers – everybody busy doing the best under the circumstances.

9th.   Selected mules, taking care to use those that are broken to ride, including saddle mules belonging to teams, and the teamsters are breaking others. Except

a few Mexicans, I have not a man who is a practical
packer; among the soldiers there are none. With the
Mexicans I established a sort of school, but they are
hardly able to impart to others what they know themselves; however, they are much help to the officers, who
want a few men instructed.

10th, 11th and 12th.   To sum up: One hundred and
eighty pack and riding mules, 170 blind bridles, and
all saddles and saddle-blankets belonging to train turned
over to Lieutenant Wheaton,[27] acting quartermaster
and commissary of the expedition.

13th.   With best six-mule teams I could rig up,
crossed the packs and infantry to south side of river
without accident, and returned to camp. Before parting,
the Colonel complimented me on the good work done,
told me what he expected in future, and as he shook my
hand, said that my pay had been increased twenty-five
dollars per month from the first of June. I was to
return to Laramie, 150 miles, turn in all surplus wagons
and harness, refit the train, and make as many six-mule
teams as I could, load the wagons with corn and commissaries, and meet him at Beauvais' Crossing of South
Platte, where we crossed coming out, by the first of
August, 175 miles from Laramie.

And now the "good-byes" are said and the command
is gone. Lieutenant Riddick is left acting commissary
and quartermaster of the train and in command of about
fifty men on their first campaign, who, having bunged
up their horses or themselves are no longer of any use
to the Cheyenne expedition, and are left dismounted
with the train. I immediately proceeded to fix up

---

[27] Frank Wheaton, of Rhode Island, became a 1st Lt. in the 1st Cavalry in
1855. He served with distinction in the Civil War and thereafter continued
in military service, reaching the rank of major general before his retirement
in 1897.– Heitman, p. 1022.

teams, and found myself with 109 wagons, twenty-five six-mule teams, eighteen five-mule teams, sixty-six four-mule teams, equal to 504 mules, Riddick's horse and mine, and a few broken-down cavalry horses, which we will turn in at Laramie. Not a saddle nor saddle-blanket for the teams, 170 bridles short. I had been preparing for this condition of things, and had men breaking in leaders and saddle-mules all the time that we had been here; also had to rig out bridles, using ropes and straps for that purpose. By noon we were straightened out, traveled twelve miles and camped above Cottonwood Grove on the Platte. Lieutenant Riddick found the remains of Daugherty on an island a little below camp and had them buried, and called the place "Daugherty's Island."

Mr. Beery went with pack train as chief "muleteer," and took Slim Routh and his pick of other men in the train. The Colonel left the "white guide" with the train, to be discharged on arrival at Laramie. I may as well dispose of him now. He was well-behaved and of rather good disposition – a pleasant man to get along with. The day after our arrival at Laramie he married a young Sioux Squaw – that is, he tied four ponies to the tepee of a warrier, they were accepted by said warrier, and the girl, his daughter, became the bride of the guide. Four years later I saw this same man married in due form to a white woman by a clergyman in Denver, while the squaw bride witnessed the ceremony through a window as she stood upon the porch.

19th. Camped one mile above Fort Laramie. Reported here that General Harney was to have left Fort Leavenworth on the 15th en route to Utah.

20th. Turned in twenty-nine wagons, traveling-forge and surplus harness, and found myself with eighty six-mule teams complete (including saddles, blankets, bridles and a few inferior surplus mules which we drew from the quartermaster here). Drew commissary, medical and other stores and loaded everything but corn.

21st.   Loaded 130,000 pounds of corn, drew fifty rifles and two boxes of ammunition for the same and eight boxes navy pistol cartridges, issued rifles to teamsters and made ready for start in the morning. One wagon was loaded exclusively with supplies for officers when we should meet at crossing of South Platte. Jimmerson was the teamster in charge of this wagon and, strange to say, none of its precious contents were lost, stolen or *evaporated*.

22d.   Passed Bordeaus' trading place [28] and camped below Major Dripp's trading house,[29] nineteen miles from Laramie.

23d.   Fifteen miles and camped at mouth of Horse Creek. We are told by Mr. Reynolds, an Indian trader, that the Cheyennes are but three days' travel south.

If Colonel Sumner meets and whips them, they will likely go north, Reynolds thinks, and may meet us. The management of the train is left to me and I take no chances. The camp is, and will be while traveling along the river, by making the train form three sides of a square, river forming the fourth — say twenty-six wagons fronting west, twenty-six south and twenty-six east — wagons about twenty feet apart — river forming north line of the camp where the dismounted soldiers and their mess wagon and my mess wagon will camp. Mules herded outside of the square until an hour before sunset and then picketed on half lariat inside. Lieutenant Riddick places sentinels pretty well out from the

[28] Trading post of James Bordeau, on the North Platte, eight miles below Fort Laramie.

[29] Presumably a station used by Andrew Drips, famous trader with the Indians.

wagons. I make a regular detail of teamsters, with a wagonmaster and assistant in charge, who divide the night between them, and I am to be called at any and all times that the man in charge sees or hears anything suspicious, or that he does not understand. The detail for sentinels is twelve teamsters each night – half being on post the first half of the night and half the last part. This gives two sentinels on the west, two on the south and two on the east – the roster kept so that each man will do his fair share of guard duty. From my experience as a dragoon I send two or three men mounted on mules to highest points in the vicinity of camp, there to dismount and let the mules graze while they keep a look out and keep me informed of everything of interest from the time we camp until sunset.

24th to 27th.   Camped each night on Platte.

28th.   Soon after leaving camp, saw a party of Indians on the opposite side of river, supposed to be Sioux. Indians seen along bluffs about two miles from camp. We saw some Sioux squaws along the bluff between Indian camp and ours, and Riddick and I rode out to see what they were hunting for, and found they were after rattlesnakes, and they found them plentiful. I dismounted and watched one squaw for half an hour, during which she got three. With a forked stick in left hand and butcher knife in the other, she crept towards the snake until he was ready to "strike," when quickly and skillfully she pinned him down by placing the forked stick close to his head, pressing down firmly and amputating the head. By killing them in this way they had no chance to bite themselves, which they do when hurt or angry. When they do not bite themselves, thereby poisoning the meat, it is good to eat, and that is what the squaws wanted them for. Having severed the head from the body, the squaw caught the latter and thrust it into the folds of her blanket next to her buckskin shirt.

Arrived at Ash Hollow at 10 o'clock and camped. Storm subsided and left a bright, sunny day. After lunch mounted my horse, and with "Billy" Daniels for a companion, went in search of a road out of Ash Hollow to avoid the one already in use, which is altogether impracticable for us with our heavy loads – 3,500 pounds in each wagon.[30] The teams could no more than pull up the empty wagons, and we should have to double teams and haul up a little at a time, straining mules and breaking chains. We found and staked out a route that can be traveled without much difficulty – five hours' hard riding to find a route three miles through the bluffs.

30th.   Off at 5:00, took the new route and at 8:00 o'clock all wagons were at the top of the hill in safety, with no accident except upsetting one wagon by carelessness.

Having fairly straightened out the train at the top of the hill, a band of Indians came in sight from the east at a fast gallop. I started the train into corral, giving the sign by riding my horse in a circle; the movement was quickly commenced, wagon-masters and teamsters moving with a will. Riddick quickly formed his soldiers in line ready for business, while I rode to a high point, with Manuel for an interpreter, and motioned them to stop. They came down to a walk, and when within hailing distance were told to stop and let their chief come up. This they did, "Man-afraid-of-his horse" [31] approached, "Howed," shook hands, and asked for

---

[30] Most of the travel heretofore had been west-bound, with the problem only the comparatively easy one of descent. But difficulty had been experienced by some trains in getting their wagons down the steep incline into Ash Hollow.

[31] Prominent Sioux chief.

something to eat. I cut the talk short by telling him that we must keep all we had for Colonel Sumner's command, which was after the Cheyennes and would be very hungry when we met. The chief promised not to come any nearer and I shook his hand, galloped to the train and straightened out on the road. The Indians had no hostile intent.

Fourteen miles brought us into camp one mile above crossing of South Platte. Immediately after lunch, about 1 o'clock, I retired to my tent to sleep off the fatigue of yesterday, and told my cook not to allow any one to disturb me unless for some good reason. At 5 o'clock he woke me and said that Lieutenant Riddick wanted me to come to the river bank; there were Indians on the other side. I took no arms, contrary to my habit of always being ready. There were four Indians, and I sent a man with a white towel for a flag to a small island to wave it as an invitation to come over, hoping to hear something from Colonel Sumner. As soon as the man beckoned them to come over, one galloped off up the river and the other three took off their saddles and commenced to cross bareback. It was easier and safer to cross without saddles. They were soon in camp, claimed to be Sioux but proved to be Cheyennes. I advised taking them prisoners, which Riddick agreed to, and I explained to him the difficulty of doing so without injuring them, which we must avoid if possible.

The teamsters were now bringing in the mules and picketing them on half lariat between us and the river. The soldiers had been cleaning their guns for inspection, and stood idly by. Having arrived at my tent, Manuel Vijil, a Mexican who had lived with the Sioux and understood the Cheyenne language, especially the sign language, was called to act as interpreter. The

Indians seemed frightened on seeing the soldiers, but
were assured that no harm would come to them; that
we would feed and take care of them, etc. We all sat
upon the ground, Riddick facing one Indian, I another,
and Manuel the third. At Riddick's request, I played
the part of "White Chief," and did the talking. They
were asked why they came into our camp and replied
that, being very hungry and thinking it a freight or
emigrant train, they hoped to get something to eat.
Asked where their people were, they said that some of
them were on the South Platte, near the mouth of Pole
Creek, about twenty miles above us. This corroborated
my suspicion that the fourth Indian, who rode off up
the river, had gone to some camp. Asked if they knew
where Colonel Sumner's command was, the big brave
said that they did, but did not want to talk about that.
They were then informed that this was Colonel Sumner's supply train, and that they were prisoners; that
they would be well treated and fed; that we would
take care of their arms and ponies until Colonel
Sumner's arrival, which would be in a day or two. To
this their leader, a large powerful fellow, six feet four
inches high, and strongly pock-marked, appeared to
agree, but said something very low to the others, which
Manuel afterwards interpreted to be: "You young men
can do as you please, but I am no longer a boy to give
up my bow." It was a trying moment. I realized that
their compliance with my request would come only
after a physical struggle. We did not want to do
violence to these three Indians in a camp of 150 men;
it would seem shameful; yet we must keep them prisoners. We all stood up, fifty men standing around, half
of them with loaded rifles. Quick as thought the big
fellow sprang on his pony, and was off towards the
river. Twenty or more shots were fired after him, but

his pony tangled in the mules' lariats and fell, pitching the Indian into a slough separating some small islands from the main land.

All but Manuel and myself rushed after the escaping Indian, while Manuel, a big, broad-shouldered, powerful man, seized one of the others from behind, pinioned his arms tightly, laid him on the ground and there held him; I reached for the bow of the third one, when he eluded me and I struck him a powerful blow in the face, thinking to knock him down; but he only bounded like a ball, drew his scalping knife and came near stabbing me. I seized him by the wrists and held up his hands, realizing that to let go meant death to me, while he sprang into the air like a wild tiger, trying with all his might to break away, and yelling like a maniac. This lasted a minute or two until "Billy" Daniels, a fine young teamster, came to my assistance. I told him to get behind the Indian, pinion his arms and lay him down on the ground, which he did; and with both hands I took his knife, bow, quiver and arrows. His saddle, lariat, bow, quiver, arrows and scalping knife fell to me, and on my return to Fort Leavenworth I gave them to my friend Levi Wilson, who sent them to his father, Dr. Wilson, of Pittsburg, Pa.

Small rope was brought and I soon had both tied hand and foot. Then I mounted my horse and searched the small islands near shore for the big brave, thinking he must be wounded or killed; but did not find him. If he was hit, he might have sunk in the muddy stream, and one could not see a foot under water; and if not, he could lie on his back under over-hanging willows with nose far enough to breathe until dark, and then make his escape. His pony, lariat, blanket, bow, quiver and arrows were left behind. For want of proper irons we used small chains and padlocks from the front boxes of wagons to iron the two prisoners, the right hand of one fastened to the left hand of the other. We had a tent pitched for them, and a soldier sentinel placed in front and one in rear. And now the interpreter, Lieutenant Riddick, and I commenced a pumping process to find out from the young fellows all we could of Colonel Sumner. We learned that he had had a battle the day before, that some Indians were killed and wounded, as well as some soldiers, that the Cheyennes were scattered, most of them going north, crossing the South Platte near the mouth of Pole Creek. We believed these statements to be fairly correct. The Indian that I captured was a son of the head chief, and the other was his cousin, each about twenty-two years old, tall, well built, and very handsome Indians – the best type of Cheyennes.

And now the suspicion arose that there might be a large camp of Cheyennes in the vicinity of the mouth of Pole Creek. We had the chief's son, and there might be an effort made to stampede or capture our train to give the youngsters a chance to escape, and I immediately set to work to corral the wagons so as to make a solid fort, with room for men and animals inside. Setting the first wagon, the next came up and struck its left front wheel against the right hind wheel of the first, with tongue on the outside – each wagon coming up so as to make the circle more complete; when the last wagon but one was in, that one would close the mouth of the corral so that nothing could get in or out. All this we did by hand in two hours, put all of the animals inside and closed the gap with the last wagon. Then I examined all arms in the hands of teamsters, and saw that each had fifty rounds of ammunition. Riddick did the same with the soldiers. A strong guard was posted, and all was quiet.

A candle was kept burning in the prisoner's tent, and lying a few feet from the open front, without being seen, I watched them. They whispered together a good deal and seemed to be listening, wrapped in a state of expectance. There was a dismal sound of wolves howling in every direction. That was nothing new; we heard them howling every night; but one of them sent out a peculiar howl, unlike any of the others; he howled at intervals directly south across the river. To this the young chief and his fellow prisoner sat up and listened eagerly. Wolves wading across a shallow river make about the same splashing noise that a horse does, and quite a number crossed during the night. An hour had passed since I had heard the peculiar howl referred to, when it broke out again on our side of the river above the camp. I now felt convinced, as I had before believed, that this particular howl was by an Indian, by which he conveyed information to the prisoners. There was no sleep for me, for I believed that there was a large band of Cheyennes in our neighborhood, but we had no fear of the whole Cheyenne Nation, the way we were corralled. Vigilance was all that we needed.

July 31st. Camp aroused an hour before daylight in anticipation of an attack, about dawn being a favorite time with Indians to surprise still unsuspecting sleepers. Daylight came, but no enemy in sight. After breakfast, with three men mounted on mules, I scoured the country to the highest bluffs north, and then posted them as videttes on three prominent points half a mile from camp. I then rode a couple of miles up the river, but discovered nothing but the tracks of two ponies which crossed the river during the night. About 4:00 p.m. an Indian approached the river on the opposite side to within half a mile of the bank, reconnoitered a while and then rode away. About 5 o'clock an express arrived from Laramie with mail for the command, which failed to reach Colonel Sumner by a former express; it was brought by a mountaineer called "Big Phil," [32] accompanied by a Sioux Indian. No news from Colonel Sumner; mules herded close to corral under strong guard, ready to rush them in quickly if necessary.

August 1st. Videttes posted and mules herded by strong mounted guard near by corral. I crossed the river and met one of Majors & Company's trains en route to Salt Lake.[33] No news from Colonel Sumner and none from the "States." Rode five miles up the river and found plenty of Indian pony tracks. Some soldiers crossed over and found two saddles belonging to our prisoners. This shows that the Indian who escaped took his saddle for another horse, when he joins his tribe or gets a chance to steal one. No Indians seen to-day. This evening Lieutenant Riddick consented to send out two Mexican spies, Manuel Vijil (pronounced Vi-heel) and Malquis Mestos, for the purpose of ascertaining the location of the Cheyenne camp, supposed to be near the mouth of Pole Creek, perhaps twenty miles above us. Manuel was given a letter from Lieutenant Riddick to Colonel Sumner, in case he should meet him, and he was instructed to find the Cheyenne camp if possible, count the lodges, see which way they faced, take cognizance of every ravine or pass leading to the camp, etc., and to return to our camp by evening of the 3d inst. They were furnished horses, feed and arms, and passed the guard at 12:00 midnight.

---

[32] This was probably Charles Gardner, commonly called Big Phil, since he had come from Philadelphia. He carried mail between Denver and Fort Laramie during the winter of 1858-59. For an account of his career, see L. R. Hafen, "Mountain Men – 'Big Phil, the Cannibal'," in *Colorado Magazine,* XIII (1936), 53-58.

[33] Freight train of Russell, Majors, and Waddell, carrying supplies for Johnston's army of the Utah Expedition. See vol. VIII in this *Series.*

2d. The expressman, "Big Phil" and the Sioux Indian left us at sunrise. They had been permitted to talk with the prisoners, it being known that they would tell of it to any Indians they happened to meet, and by that means the safety of the prisoners would be known to their friends; and it was believed that the Cheyennes might be induced to come in and make terms for peace. Moved camp one and one-half miles up river for fresh grass. Improved this time to practice in corralling, so as always to be ready to corral quickly by driving round in a circle without confusion. A hundred men well armed inside of my corral could stand off thousands with bows and arrows.

After the videttes had been posted on high ground and I or one or two wagonmasters had explored a little, the mules are turned out to graze and kept out until within an hour of sunset, and then shut up in the corral for the night. We feed corn to wagonmasters', Mexicans' and Riddick's and my horses to keep them in condition for long rides or stampedes at any time; no other animals are fed. We save the corn for the command when it reaches us.

August 3d. Mexicans return this evening, and report having found a camp of seven lodges on the south side of South Platte, nearly opposite mouth of Pole Creek, where there had been two other camps. They found a chart in one of the camps marked on a buffalo skull, showing that the Indians had taken the route up Pole Creek to a point opposite Smith's Fork, thence north across North Platte. The Mexicans saw one Indian to-day, but could not get near him. No news or sign of Colonel Sumner. Heavy rain and electric storm during the night.

August 4th. I called for volunteers to go to the camp of seven lodges. Twenty teamsters and the two

Mexicans above mentioned got ready, armed with rifles and revolvers.

August 5th. Off at sunrise; teamsters on mules, Mexicans and myself on horses; crossed river opposite camp, up south side to the seven lodges. There they stood, but no Indians in sight, and a careful reconnaissance revealed none. Everything indicated that they had gone in a hurry, leaving besides lodges, many useful articles; live coals of a small fire still smouldering, and cooking utensils that would not be abandoned except in case of necessity. Looking across the river, up Pole Creek, we saw a band of Indians in rapid retreat two miles away. Undoubtedly my party had been seen, and the Indians were in too much of a hurry to encumber themselves with lodges. The party seemed quite large and their precipitate retreat indicated that they were greatly demoralized. The Indian trail coming from the south was broad and quite well worn, showing that many had traveled it recently, and quite a number since the rain night before last. Manuel and I were so impressed with the indications of recent Indian travel over this line, that we instinctively looked south for some portion of Colonel Sumner's command in pursuit. We saved one of the lodges, a nice small one, packsaddle and a bushel or two of kinickinick (the inside bark of red willow, dried), enough for all hands to smoke for a month, piled everything else together and burned it. Placing sentinels on several high points, with the Mexicans and "Billy" Daniels, I rode to the camp two miles above; found a chart on a buffalo head and everything to corroborate Manuel's statement; had him bring the head to camp. To me it revealed the fact that the scattering bands were going to concentrate somewhere north of North Platte, and it might be valuable information for Colonel Sumner. Returned to my party and thence to camp without incident, except plentiful signs of Indians having traveled up and down the river opposite our camp — surely Cheyennes. There were tracks of two American horses, with shoes on, that had passed the camp both ways since the rain, indicating that Colonel Sumner may have lost some horses.

August 7th and 8th.   Nothing new. Several false alarms. Each sunny day the wagon covers are thrown off so that the sun may dry out any dampness that may have accumulated. If rain has beaten in, the loading is taken out and repacked. Damp commissaries and corn soon spoil under wagon covers exposed to the hot sun. Many horses and mules die of colic caused by eating corn thus exposed. It gathers dampness, swells, heats, gets musty, moldy and finally rotten, unfit for any animal to eat. There is nothing so demoralizing for men as idleness, and examining loads, unloading and re-loading wagons is a great benefit to men and stores.

The Indian prisoners seem to have outgrown their fears of violence, and to have overcome their aversion to Manuel and myself, who were the prime cause of their captivity; in short, they have become quite communicative. The one who fell into my hands says that after the fight the Cheyennes scattered, agreeing to go North and meet from time to time at some point north of the North Platte. When told of what we found near the mouth of Pole Creek, the buffalo head with chart having been shown them, they said that that camp was a sort of depot of supplies and information to assist those going north. Being closely questioned, the young chief said the wolf that made the peculiar noise the night of their capture was his father, and that two other nights he had heard his father. He thought the Cheyennes too much scattered to attack our train, and thought his father would not do so for fear of what

might happen to them; in fact sufficient assurance had
been given through the peculiar wolf howl, that they
would not disturb the train. And we believed that their
captivity would have a strong influence in including
the Cheyennes to come to terms and sue for peace.

August 9th.   This morning one of Childs' ox trains
passed en route to the "States." By it we learned that
the mail passed west during the night. Sent two men
and caught mail at Ash Hollow.

August 10th.   Crossed train over river without accident, and camped one mile below where we had so
much trouble in June. Water is low; half the river bed
a dry sand bar; Lieutenant Riddick took 211 sacks of
corn from one of Major Russell's trains en route to
Laramie, believing that Colonel Sumner's command
would soon be here. Some Indians seen this evening
supposed to be Sioux.

August 11th.   This morning a band of Sioux, under
"Man-Afraid-of-His-Horses," crossed from north to
south side of the river. Only the chief allowed to come
into camp. He was told to keep away from the mule
herd, and not to allow his men to come near. In the
meantime the mules were corralled. The Indians soon
left, and the mules were again turned out. A wagonmaster or his assistant is with the herd all of the time,
and he is instructed to corral on the appearance of
Indians, whether there seems to be danger or not. One
of the herders leads a horse with a bell on his neck,
and when the herd is to be corralled, he rattles the bell
violently and gallops for the corral. The passageway is
always kept clear when mules are out. The mules have
now gotten so used to this that they run for the corral
when the bell is rattled, and could hardly be kept from
it. About noon a train came in sight down the river. Of
course we are all expectancy, hoping that every outfit

that comes in sight may be ours. I rode out and met Colonel M. F. W. Magraw [34] and his surveying party, en route to California, with "Tim" Goodale, the celebrated mountaineer, as guide.[35] I had met him here in 1851. Major Johnson, Sixth Infantry, en route to Laramie, is with Magraw. Magraw with his fifty wagons camped near us, and half the night was spent in gathering the news from him, Goodale and Johnson. They left us a few old papers.

August 12th.   Magraw's train crossed the river and camped on north bank. He, Goodale, and Major Johnson dined with us. Goodale belonged to the class of mountaineers who ranked with Sublett, Fitzpatrick, Bridger, etc., with Carson as the recognized head – reliable characters, unmixed with false heroism, intelligent and trustworthy. The young Cheyennes knew him, and he learned from them about what they had told us, and he thought the information pretty correct. Of course Goodale knew nothing of Colonel Sumner's fight, but judging from what the prisoners said, it was forty hours afterwards that they came to my camp, and he thought the Cheyennes were sure to retreat north; they would not be likely to go south or west, and surely not east; they could get north of the North Platte more easily, and soon be in a comparatively safe country, at that time almost unknown to the whites. We wondered why Colonel Sumner was not hot after them, as they passed within twenty miles of his supply train, and some of them much nearer, unless he was himself too

---

[34] Magraw was engaged in a wagon road building project. For a full treatment see W. T. Jackson, *Wagon Roads West, op. cit.*

[35] Goodale, long an associate with Carson and other trappers and traders, was well known in the West. When he visited Denver in 1861, the *Rocky Mountain News* said he had been familiar with the country for some thirty years past.– Issue of May 18, 1861. See report from Goodale in the Introduction, above.

much crippled to follow; at any rate, if the Cheyennes were whipped anywhere on the branches of the Kaw River they would retreat north if possible; and we had ample proof that the chief (whose son and nephew were our prisoners) and most of his people did go north. Any one who knew the country north of North Platte would know they would do that, and then old "Tim" expressed the opinion that Colonel Sumner's guides knew nothing about the haunts of the Cheyennes in the northern country.

Mr. R. M. Peck, of Whittier, California, has written an interesting account of the Cheyenne expedition, as he remembers it;[36] and as a soldier in the First Cavalry he participated in the battle and in pursuit of some of the Cheyennes, the command going to the Arkansas afterwards, undoubtedly opposite to the route taken by most of them.

13th.   Went with Colonel Magraw to Ash Hollow. He passed his train over my new route without difficulty, and named it "Lowe's Route Avoiding Ash Hollow Hill."

14th.   In the evening one mule left the herd and ran down the road, followed by Assistant Wagonmaster Stanley and two teamsters. They soon returned and reported that they saw Indians on the north side of the river. Messrs. Patrick, Cecil and I went in pursuit as far as Nine Mile Tree, where we found Captain Van Vliet,[37] quartermaster of the Utah army, camped. His men had caught my mule. Captain Van Vliet is on the way to Salt Lake, to return immediately. He informed me that while Colonel Sumner's whereabouts are unknown, four of the six troops of cavalry now with him

---

[36] Published next below, as Section c.

[37] Capt. Stewart Van Vliet was on his mission to the Mormons to obtain information and supplies for the army. See vol. VIII in this *Series*.

are to go to Utah, while the Colonel with the other two troops returns to Leavenworth. The three companies of infantry now under Colonel Sumner (C, D and G, Sixth), with the company at Laramie (B, Sixth), are also to go to Utah. Colonel Alexander, Tenth Infantry, with advance troops for Salt Lake, expected in a day or two. Returned to camp at midnight.

15th.   Captain Van Vliet passed this morning. I led the command over the river, as I did every other military outfit while we were camped near the crossing, and was able to serve many of them to good advantage.

17th.   An express from Laramie, "Big Phil" arrived at sunrise. Received several letters from friends. No news from Colonel Sumner. A party of returning Californians camped near by. The party was managed by Mr. D. O. Mills, a banker of San Francisco, and a sea captain whose name I have forgotten. They stopped in Salt Lake several days. Mr. Mills and Captain ―― seemed to be very superior men and not inclined to talk romance. This is the D. O. Mills of New York whose name is honored throughout the financial world. They camped near us two days. They needed rest and took it while they could safely do so near our outfit.

21st.   Colonel Alexander crossed over and camped on the north side.[38] I led the train and gave him full information of route to Laramie. Saw Mr. Andrew Garton and son, beef contractors of Clay County, Missouri, who are driving a large herd of cattle for delivery at Laramie under escort of the Tenth. Lieutenant Bryan's party arrived from Bridger's Pass and camped near us.[39] Dr. Covey joined us from Lieutenant Bryan – quite an acquisition to our mess.

[38] Col. E. B. Alexander, of the 10th Infantry, was leading the advance troops of the Utah Expedition. Col. A. S. Johnston, commander of the forces, had not yet come up.

[39] Lt. F. T. Bryan had been surveying various routes. See vol. VIII of this *Series*, pp. 111-12.

22nd.   Colonel Alexander marched early. Lieutenant Bryan's party left en route to the States.

Captain Dixon, quartermaster,[40] and Captain Clark, commissary, [41] arrived and crossed the river en route to Utah. They bring news that Colonel Sumner had a fight with the Cheyennes on the 29th of July. Large body of Indians formed in battle array, and the cavalry charged with drawn sabers. Twelve Indians were left on the field and many wounded; cavalry lost two men killed, and Lieutenant Stuart and eight men wounded. Captain Foote with his company of Sixth Infantry bringing the wounded to Fort Kearney. The fight is said to have taken place on Solomon's Fork of the Kaw River. Colonel Sumner followed the Indians, burned their lodges and other property, and then followed their trail, as he supposed, en route to the Arkansas. Colonel Sumner established a camp on Walnut Creek, leaving two companies of infantry there, under Captain Ketchum. Sent Lieutenant Lomax to Fort Riley after supplies. This is the first news of Colonel Sumner's command except what the prisoners gave us. Moved camp five miles up river. We think the chances much against Colonel Sumner ever coming to us. For sanitary reasons one camp should not be long occupied; it becomes filthy and the corrals muddy and unclean.

August 24th.   Fifth Infantry camped nine miles below crossing en route to Utah. More than half of the regiment said to have deserted since leaving Florida, two months ago.

25th.   Fifth Infantry crossed river. Animals in good condition, the credit of which is largely due to my friend "Jim" Miller, the head wagonmaster, who

---

[40] Capt. John H. Dickerson; see vol. VIII of this *Series*, pp. 83, 103, 111, 134.

[41] Capt. H. F. Clarke, *ibid.*, pp. 35, 111, 134, 165, 174.

always herds mules and never starves them at the lariat. He came to me at Riley in the fall of 1855 with the Second Dragoons from Texas, and is one of the very best in his line.

28th. Express arrived from Kearney bringing letters from Captain Foote and Lieutenant Stuart to Lieutenant Riddick, and orders from Colonel Sumner to Lieutenant Riddick for the train to proceed to Kearney, turn in all stores not necessary for use, and proceed to Fort Leavenworth. Colonel Sumner gone to the Arkansas, and will go from there to Fort Leavenworth, where he will probably arrive as soon as we do. Though there has been no hardship in our stay here, there has been a good deal of anxiety. The long suspense is very monotonous, and all are glad to move.

29th. En route to Kearney. When nine miles below the crossing an express arrived from General Harney at Leavenworth, ordering that the train proceed to Ash Hollow and there remain until the arrival of four troops of the First Cavalry and three companies of Sixth Infantry en route to Utah. The order presupposes the train to be at Kearney, and directs Lieutenant Riddick to take supplies from the post sufficient to subsist the four troops and three companies to Laramie. As he has not sufficient supplies, Lieutenant Riddick determined to proceed to Kearney and procure them, and, unless otherwise ordered, return to Ash Hollow and remain as directed. Camped at Nine Mile Tree.

31st. Camped below O'Fallon's Bluffs at Freemont Spring, the head of big slough that runs parallel with the South Platte, twenty or more miles. When coming into camp, an Indian and two squaws with pack-pony dragging lodge and poles crossed the road from the south going north. The "buck" said that they were Sioux; I thought them Cheyennes. When in mid-river, becoming frightened, they cut away their packs and ran, which confirms my belief that they were Cheyennes. I was sorry to see their effects thus thrown away. The poor squaws were safe enough.

September 7th.   Camped at Fort Kearney. And now we must part with our Indian prisoners, of whom I have become quite fond, though glad to be rid of the responsibility of holding them. Lieutenant Riddick turned them over to the commanding officer, and they were confined in the guard house. Thirty-nine days they have been with us, and while we have been obliged to be a little severe in keeping them safely ironed, they have been well fed and safely cared for.

9th.   We started to return west and camped seventeen miles above the fort on Platte. Dr. Covey accompanied us. The Doctor and I went after buffalo about sunset and killed one each. Dr. Summers, post surgeon, and John Heath, post sutler, arrived from the fort on a buffalo hunt and spent the night with us.

13th.   Camped one mile below O'Fallon's Bluffs on head of Freemont's Slough. At 6:00 this evening an expressman arrived from Kearney with orders from Colonel Sumner for the train to remain at Kearney until the arrival of Major Sedgwick's four troops of cavalry and two companies of infantry. The order was sent under the belief that the train was then at Kearney.

14th.   On the back track en route to Kearney.

16th.   Short distance from camp killed a buffalo while crossing road ahead of train, and before going into camp Messrs. Stanley and Eskridge killed another; saved abundance of fine meat. Met George Cater, an expressman, en route to Laramie. Lieutenant Riddick received letters stating that all of the cavalry and infantry that were ordered from the Cheyenne expedition to Utah are now ordered to Leavenworth. Camped on Platte.

17th. Camped on Platte. Killed nine prairie chickens with pistols in camp before train came up. Lieutenant Marmaduke,[42] with detachment of recruits for Seventh Infantry, en route to Laramie, arrived and camped with us.

18th. Lying by. Rained all forenoon. In the afternoon Marmaduke and I "still hunted" (hunted on foot) buffalo, but did not kill any. His transportation consisted of two dilapidated wagons, each drawn by six broken-down-pack-mules that Captain Foote had brought into Kearney with the wounded men from the Cheyenne campaign. We were going in, and could exchange and give him fine teams and wagons, which we did, and turned over to him another team and wagon for which he receipted; and with it I turned over an experienced man capable of looking after all of the teams; knew the camps, and would take him to Laramie all right. I never saw a better pleased man than Marmaduke – a future major general in the Confederate Army, and later Governor of his native State of Missouri. We invited Marmaduke to join our mess while camped near us, which he did. He had some potatoes, something we had not seen in four months. I would only accept enough for one dinner, which, with my prairie chickens, made a fine feast.

19th. Lieutenant Marmaduke and party went on west and we east. Met "Sim" Routh and Sarcoxie, a Delaware guide, with letters, by which we learn that Major Sedgwick's command of four troops of cavalry

---

[42] John S. Marmaduke, of Missouri, graduated from West Point in 1853. He was made a 2nd Lt. in the 1st Infantry in July, 1857. He served the Confederacy as a major general, and died Dec. 28, 1887.– Heitman, p. 689.

and two companies of infantry are waiting for us thirty-two miles below Kearney. Arrived and camped at Kearney. Found Lieutenants Wheaton and Bayard at the fort with orders for Lieutenant Riddick to turn over the train and all other property to Lieutenant Wheaton. We left here all commissary stores not necessary for troops going in to Fort Leavenworth.

20th. Finished turning over property and started down the river at noon. Met Beauvais'[43] and Bisonet's[44] traders' trains for their trading posts near Fort Laramie.

21st. Camped with Major Sedgwick's command on Little Blue.

22d. Camped on Little Blue. Turned over four teams to Captain Ketchum's command. Feed half rations of corn to horses and mules.

23d. When leaving camp this morning met Colonel Albert Sidney Johnston, of the Second Cavalry, in command of the Utah Expedition, and his adjutant-general, Major Fitzjohn Porter, with a train of twenty-four mule ambulances, several officers and an escort of the Second Dragoons, en route to Utah.[45] I received orders to select twenty-five of my best mule teams to be left with an escort of cavalry to await the arrival of

---

[43] James P. Beauvais, long a western trader, had sent a wagon train with some 6,000 pelts from his trading post near Fort Laramie down to the Missouri River. The *Elwood Weekly Advertiser* of July 30, 1857, reports the arrival of the furs at Elwood, Missouri. The u.s. census of 1860 gives his age as 44.

[44] Joseph Bisonet, or more properly Bissonnette, is listed in the u.s. census of 1860 as a trader, 50 years old. He was met in the Fort Laramie region and mentioned by Francis Parkman, James Clymen, Lt. J. H. Carleton, Capt. Howard Stansbury, and others.

[45] See vol. viii of this *Series*.

Colonel Cooke, en route to Utah.[46] Colonel Johnston and Major Porter were waiting by the side of the road, and saw the teams go by. I was sent for, and Colonel Johnston said: "I am told that this is the finest train on the plains." To which I replied that we had exchanged a few good teams for brokendown ones from the Cheyenne campaign; otherwise, the teams and equipments were complete. "Well," said he, "we want the best; we will need them," and he got them. Traveled eighteen miles and camped on Little Blue. Unloaded twenty-five wagons, fitted up the best teams and equipments throughout, got volunteers to drive them, drew rations for the men, and have everything ready to turn over in the morning.

24th. Turned over the twenty-five wagons for Colonel Cooke's command to Lieutenant Perkins, and two wagons for himself and escort — a small detachment of cavalry. Mr. Patrick took charge of train as wagonmaster; he was an excellent man and very competent. "Billy" Daniels went as assistant wagonmaster — a well earned promotion. Camped on Little Blue. An expressman left this morning and another this evening en route to Fort Leavenworth.

26th. Camped on Snake Root Creek. Express arrived this evening from Fort Leavenworth. Colonel Cooke's command of six troops of Second Dragoons said to be at Big Blue. The troops of Major Sedgwick's command to be stationed at various points in Kansas for the present.

---

[46] Philip St. George Cooke, a native of Virginia, graduated from the U.S. Military Academy in 1827. For his distinguished career see Otis E Young, *The West of Philip St. George Cooke, 1809-1895* (Glendale, Arthur H. Clark Co., 1955).

27th.   Met Colonel Cooke's command three miles
west of Big Blue. Lieutenant Buford, acting quartermaster for the command, had an order to change all
the mules he wanted to, taking our best and leaving his
worst, which he did, leaving us nothing but a bad lot
of mules to go in with. The last of my beautiful train
was gone. We were going where forage was plentiful;
they were approaching winter, where forage of all
kinds would be scarce. Buford trusted to me, and I gave
him the best. Crossed Big Blue and camped on Spring
Creek. I heard that there were eighty desertions from
dragoons since leaving Fort Leavenworth. Captain
Ketchum, with his two companies of infantry, remains
here (Marysville) until after election – first Monday
in October, or until further orders.

28th.   Arrived and camped at Ash Point, twenty-
five miles.

29th.   Camped on Nemaha, Seneca is the town (now
county seat of Nemaha County, Kansas). Captain
Sturgis and Lieutenant Stockton arrived from Fort
Leavenworth. G Troop First Cavalry to remain here
until after election, B Troop to go to Palermo, A Troop
to Claytonville, E Troop to Atchison. I go with twenty-
nine teams and all the extra animals to Fort Leavenworth. Twenty-nine years old to-day, and gray enough
to be fifty.

30th.   Off for Fort Leavenworth at the same time
that the command starts down the Atchison road. Four
days later, with Lieutenants Wheaton and Riddick, I
arrived at Fort Leavenworth and turned over the
remnant of property in my charge; the Cheyenne campaign had ended, but the troops were still in the field,
keeping peace at the polls, a more irksome business for
soldiers than fighting Indians.

The day after my arrival Colonel Sumner sent for

me and inquired particularly about what I saw of the campaign; said he had heard a good account of my part in it from various sources, and especially from Mr. Riddick; said that my train had the reputation of being the finest ever seen on the plains, and the best managed; in short, he was very profuse in his praises. He was especially interested in knowing my idea of the flight of the Cheyennes north, after his battle with them; I told him how things looked where I burned the camp, and all information gained from the Indian prisoners and by scouting in the neighborhood, but I did not venture an opinion, nor did he ask me to. He had probably made history that would redound to his credit, and whether he followed the right or the wrong trail after the battle, he did the best that an earnest persevering commander could do, with the light before him; and I think that the general verdict of his command was that he did well, and that is the highest court by which a man can be tried.

After Colonel Sumner's command was "sifted" where he left us on the South Platte, he went into the field with as fine a set of officers and men as I ever saw. The civilians with his pack train –"Big Nick" Beery at the head – were the best we had.

The civilians who were with me four-and-a-half months were from all parts of the continent and some from Europe. Probably one-third of them born in the United States, representing a dozen States and Territories, most of them from Missouri and Kansas. Then there was the hardy, cheerful, untiring "Canuck" (Canadian) – more than twenty of them – always skillful and willing, wet or dry, feasting or fasting; and the Mexican, patient and uncomplaining always – he will squat over a fire no larger than his hand with his serape about him, smoke his cigarette or munch his "hard tack" cheerfully. A few Germans, careful of their teams, always ready and willing – and the never failing Irishman with his unbounded energy and snap. In short, as I look back in memory to the motley crowd I see more than an average set of men.[47]

I am told that Mr. Beery still lives in Montana. Except him I know but two living – Mr. K. B. Cecil, a wealthy farmer of Platte County, Mo., and "Sim" Routh of Easton, in Leavenworth County, Kansas – always a good citizen and prosperous. Of all the officers of that expedition, I do not think there is one living. Of the enlisted men I know of but one, Mr. R. M. Peck of Whittier, California. Probably there may be others.

---

[47] This is in contrast to Capt. Phelps' estimate of his soldiers. See his diary in vol. VIII of this *Series*.

C: R. M. PECK'S ACCOUNT
OF THE SEDGWICK DIVISION [1]

The Cheyenne Indians had been on the war-path for a year past, committing all sorts of depredations on the overland routes through Kansas and Nebraska, and orders had been sent out by the war department for Colonel Sumner to take the field in person during the coming summer, hunt the hostiles down, and bring them to terms, or chastise them properly. I will here take occasion to remark that such orders from Washington to punish hostile Indians were generally neutralized by a clause admonishing the commander of the expedition that he must first exhaust all means of conciliation before beginning hostilities. . .

Our Cheyenne expedition was to be divided in two commands. Four companies of the First cavalry, commanded by Major Sedgwick,[2] were to proceed by way

---

[1] From *Transactions of the Kansas State Historical Society, 1903-1904,* etc., VIII, pp. 486-506. Robert M. Peck was living at Whittier, California, when he wrote these recollections. He lived in Kansas for some years after the close of the Civil War.

[2] John Sedgwick was born in Connecticut on Sept. 13, 1813. He graduated from the U.S. Military Academy in 1833. He became a 1st Lt. in 1839, a captain in 1849, and a major in the 1st Cavalry in March, 1855. He was decorated for gallant service in the Mexican War and fought in many battles of the Civil War. He commanded the V and VI Corps of the Army of the Potomoc, and was killed by a sharpshooter at Spotsylvania on May 9, 1864. He is honored with a bronze plaque at West Point, and statues at Gettysburg and his native town of Cornwall Hollow, Conn. He never married.– Heitman, p. 872; the *Dictionary of American Biography,* XVI, p. 548; and *Correspondence of John Sedgwick, Major-General* (2 vols., privately printed, 1902-03).

of the Santa Fe road and upper Arkansas River to the foot of the mountains, unless the Cheyennes were sooner found; thence over to the South Platte and down that river till meeting Colonel Sumner's command, which, consisting of the remaining two companies of the First cavalry and four of the Sixth infantry, were to go from Fort Leavenworth to Fort Kearney, thence on to Fort Laramie, and then back across to the South Platte to form a junction with Sedgwick. If the hostiles had not been found by either command in this time, a pack-mule expedition was to be fitted out by the two commands united, to scour the country between the South Platte and Arkansas in search of them. Each of these three commands was reenforced by a couple of twelve-pounder mountain howitzers, drawn by four mules to each piece, and manned by detailed dismounted cavalry-men.

On the 18th of May, 1857, Sedgwick's command, four companies of the First cavalry, marched out of Fort Leavenworth, starting on this expedition. The company I belonged to, E, (Capt. S. D. Sturgis) was with Sedgwick, and Sturgis was the ranking captain of Sedgwick's party.[3] Next day Lieut.-col. Joe Johnston started on the boundaryline expedition.[4] A day or so later Colonel Sumner's command, the other half of our Cheyenne expedition, took the road for Fort Kearney.

As we (Sedgwick's command) marched westward, we found the settlements of Kansas few and scattering, generally being confined to the timber along the water-courses, most of the prairie land being yet unoccupied. Easton, on the Little Stranger creek, and Osawkee, on

---

[3] See the biographical note and the report of Sturgis' campaign of 1860 in Part III, below.

[4] See fn. 27, in Part I, A, of this vol.

the Grasshopper, were mere hamlets, of probably a dozen houses each. At Hickory Point, where there was but one dwelling-house and a blacksmith shop, the property of a Mr. Lowe, a cannon-ball hole in the shop was pointed out to me by one of the old soldiers as having been recently made in a "scrap" between the proslavery and freestate men.

Passing through Indianola, on Soldier creek, we crossed the Kaw river a little beyond, fording the river on our horses, but ferrying our wagons over, one team at a time, on a flatboat, pulled back and forth by means of a rope stretched between trees on opposite banks, entering the old Santa Fe road just after crossing the Kaw, a few miles west of Topeka.

Council Grove, a small village at this time, was the farthest western settlement on the Santa Fe Trail in Kansas,[5] except Allison's ranch, at the mouth of Walnut Creek, five miles west of the Big Bend (the point where the Santa Fe road first strikes the Arkansas going west), and Bent's Fort on the upper Arkansas, where Fort Wise [6] was afterwards built. Just south of Council Grove the government had established a reservation, agency and mission for the Kaw tribe of Indians, where teachers, preachers, farmers and mechanics were trying to teach them the arts of peace – more particularly, how to earn their bread by the sweat of their brows – but with indifferent success; for Mr. Lo [7] invariably

---

[5] An important station of the Trail, located on Neosho River. The Santa Fe Trail, which the party follows to Bent's Fort, is too well known to require identification. For the Peoria Party journey over the Trail see vol. III of this *Series*. Recently published descriptions are cited, p. 28.

[6] The establishment of Fort Wise is described in Part III.

[7] A term then commonly applied to the Indians; taken from the verse:

Lo! the noble Indian whose untutored mind
Saw God in the forest, and heard him in the wind.

Westerners composed various parodies of the lines.

develops an inherent horror of labor, and would sooner
raise hell and hair any time than corn. After passing
Council Grove we were fairly on the plains and saw
little more of timber, consequently had to depend
mostly on buffalo-chips for fuel; and the prairie
chickens, which were so numerous in the Kansas settlements that they were a great nuisance to the farmers,
were seen no more after we struck the plains.

At Cottonwood Creek, about fifty miles west of the
Grove, we saw the first buffalo, a few scattering small
bands appearing at a distance; but from there on their
numbers increased amazingly, and, when in the thick
of their range, we were often in great danger from the
stampeding of the vast swarms of these animals that
covered the prairie in every direction, for when those
immense herds started on a run it was impossible either
to stop or turn them out of their course. Of late years
I hesitate to tell people of the vast numbers of buffalo
I have seen at one sight on the plains in those early
times, for when doing so I often find my listeners
looking at me with an incredulous smile, that seems
to say: "He is another one of those old frontier liars
we've heard about." One who has never seen them can
scarcely comprehend the vastness of those herds. Some
seasons they would be found ranging farther east or
west than others, the distance through the herds east
and west varying from 150 to 200 miles. They drifted
north in summer and south in winter.

The first settlement of prairie-dogs that I noticed
was at the Little Arkansas, but from that time on
throughout the trip we were seldom out of sight of these
interesting little animals.

As we were approaching the Big Bend, crossing the
level stretch of eight miles between the Plum Buttes

and the Arkansas River, with our beef herd and a train of about fifty six-mule teams strung out behind us, we had an exciting bit of experience in a buffalo stampede, a description of which may assist the reader to realize the immensity of the herds of these animals near the center of their range. This stampede might have resulted in a direful calamity to us but for the prompt action of Captain Sturgis, who, having been in such a predicament before many times, knew just what to do and how to do it.

Sedgwick, though an old officer in the service, had never had much experience on the plains, having been in the artillery for nearly twenty years, and the sight of that brown mass of animals – so vast in extent that we could see no end in flank or depth – thundering towards us in an irresistible torrent, made him turn pale, as he appealed to Sturgis: "Sturgis, what'll we do?"

"Time is too precious for explanations now, Major," replied the Captain; "better turn the command over to me for a little while – I'll steer you through it."

"Take command, Captain, take command, and give your orders," replied Sedgwick, eagerly.

Before the last word was out of Sedgwick's mouth Sturgis was giving his commands: "Orderly bugler, give my compliments to company commanders and say that Captain Sturgis is in command. Then hurry on back to the train as fast as you can go, and give my compliments to the quartermaster and tell him to corral his wagons quickly, in as small a space as possible, teams heading south, with the beef cattle inside the corrall."

The buffalo were coming from the north. In another moment Sturgis had us headed about and going back to the train on a gallop. At the start of the stampede the buffalo had been probably two miles or more from us. On reaching the train, which was being hurriedly formed in corral, with the beef herd on the inside, as ordered, Sturgis halted us and commanded: "Dismount, to fight on foot!" This leaves each No. 4 holding the horses of the other three men of his set. We quickly "formed ranks," after dismounting, and were then marched out, on "double quick," about a hundred yards to meet the buffalo. Our flanks were then thrown back, forming us in the shape of a huge V, with the point towards the coming herd, and the open ends of the V enclosing our horses and train.

The stampede was now coming near, driving right at us, making the earth tremble, presenting a solid front as far as we could see, right and left. To me it was a fearful sight, for I thought, "What will be left of us when that dense avalanche of horns and hoofs sweeps over us?" I had been told that we were to split the herd by firing into them, but could not see how they could find room to divide, they were crowded so closely together. However, when the command was given, "Commence firing," we poured into their faces such a sheet of fire and lead from our Sharp's rifles that they did the impossible, splitting, by crowding savagely to the right and left, actually climbing over each other in their frantic efforts to avoid our withering fire, thus making an opening that cleared our train and horses; but that torrent of brown wool went right on without any perceptible check in its speed.

We stood there loading and firing as fast as we could work our pieces, boxes of cartridges being brought up from the ammunition wagons and placed in rear of each company to keep us supplied, and it seemed at times that in spite of our efforts we were doomed to be overwhelmed by that living tornado; the dust they kicked up was often blinding to us, as well as to the buffalo, and we had been crowded back, inch by inch, till we were closely packed about our horses and wagons, when we were greatly relieved to perceive a thinning and straggling in the threatening mass, and were glad to hear the command to "Cease firing." The danger, with the buffalo, had passed, leaving the ground around us covered with dead and badly crippled buffalo, while many wounded ones went limping on after the stampeders. I heard one of the officers say, as he looked at his watch, that it lacked but a few minutes of half an hour from the command "Commence firing" to "Cease firing," with the buffalo going on a steady lope all the time.

We cut up and stowed away in our wagons the choicest meat from some of the young and tender buffalo, and leaving the rest of the killed and crippled for a grand feast for the wolves, we moved on to the Big Bend, camping on the bank of the river. Next morning we passed Allison's ranch,[8] at the mouth of Walnut Creek. Be it understood that these frontier "ranches", as they were called, were mere trading-posts, no efforts being made by the proprietors at any agricul-

---

[8] At the mouth of Walnut Creek, near the site of Great Bend, Kansas. Upon reaching this point on Oct. 1, 1858, David Kellogg wrote in his diary: "Bill Allison, a one-armed plainsman, has a stockade here and trades with the Indians."–"Across the Plains in 1858, Diary of Daniel [David] Kellogg," in *The Trail* (Denver, Colo.), v, no. 7, p. 7.

A. E. Raymond reports in his diary on May 5, 1859, that Allison's Ranch was "built of Poles inclosed with Sod. The roof is nearly flat one story high. The Stone Walls and Sods inclose about an Acre of Land. This affords a strong protection against Indians. Here is a Mail Station, Store, Tavern, Corn & Hay, etc."–Raymond's diary, MS. in the State Historical Society of Colorado Library. See also L. R. Hafen, *Pike's Peak Gold Rush Guidebooks of 1859* (Glendale, Arthur H. Clark Co., 1941), 175.

tural pursuits or stock raising. They were there to catch
the trade of travelers and Indians, and usually kept a
small stock of such goods as the trade demanded. They
also made profitable speculations in trading for the
lame or give-out animals of passing trains or emigrant
outfits, and after recuperating, selling them again to
other travelers.

As a necessary precaution against Indian attacks,
these ranches were always enclosed by walls or pali-
sades, the ranch buildings being strung around the
inside of the enclosure, leaving an open court or corral
in the center of sufficient capacity to contain all the
animals belonging to the establishment. For traffic with
Indians a long, narrow opening, about waist-high, to
be closed when need be by a drop-door on the inside,
was made in that side of the storeroom that formed a
part of the enclosing wall, and through this slit all
trade with the red-skins was conducted, thus avoiding
the risk of admitting them to the enclosure. A watch
tower was frequently built on a prominent corner of
the wall, and in dangerous times a lookout was maintained day and night.

Our road from the Big Bend westward lay along the
north bank of the Arkansas River, sometimes several
miles off, sometimes close in.

Old Fort Atkinson, at the western junction of the
"dry route" and river road, had been abandoned by the
government several years previous to our trip, and
nothing was left standing of it but some of the corners
of the old 'dobe walls, about as high as a man's
shoulders.[9] The nearest timber to Fort Atkinson was
fourteen miles north, on a branch of Pawnee Fork, that
has since been named Sawlog Creek. Previous to its
occupation as a military post by the government, the

---

[9] For an account of Fort Atkinson see fn. 11, Part I, A.

site of Fort Atkinson had been held by a trading post, conducted first by one Mann, and subsequently by one Macky, and the place was frequently spoken of by old plainsmen as Mann's Fort, or Fort Macky, and these names were used to indicate the place about as often as Fort Atkinson.

About fifteen or eighteen miles west of the ruins of old Fort Atkinson was the Santa Fe crossing of the Arkansas. The crossing was opposite – almost under – a high bluff, that overlooked the ford and surrounding country for some distance. In recent historical sketches, I have noticed some diversity of opinion between writers as to the relative location of and distance between old Fort Atkinson and the Santa Fe crossing, varying from eight to twenty-six miles. I have traveled the road and camped many times at both places, and we always considered it a short day's march between them, and we usually called the distance fifteen or eighteen miles, but I never knew the exact measurement.

We had passed the western limit of the buffalo herds that season when we reached old Fort Atkinson, and saw no more of them beyond there. At the Santa Fe crossing, of course, we parted company with that famous old trail, and traveled along the north bank of the river on a well-worn road, then called the California trail.[10]

The Santa Fe road, from the Arkansas to the Cimarron, then ran about due north and south on the sixty-mile stretch, without water, called the "journeda," for I remember to have noticed, in traveling it afterwards by night, coming from the Cimarron to the Arkansas, that we were going towards the north star all night.

All the freight for the western country was then

---

[10] Or the "Mountain Branch" of the Santa Fe Trail, as far as Bent's Fort.

transported across the plains in wagon trains, sometimes of mule teams, sometimes oxen. We had met
several of these outfits from New Mexico, going into
the states for goods, their wagons being usually empty,
but sometimes carrying light loads of wool in huge
sacks, that being about the only commodity that New
Mexico exported. We had also overtaken and passed
some freight trains going out loaded, and several
emigrant outfits *en route* to California. The teamsters
employed in the New Mexico trains were mostly
Mexicans.

Frequent graves were to be seen along the roadside,
many of them being marked by rude wooden crosses.
Such almost invariably indicated the last resting place
of some Mexican, who is always a Catholic. I had
noticed, too, but thought it the result of carelessness in
placing the crosses on the graves, that nearly all these
cross-pieces were in a slanting position, but on mention-
ing this peculiarity to one of the old soldiers, he informed me that when the horizontal piece was slanted
it meant, "died with his boots on," or a violent death –
usually killed by Indians – and that where the cross-
piece was fastened at right angles to the upright (and
these were few, for people seldom die of disease on the
plains), it signified, "died on the square," or a natural
death.

Major Sedgwick had employed at Leavenworth, as
guides, scouts and trailers for the expedition, a half-
dozen Delaware Indians from their reservation on the
Kaw river, near Lawrence. They were under the command of old Fall Leaf,[11] a noted chief of their tribe.
The Delawares had then adopted white men's garb and
ways to a great extent, and were far superior to the

[11] See fn. 23, in Section B, above.

plains Indians. They did us excellent service throughout the trip.

The Arkansas River, from where we first struck it,
at Big Bend, to some distance west of the Santa Fe
crossing, was a broad, shallow stream, showing many
sand-bars and islands, but no timber except a few
scattering trees now and then on some of the islands,
but as we approached the mountains we found more
timber along the river banks and the stream grew
narrower and deeper.

Bent's Fort,[12] on the upper Arkansas, was the second
white man's habitation we struck after leaving Council
Grove. It was admirably located on a high bluff that
overlooked the river and adjacent bodies of timber,
and commanded a view of the surrounding country for
miles. It was a typical frontier trading post, and, with
its motley crew of retainers and hangers-on of Mexicans, Indians, French-Canadian and white trappers,
and their various equipments and appurtenances, made
quite an interesting picture of frontier life. There had
originally been three of the Bent brothers engaged in
trapping and Indian trading on the frontier – William,
Charles and Robert[13]– and, although I subsequently
became well acquainted with "Colonel" Bent,[14] who
was the only survivor of the three, and the proprietor
of Bent's Fort at the time of which I write, yet I cannot

---

[12] This was Bent's New Fort, constructed by William W. Bent in 1852,
after he had abandoned his more famous original fort, built in 1833-34, and
which was located about 35 miles west of his New Fort. The original fort
was built of adobes, the new one of stone.

[13] Also George Bent.

[14] Note to Peck's article: "Wm. W. Bent was agent for the Cheyennes and
Arapahoes in 1859 and 1860, making a report the former year. He was also
one of the commissioners for the United States in the treaty with the
Comanches and Kiowas on the Little Arkansas, near Kansas, October 18,
1865. See note about the Bent brothers, *Historical Society Collections,* vol.
VII, p. 327."

recall his Christian name. We usually addressed him as "Colonel," or spoke of him as "Old Bent." He had held the position of Indian agent under the government for several years, hence his title of "Colonel," it being customary to confer the title "Major" or "Colonel" on Indian agents as a matter of courtesy.

Bent was then (1857) out of office, but the agency of the five tribes – Cheyennes, Arapahoes, Kiowas, Northern Comanches, and Prairie Apaches – was still maintained at his post, "Maj." A. B. Miller having succeeded Bent as agent.[15] Bent had a Cheyenne squaw for his wife, and quite a flock of half-breed children. The three older ones, Charlie, Bob and Mary were nearly grown, and had been educated in a Catholic school in St. Louis, Mo. Charlie Bent, a few years later, became notorious as a leader of the hostile Cheyennes, and gained the reputation of being one of the worst Indians on the plains.[16]

Shortly after passing Bent's Fort, following the California trail up the river, we got our first sight of the snow-covered summit of Pike's Peak, resting on the western horizon like a small white cloud, which many of us thought it really was; but day after day, as

---

[15] Another Peck note: "Three years later (1860), the government, through Major Sedgwick, bought Bent out and we (Sedgwick's command) built Fort Wise (name afterwards changed to Fort Lyon) in the low flat, on the river bank just above, using Bent's old establishment on the hill as a commissary and quartermaster's store. The selection of that low bottom, which had only about eight feet elevation above the low-water stage, as the sight for locating a permanent post, always seemed to me to show very poor judgement in Sedgwick and his officers, for they ought to have known that the annual 'June rise' in the Arkansas River was liable to inundate that low ground and compel its evacuation, which acctually occured a year or so later, and was the cause of the abandonment of the post, the government again buying Bent out, and building new Fort Lyon, twenty-five miles up the river."

[16] Charlie and Robert, sons of William W. Bent, both took the side of their mother's people in the Indian troubles of the middle sixties.

we marched towards it, the white cloud grew larger, higher, and plainer, other mountains on each side of it coming into view, till in a few days it seemed like we were running up against the whole Rocky Mountain range.

Near the mouth of a creek called Fountain que Bouille,[17] we turned off from the Arkansas and struck over the divide for the head of Cherry Creek, passing through some fine bodies of pine timber.[18] At a point shortly before leaving the Arkansas, a small collection of 'dobe shanties on the opposite bank of the river had been pointed out to me as Pueblo, then a small settlement of Mexicans and trappers.[19]

Soon after reaching Cherry Creek, while marching down it, we met a party of six or eight men – Missourians, and all afoot – with a little old wagon drawn by a single yoke of steers, driven by a big "buck nigger," the slave of one of the men, on their way back to Missouri. *These men were the first discoverers of gold in the Pike's Peak region.*[20] I have always been sorry that I did not ascertain their names, and more about them, in order to give them the credit to which they are entitled, for giving to the country so important a discovery. The honor of this discovery has been claimed by others, but I am satisfied that those Missourians were the first to make known to the public the presence of gold in that part of the country. Remember this was all Kansas territory then.

[17] Fountain Creek, which runs through Colorado Springs.

[18] The Black Forest area on the divide between the Arkansas and South Platte drainages.

[19] The Pueblo, or Fort Pueblo, built of adobes by trappers and Mexicans in 1842. Jim Beckwourth and J. B. Doyle both claim to have been founders.

[20] Gold had been discovered in 1850 by California-bound Cherokees. See the "Historical Introduction," in L. R. Hafen, *Pike's Peak Gold Rush Guidebooks of 1859, op. cit.,* for an account of discoveries made prior to 1857.

Those men had a wounded comrade lying in their wagon who had accidentally shot himself through the hand, in pulling his rifle out of the wagon muzzle foremost, a day or so before we met them; the wound had reached the gangrene stage, and they halted to ask surgical aid from our doctor. Our surgeon decided that it would be necessary to take the man along with us, and while halting to bring up a wagon and transfer the man, we got a chance to talk to them a little, and they told us their troubles. I think they had been in the mountains between the mouth of Cherry Creek and Pike's Peak all winter and spring prospecting, and had found plenty of gold, some of which they showed us, put up in bottles and little buckskin bags.[21]

They had originally intended to keep the discovery of gold a secret, but the Indians had run off all their stock except the yoke of steers, and had otherwise made life such a burden to them that they finally concluded the only way to make mining safe and profitable was to go back to Missouri, proclaim their discovery, make up a strong party that would be able to hold their own against the Indians, and return determined to have "the dust."

We parted company with them – they continuing on towards the States, and we moving on down to the mouth of Cherry Creek, where Denver now stands, and camped, on the 29th of June, 1857. The next day being our regular bimonthly muster day, we laid over at this camp, and were mustered for two month's pay.[22] Our

[21] Some of this gold, or some other "dust" procured by Fall Leaf independently, was taken back to Kansas in the fall of 1857 and helped bring on the Pike's Peak gold rush.

[22] Peck's note: "Wherever we happened to be on the last days of February, April, June, August, October, and December, we were always mustered for two month's pay at a time. This did not necessarily imply pay, for we would not get the money until we got back to Fort Leavenworth, or in reach of a paymaster somewhere else."

surgeons, Doctors Covey [23] and Brewer,[24] amputated the wounded prospector's hand at this camp, and a few days later found it necessary to take his arm off above the elbow.

The California trail, which we had been following, crosses the South Platte here, just below (north of) the mouth of Cherry Creek, and seems to take through the mountains, while we leave it and follow down the right bank of the river on a dim wagon-trail that did not appear to be used much.

This part of Kansas Territory was literally a "howling wilderness," with little indication of its having been occupied or traversed by white men, except the old wagon-road we had been traveling, with here and there a stump and a few chips by the roadside, as the mark of some California emigrant. Game was very abundant, and comparatively tame. Herds of elk, antelope, and deer were frequently seen from the trail as we marched along, and occasionally a bear. Old Fall Leaf and his Delawares proved to be expert hunters, as well as good guides and trailers, for they almost kept the command in fresh game meat while we were traveling through this foot-hills country.

We had one or two desertions shortly after leaving Cherry Creek, and our officers seemed to fear that the reported gold discovery had caused these men to abscond for the purpose of going into the mountains prospecting. For fear of others being led to desert to go gold hunting they caused to be circulated through the camp reports that the rumored gold discovery was

[23] Peck's note: "Edward N. Covey, Maryland. Assistant surgeon, August 29, 1856; resigned June 1, 1861. Died September, 1867."

[24] Peck's note: "In special order No. 59 of Lt. Stephen D. Lee, dated Fort Leavenworth, April 27, 1858, naming troops to be sent to Fort Scott, on the requisition of Governor Denver, is the following paragraph: 'V. Assistant Surgeon Chas. Brewer, medical department, is assigned to duty with this command.'"

a fake, and instructed the wounded prospector to con-
tradict his first statements and deny the discovery of
gold in paying quantities.

On the Second day's march down the South Platte,
after leaving the mouth of Cherry Creek, we passed
the ruins of three old abandoned trading posts, a few
miles apart, which I was told were formerly called
respectively: Forts Lupton, Lancaster and St. Vrain,
after their several owners.[25] They seemed to have been
abandoned several years, nothing remained but the
crumbling 'dobe walls. Inside the walls of one we found
a small cannon, apparently about a four-pounder, without carriage, half buried in the crumbling dirt. This
piece had probably been disabled and left by the
proprietor when he abandoned the place. We left it as
we found it.

On the Fourth of July we laid over on the bank of
the Platte, and, with our two howitzers, fired our
national salute of thirty-two guns in honor of the day.

We had now got clear of the foot-hills and timbered
country and were back again on the plains. We had
expected also to form a junction with Colonel Sumner's
command somewhere in this part of the country, but
had not heard a word from them since leaving Fort
Leavenworth. As the echo of our last gun died away
we were cheered by the answering boom of cannon from
down the river and distinctly counted thirty-two guns.
Of course, we understood that this must be from Colonel
Sumner, and Major Sedgwick immediately dispatched

---

[25] There were the ruins of four forts: Lupton, Vasquez, Jackson, and St.
Vrain. For the history of these fur trade posts see L. R. Hafen, *Colorado and
its People* (New York, Lewis Historical Publishing Co., 1948, 2 vols.), I, pp.
74-80; and the following articles by Hafen in the *Colorado Magazine:* "Fort
Jackson and the Early Fur Trade Posts on the South Platte" (V, pp. 9-17);
"Old Fort Lupton and its Founder" (VI, pp. 220-26); "Mountain Men –
Louis Vasquez" (X, pp. 14-21); and "Fort St. Vrain" (XXIX, pp. 241-55).

one of Fall Leaf's young Delawares to the colonel's camp, which was found to be about fifteen miles down and on the opposite side of the river, near the mouth of Crow creek.

Next day we moved down opposite the colonel's camp, and in fording the river to join him got a lot of our horses and mule teams mired in the quicksands,[26] but finally got over without the loss of an animal.

Sumner's command, two companies of cavalry and four of the Sixth infantry, had come by Fort Kearney, and then went on to Fort Laramie, on the North Platte, and hearing nothing of the Cheyennes in that direction, he had come across from Fort Laramie to this camp. At Fort Kearney the colonel had hired a squad of Pawnees for guides and trailers, judging that their hereditary enmity for the Cheyennes would prompt

[26] Peck's note: "Here, in the middle of the South Platte, was the first time and place that I ever remember to have seen P. G. Lowe, Colonel Sumner's chief wagon-master, who there assumed control of our trains. One of Wagon-master Cecil's teams had bogged down, and Cecil was sitting there on his riding mule looking bewildered and helpless, and seemed afraid of getting himself wet. Lowe came riding up on a horse, and – well, the language he used to Cecil I'm sure he never learned in Sunday school. It was both emphatic and persuasive, for he made Cecil get down in the water, nearly waist-deep, and hold up above water the head of a mule that was about to drown, until he could get help enough to work the team out. It was a way Lowe had of exhorting bashful wagon-bosses and teamsters. I afterwards served as assistant wagon-master under him at Fort Leavenworth during the war, and got so I could understand his language perfectly.

"(Percival G. Lowe still lives in Leavenworth, and has attained great prominence, in Kansas public affairs. For biographical sketch see vol. VII, p. 101. He has written several chapters of early recollections for the State Historical Society, notably, 'Kansas, as Seen in the Indian Territory,' vol. IV, p. 360, and 'Recollections of Fort Riley,' vol. VII, p. 101. He is now publishing in the Journal of the United States Cavalry Association, Fort Leavenworth, a series of articles entitled, 'Five Years a Dragoon.' A marvellous interest attaches to the days when the solitude of these prairies was broken only by the Indian and the buffalo. Mr. Lowe's story is five years preceding Mr. Peck, or from 1849 to 1854.– Secretary, Kansas State Historical Society)."

them to a vigorous pursuit of the enemy, but they proved to be inefficient and not at all comparable to our Delawares. We lay at this camp five days, preparing for a pack-mule expedition across the country from the South Platte to the Arkansas in quest of the Cheyennes.

On the 13th of July, with twenty days' rations on our pack-mules and otherwise lightly equipped, we crossed the river, leaving our trains of six-mule teams under charge of P. G. Lowe, chief wagon-master, escorted by a company of the Sixth infantry, to return to Fort Laramie for a supply of rations and forage, and then again to come back to the South Platte, about the old Salt Lake crossing, and there await orders from Sumner.

The wounded gold prospector, whom I have mentioned, was left with our train and I never heard of him again, but suppose he recovered and returned to his home in Missouri.

I think most of the officers and soldiers of our pack-mule outfit fully expected that we would find and clean out the Cheyennes and get back to our supply-train within the twenty days for which we were rationed. But I doubt whether Colonel Sumner and the more experienced men anticipated such an easy job, for it was said of the "old bull o' the woods" that whenever he started on such a trip he never expected to get back in twice the time of his rations, and during the last half after rations had run out, his command was liable to have to subsist on their pack-mules or horses, if he struck a warm trail.

We left all extra luggage with our wagons, such as tents, blankets, and overcoats, taking no clothing but what we wore, and no bedding but our saddle-blankets, lightening ourselves and our horses of every pound that could possibly be dispensed with. We took no wheeled vehicles except one two-mule ambulance for the use of the sick, and the four mountain howitzers, which were united in a four-gun battery under command of Second Lieut. Geo. D. Bayard, of G company. We were *entirely* without shelter. The colonel took along a tent-fly, to use for headquarters and adjutant's office, and one fly was allowed for the hospital.

After crossing the river we followed down the south bank of the South Platte, eastward, for three or four days, and then bore away in a southeast direction. Our guides seemed to have ascertained or guessed something of the whereabouts of the Cheyenne village, and led us as though they knew where they were going; though the old lodgepole trail we were following was by no means fresh – apparently not having been used for a year or more.

On the sixteenth day from the time of leaving our train, on the 29th of July, traveling generally in a southeast course, we found the Cheyennes, and thought for awhile that we had "found more Indians that we had lost." During the previous day our Delaware scouts, who usually kept the country explored for ten or twelve miles in advance and on each flank, had found some fresh signs. The country being somewhat broken in many places, for we were near the headwaters of Solomon River, Colonel Sumner had taken the precaution to march the command in three columns, *"en echelon"* (a sort of stair-step formation), from which they could be brought quickly into line, to meet an attack from the front, rear, or either flank. Our pack-mules were kept close in our rear. The three infantry companies, and sometimes the battery, would unavoidably drop to the rear in rough ground, but we made frequent short halts to allow them to close up. Be it remembered that this was all a treeless prairie, with seldom even a bush to be seen.

On this day (July 29), about ten o'clock a.m., old Fall Leaf sent one of his Delawares galloping back from the front to report to Colonel Sumner that his trailers had sighted a small party of Indians, some distance ahead, who seemed to be retreating as our scouts advanced. This proved to be a reconnoitering party of Cheyennes who had been sent out to watch us, and were falling back on the main body as we approached. Colonel Sumner seemed to fear that the Cheyennes were all on the retreat and might escape us; so he determined to push on with the six companies of cavalry, and try to bring the enemy to a fight, even if he had to leave the infantry and artillery behind. And it is probable that the Indians had planned to draw us out in a rapid pursuit of that decoy party, and after getting us well strung out to fall on us with their whole force and clean us up in detail; for, as we afterwards learned, they had no notion of running from us. Instead, they had come out fifteen miles from their village, selected their ground to fight on, and were coolly awaiting our approach apparently so confident of defeating us that they had made no preparations for moving their village, a precaution they seldom neglect when they are about to have a fight near their camps.

As soon as the colonel got the word that the Indians had been sighted, he halted the command and sent orders to all company commanders to see that their men were prepared for action. At the command, we dismounted, tightened up saddle-girths, and examined arms and equipments to see that everything was in fighting order. Little preparation was necessary, however, for we had frequently been admonished on the trip to keep our "kits" in good shape, and were always ready for a call. As soon as the captains remounted their companies and reported ready for action, the "old man" rode out in front of the center column and made a little speech. He had a very loud, strong voice, and I think this, together with his well-known fighting proclivities, had probably earned for him the name "Bull o' the Woods," by which sobriquet his men were fond of speaking of their old white-headed, white-bearded fighting colonel. His speech on this occasion was about as follows: "My men! the enemy is at last in sight. I don't know how many warriors the Cheyennes can bring against us, but I do know that if officers and men obey orders promptly, and all pull together, we can whip the whole tribe. I have the utmost confidence in my officers and soldiers. Bugler, sound the advance!"

As the clear notes of the bugle rang out, followed by the captains' "Column forward! march!" we again struck the trail, and all seemed encouraged by the colonel's confidence. This was the first bugle-call we had heard for several days, Sumner having dispensed with those signals lately, lest the sound might be borne to the ears of some scouting Cheyenne; but now there was no longer any use for such precaution. A few minutes after we had resumed the march the notes of "Trot!" reached us from the colonel's orderly-bugler, and each captain commanded: "Trot! March!" Our pack-mules were also put in a trot, and kept close in our rear. The infantry, of course, now dropped behind. Lieutenant Bayard's battery kept up with us for a little while, but soon, in crossing a miry little creek, some of his mules bogged down, and we left them floundering in the mud, with Bayard swearing a blue streak at the unfortunate detention. We saw no more of the infantry or battery until after the fight.

It seemed a little reckless of the colonel to scatter his command this way, and attack an enemy of unknown numbers on their chosen ground with only a part of his force, but he had probably estimated all the chances and was so much afraid that the Indians would get away from us that he decided to try to bring them to a fight and take the risk of either whipping them or holding them till our reenforcements came up. Deducting the "sick, lame, and lazy," who had been left behind with the train, and the men on detail manning the battery and attending to the pack-mules, we had scarcely an average of fifty fighting men in the ranks of each company of cavalry – a little less than 300 men all told – ready to go into action.

As we came down a hollow from the upland prairie, debouching onto the Solomon River bottom, and rounded a bluff-point that had obstructed our view to the eastward, before us and extending down along the north bank of the river, was an almost level valley of several miles, at the lower end of which stood a few scattering cottonwood trees. About these trees we could see a dense mass of moving animals that at first looked like a distant herd of buffalo. But we had been told by our guides that we were more than two days' march west of the buffalo range. Several of the officers halted long enough to take a look through their field glasses, and promptly announced: "They are Indians, all right, and a swarm of them, but no sign of lodges; they seem to have been halted about those trees, and are now mounting and moving this way."

Soon we began to see the glint of a rifle barrel or lance point here and there, reflecting the rays of the sun. We afterwards discovered that the Cheyennes had been awaiting our arrival several hours, in the vicinity of the trees, had coolly unsaddled and turned their horses out to graze, and they and their mounts were well-rested and fresh when the fight began, while we and our horses were quite jaded. We found near those trees, after the fight, a number of their saddles, blankets, and other impedimenta that they all had discarded; for, on going into battle, the Indian warrior wants the free use of every limb and muscle, usually dispensing with everything in the way of clothing but his "gee-string," leggings, and moccasins, often doffing even his leggings, many times throwing off his saddle and riding bare-backed, to give his horse more freedom of action.

When the Indians had approached near enough that we could make a rough estimate of their numbers we saw that they greatly outnumbered us, and noticed that they were advancing in a well-formed line of battle, but differing from our formation in being several ranks deep, and preserving sufficient intervals between the men to give each perfect freedom of action. And all the time they were yelling as if

> All the fiends from heaven that fell
> Had pealed the battle-cry of hell.

Things happen pretty lively and thought flies like lightning at such a time. I remember to have thought, as I made a mental estimate of our chances, while we got into line, "Of course we'll have to whip them, for it's a groundhog case; but I wish the infantry and battery were here, for I'm afraid 'Old Bull' has bit off more than he can chew." If the colonel thought anything of the kind there was no sign of it, for he never hesitated, but went right ahead as though the prospect just suited him. The men used to say they believed he would fight a buzz-saw.

Just when we were nearly in rifle range of the enemy we saw our old Delaware chief, Fall Leaf, dash out from our line till he got about midway between the two bodies, when he suddenly halted his horse, raised his rifle, and fired at the Cheyennes. As he turned and rode back, followed by several shots from the enemy, we heard Colonel Sumner say in a loud voice to Lieut. David Stanley,[27] who was beside him: "Bear witness, Lieutenant Stanley, that an Indian fired the first shot!"

It is probable that he had been hampered by one of those milk-and-water orders from Washington, to "first exhaust all means to conciliate the Indians before beginning hostilities," and he seemed relieved to be able to establish the fact that an Indian fired the first shot, pretending not to have noticed that said first shot was fired by one of his own Indian scouts and not by a Cheyenne. Up to this time the colonel was possibly expecting that the Cheyennes might halt, display a white flag and request a "pow-wow," but now that he could establish the fact than an Indian begun hostilities, he was under no obligations to wait longer for peaceful overtures from them to satisfy the demands of the weak-kneed sentimentalists of the East.

When the Cheyennes were almost in rifle-shot they were outflanking us both right and left. Our right was moving along the bank of the river. A large party of the Indians had crossed the river, and, after passing our right, was about to recross and come on our pack-train in the rear. They were also turning our left, all the while keeping up that infernal yelling. Noticing that the Cheyennes were turning our left, the colonel

---

[27] David Sloan Stanley, of Ohio, was a graduate from the U.S. Military Academy in 1848. He became a 1st Lt. in the 1st Cavalry in 1855. He served with distinction in the Union Army and died March 13, 1902.

ordered Captain Beall (the left company) to deploy
his company to the left and head them off. He seemed
to have determined to offset the disparity of numbers
by a bold dash that would create a panic in the enemy's
ranks, and roared out, "Sling – carbine!" then immediately, "Draw – saber!" and we knew the old man was
going to try a saber charge on them.

I noticed with some surprise that when the command
"Draw – saber" was given (which I then thought was
a serious mistake in the colonel) and our three hundred
bright blades flashed out of their scabbards, the Cheyennes, who were coming on at a lope, checked up. The
sight of so much cold steel seemed to cool their ardor.
The party that had started to cross the river after
passing our right also hesitated, and Captain Beall,
with his company deployed to the left, easily turned
back those that were turning our left flank. I then said
to myself, "I guess 'Old Bull' knows what he is doing,
after all; he knows the Indians will not stand a saber
charge." And so it proved.[28]

At their first checking of speed, a fine-looking warrior
mounted on a spirited horse, probably their chief,
dashed up and down in front of their line, with the tail
of his war-bonnet, flowing behind, brandishing his
lance, shouting to his warriors, and gesticulating wildly,
evidently urging his men to stand their ground, when
he saw symptoms of a panic among them. Many of us
found time to admire his superb horsemanship, for he
so presented a splendid sight as he wheeled his horse,
charging back and forth, twirling the long lance over
his head now and then.

The Indians had almost ceased their yelling, had

---

[28] For an explanation of the Indian reaction to the sabre charge, see above,
in the report of Indian Agent Miller.

slowed down almost to a walk and were wavering. We had kept a steady trot, but now came the command in the well-known roar of "Old Bull," "Gallop – march!" and then immediately "CHARGE!" and with a wild yell we brought our sabers to a "tierce point" and dashed at them.

All their chief's fiery pleading could not hold them then, for every redskin seemed suddenly to remember that he had urgent business in the other direction, but as they wheeled to run they sent a shower of arrows toward us, by way of a "parting shot" as it were. Few of the missiles, however, took effect. They scattered as they ran, some going to the north, some east, but by far the greater number struck across the river and went south; and these, as we afterwards discovered, were heading for their village, which was about fifteen miles south of the Solomon, on the next creek.

Our men, of course, became much scattered in following them, fighting occasionally, when a party of the Indians could be overtaken and brought to bay, but their horses were fresh and well rested, while ours were jaded. It was a running fight, mostly a chase, for about seven miles, when the colonel had "recall" sounded, calling us back to the Solomon where the fight began. Our pack-mules had been ordered halted there when the charge was made to await the result.

It was estimated that about thirty Cheyennes were killed, though they were scattered over the country so far and wide that it was almost impossible to count the dead correctly. If it had not been for the fact that a number of their horses had stuck in the quicksands while crossing the river, we would have got but few of them. Some ten or twelve Indians who had been compelled to abandon their mired horses in the river, and who had reached the further side afoot, were soon overtaken and killed on the slope of the hill after crossing. They fought like devils as long as there was breath in them, never seeming to entertain the idea of surrendering, for they generally believed that if taken alive they would be tortured to death the same as they would have served us if taken prisoner by them. It was here on the slope of the hill, after crossing the river, that most of their casualties occurred. Quite a number of the dismounted Indians escaped by being taken up behind others of their comrades who had got through with their horses, but many of these were overtaken on account of the double load.

Besides the dread of torture, Indians consider it a great disgrace to surrender while yet able to fight. As a rare instance of disregard of this rule, one strapping big Cheyenne, who had lost his horse, but was not wounded at all, surrendered to a party of our men, without offering any resistance, seeing that there was no chance of escape.

When I got back to the Solomon River, after the "recall" had been sounded, I found the colonel establishing camp on the south bank, about opposite the ground where we made the charge. The three companies of the Sixth infantry and Lieutenant Bayard's battery were just crossing the river, coming into camp, all cursing their luck at being left behind. The hospital tent-fly had been hastily put up to shelter the wounded from the hot sun, and I went there immediately after finding my company's camp and unsaddling and picketing out my horse, anxious to learn who had been killed or wounded. At the corner of the hospital tent my attention was first drawn to two still forms, side by side, covered by a saddle-blanket, and on turning back to the blanket I was shocked to meet the dead face of an intimate comrade, Private George Cade, of G company, and alongside of him Private Lynch of A company. A small hole in Cade's breast, over the heart, showed where a Cheyenne's arrow had gone through him, which must have killed him instantly.

Lynch had been shot several times with arrows and twice with his own pistol, and a cut around the edge of his hair, with the edge of the scalp turned back, showed that the Indians had also attempted to scalp him. He had been detailed to lead his company's pack-mules for the day, and so was occupied just before we came into line to make the charge. Seeing his first sergeant passing near, Lynch called to him to ask if he couldn't send another man to relieve him, as he wanted to go into the fight. The sergeant replied: "No time for any change now, Lynch; you'll have to stay and hold the mules," and then rode on to join his company. Just then the charge was ordered. Lynch was heard to exclaim, indignantly; "Hold hell in a fight! Does he suppose I've come all this way out in the wilderness to hold pack-mules when there's a fight going on?" And with that he dropped his leading strap, drew his saber and charged with his company. After crossing the river, Lynch's horse – a fiery, hard-mouthed thing – took the bit in his teeth and ran away with him, outrunning his company, overtaking a party of the Indians who shot him with arrows until he fell off his horse; then, halting and dismounting quickly, they drew Lynch's pistol out of its scabbard, shot him twice with it, and one Cheyenne had boldly begun scalping him when our men overtook them and killed several near where he lay. His revolver was found in the hand of one of the dead Indians, but his horse had continued running with the fleeing Cheyennes, and we never saw it again.

Cade and Lynch were all the killed, but under the tent-fly were twelve wounded. Among the number, First-lieut. James Elwell Brown Stuart had received a pistol ball in the shoulder from an unhorsed Cheyenne whose life Stuart was trying to save; it is possible that the Indian had misunderstood his intentions. None of the wounded was mortally hurt. One of the most seriously injured was Private Cook, of G company, who had had an arrow through his breast, very similar to the wound that killed Cade, but, though spitting blood occasionally, Cook seemed determined not to die, and finally recovered and served out his time a hearty man. The wounded were being attended to as well as could be under the circumstances, and Colonel Sumner was circulating among them, examining their condition, speaking cheerfully to each, and giving directions for making them more comfortable.

It was estimated that there were about 900 or 1000 of the Cheyenne warriors. If Colonel Sumner had known that we were almost in sight of their village when he gave up the pursuit, it is probable that he would have gathered his men and followed them right on, but we did not discover that their camp was so near in time to take advantage of the opportunity to inflict further punishment on them. The fact was we were all pretty well tuckered out, as were our horses, also; and probably our Delaware scouts were in a similar condition, and, on that account, had failed to penetrate the country far enough in advance to detect the Cheyenne village.

Old Fall Leaf and his Delawares went into the fight with us, and did good service, but the cowardly Pawnees, that Colonel Sumner had brought with him from Fort Kearney, only followed in our wake, scalping the dead Cheyennes, and gathering up their abandoned ponies, of which they had collected about sixty head, which the colonel agreed to let them keep as part pay for their services.

As I have before mentioned, some of our men had taken one Cheyenne prisoner. On hearing of this, after the fight, the Pawnees went in a body to Sumner's headquarters and tried to buy the prisoner off him, in order to have a grand scalp-dance over him, and put him to death by torture, offering to surrender to the colonel the sixty captured ponies, and also to forfeit the money that was to be paid them on their return to Fort Kearney, if he would only give them that Cheyenne, and they seemed fairly wild with a fiendish desire to get him into their possession. Of course, the old man would not listen to any such a barbarous proposition, and promptly ordered them back to their own camp, on the outskirts of ours. They went away, very angry at his refusal. The "Old Bull" was so disgusted with the conduct of the sulking Pawnees this day that he immediately discharged them, and they started next morning back to their village, near Fort Kearney.

I have always felt sorry that we could not have managed some way to turn that Cheyenne over to the Pawnees, in order that I might have been enabled, by witnessing the "hop," to write a description of the ceremony, for few white men have seen such affairs and lived to tell it; and in such matters I have always felt that I would sooner that an Indian was given the "post of honor."

We had probably been a little improvident with our rations on this trip, at least in my mess, for, although this was only the sixteenth day since we left our train, we ate the last of our twenty days' rations this day. It began to look like hungry times ahead. We had been driving a small herd of Texas steers along, from which to draw our fresh meat, but now, for fear we would soon exhaust that supply, Colonel Sumner thought best to cut down our allowance of beef from one and one-fourth pounds a day to the man, which is the full ration, to three-fourths of a pound.

From the place where we had left our supply train, at the mouth of Crow Creek, on the north side of the South Platte, to the battle-ground on Solomon Fork, we had been traveling about southeast. After the fight, we followed the Cheyennes' trail nearly due south, or a little east of south, coming out on to the Santa Fe road and Arkansas River, on the 9th of August, at old Fort Atkinson; not seeing a buffalo or any other game, except an occasional coyote, in the whole distance.

On leaving our train, Colonel Sumner had directed his chief wagonmaster, P. G. Lowe, to take the outfit back to Fort Laramie, load up with commissaries and grain, return to the South Platte, and wait about the Salt Lake crossing until he heard from us, or until we joined the train there. Lowe performed his part all right, but we failed to connect with him, much to our regret; for the colonel had been disappointed in not getting to give the Cheyennes such a chastisement as he had wished to, and still hoped to be able to overtake them and give them another drubbing; and accordingly decided to make the effort to catch them again, even with the prospect of having to subsist on our pack-mules and horses.

As we had but one ambulance, that would not hold half of them, and, with no other means of transporting our wounded, Sumner determined to leave one company of infantry here on the Solomon, to take care of them until they were able to travel, and then they were to make their way to Fort Kearney.

Capt. Rensselaer W. Foote, with his company of the Sixth infantry, was detailed to perform this service; and to prepare them to defend themselves against a possible attack of a returning party of Cheyennes, we turned to and threw up a sod-and-dirt wall about five feet high, enclosing a square plot of probably about fifty feet each way – large enough to contain the little garrison and their animals.

Next forenoon, after burying the dead, and leaving Captain Foote's party a dozen head of beef cattle, as their share of the remaining subsistence, we saddled up, about ten o'clock, and resumed the Cheyenne trail southward; and about the middle of the afternoon, at the distance of about fifteen miles from the Solomon, we were much surprised to see the Cheyenne village looming up before us, lodges all standing; but our scouts soon brought back word that the enemy had vamoosed, and in such a panic, too, that they had left their lodges and a great deal of their other property; apparently having rushed off with what few things the squaws could hastily pack up, as the defeated and demoralized warriors had come rushing back after the fight, supposing that we were following right on their heels.

We were soon riding through the deserted village, in which we found no living thing, except a few female dogs with fresh litters of pups. The evidence of the Indians' wild panic was to be seen everywhere; buffalo robes, blankets, skins of many kinds, dressed, half-dressed, and undressed, bead-worked leggings and moccasins – in fact all sorts of "Injun fixin's" were scattered about in wild confusion. It is a custom with them for a warrior to stick a slim rod in the ground, in front of his lodge, on which he strings the scalps he has taken. We found a number of these standing untouched – a plain indication of the extremity of their fright and wild rush to escape us; for the occasion must be one of the greatest urgency when they will abandon these trophies.

Their camp was well located in a horse-shoe bend of a little creek, having some few trees and bushes along its banks. Our men helped themselves to such of the Indian property as they could make use of or take along; but our transportation facilities were too limited to admit of carrying off anything but necessities. Many of the men supplied themselves with leggings and moccasins, which soon became useful, for we were getting very ragged already, and before we again got in reach of a supply of clothing, many of us had but little more to wear than an Indian in his "gee-string." The most valuable thing we found in the village was a lot of dried buffalo meat packed up in *parfleche* cases (receptacles made of half-dressed rawhide, patterned like huge letter envelopes), convenient packages for transportation on pack animals. We gladly appropriated this buffalo meat, but found nothing else in the way of food. After selecting such stuff as we could make use of we pulled down their lodges and made bonfires of everything left in the camp, and established our camp for the night in an adjoining bend of the creek.

I have an unpleasant remembrance of our experience for the next twenty-three days after the battle; of our long exhaustive marches in the hottest and driest part of the season, and almost at the point of starvation. Our miserable pittance of three-fourths of a pound of fresh beef to the man, of the poorest quality, issued each afternoon after camping (and in a day or so after the fight we hadn't a bit of anything else in the way of food, not even a grain of salt), was sometimes eked out by using the meat of a horse or mule that chanced to give out and would be shot to prevent its falling into the hands of the enemy.

We found frequently along the trail freshly made graves, showing that a number of the Cheyennes had succumbed from their wounds after the fight. It soon became evident that there was little prospect of our catching them again, for the trail showed that several parties had split off from the main body since leaving their village; and by the time we reached the Arkansas River the band we were following was small, and well in the lead of us.

On account of its historical interest I have been anxious definitely to locate our battle ground on Solomon Fork, and had hoped that the finding of the remains of our little breastwork by some of the early settlers who went into that country after the Civil War, might be the means of establishing its exact location. In 1901 I published, in the *National Tribune,* of Washington, D.C., the narrative of my five years' soldiering on the frontier, including an account of the Cheyenne expedition, and hoped that it might attract the attention of some pioneer of northwestern Kansas who might have noticed the traces of our old sod corral, and would tell us about it; but not a word has ever been heard of it. I have since corresponded with several parties whom I thought might be able to give me the desired information, but have found no one who knew or ever heard anything about it.

It has been suggested that we may have been mistaken, and that the fight was on some other stream, and not the Solomon; but I have always felt confident that it was the main Solomon – the south fork – and never heard any question raised as to its being that river; all our officers and guides seemed satisfied on that point.

Besides our Delawares we had a competent guide in a white man (whose name I have forgotten), who lived near Fort Riley, and he said that he recognized the locality of our battle-ground, for he had previously been out there with a party on a hunting trip, on which occasion he had followed the Solomon up from its mouth on the Smoky Hill. The river at the battle-ground is a broad, shallow stream, without timber, except the few scattering cottonwoods before mentioned, where the Cheyennes had been waiting for us, and it contained numerous visible sandbars and invisible quicksands.

I have understood that some settlements were made in that country as early as 1867, ten years after our sod-walled corral was built. It seems hardly possible that in that time our breastwork should have been so completely obliterated as to leave no trace. Even if leveled, it should still show an outline that would attract the attention of the first comers into that country, and excite their curiosity as to how, when and for what purpose it had been built and used.

On reaching the Arkansas, Colonel Sumner sent Major Sedgwick, with his four companies of cavalry, to follow the Cheyenne trail – which now turned westward up the river – as far as Bent's Fort (with little hope of catching them, however), and at that post to take possession of anything in the way of rations that he could find among the goods sent out by the government to be distributed to the Indians as annuities. The colonel also immediately dispatched an express-rider into Fort Riley for a train-load of supplies, to be hurried out to us at the Big Bend, to which point he moved with the rest of the command, and remained there till we rejoined him from Bent's Fort.

At Bent's Major Sedgwick got some hardtack, bacon,

sugar, coffee and salt from Maj. A. B. Miller,[29] the Indian agent; and we did not have to eat any more pack-mule steak or dead-horse stew during the season. As we had no tents or bedding, and the weather had turned rainy and chilly, we suffered considerable discomfort from this source, partially alleviated in a few individual cases by the assistance of some Indian blankets that Sedgwick appropriated and issued to us, but which had been intended for the Cheyennes, provided they had come in and promised to be good. We were sadly in need of clothing, too, many of us being nearly naked, but there was nothing among the Indian goods that would supply this want. We heard at Bent's that a party of the Cheyennes had passed there, still on the run, making for the mountains, all broken up and badly demoralized.

On our return down the river to rejoin Colonel Sumner, at a place called Grand Saline, on the bank of the Arkansas, we were nearly surrounded by a swarm of Indians, Kiowas and Comanches, who tried to provoke us to hostilities, and seemed to be fairly spoiling for a fight. Their two villages were on the move, on the opposite side of the river, *en route* to Bent's to receive their annuities from the Indian agent, but evidently thought this was too good a chance to wipe out a few of Uncle Sam's soldiers to let slip, and were willing and anxious to do it, though living under the solemn obligations of a treaty of peace with the government.

Want of space forbids my giving details of this affair, as also many incidents of the fight on the Solomon; but, as a historical fact, I feel compelled to state that, here again Major Sedgwick showed a want of nerve, as he did at several other times and places of danger while I

---

[29] See his report, Section A.

served under his command. On this occasion he seemed to be perfectly helpless, and eagerly turned over the command to my captain, Sam D. Sturgis, who, by promptness and pluck, bluffed the Indians off and saved us from a probable massacre. It is an unpleasant thing to do – and I know it will be unpleasantly received by the public – to make a statement as a historical fact that casts an aspersion on the valor of one who has subsequently gained fame and gone into history as one of the heroes of the Civil War; but I am one of those cranks who believe that history should be strictly true, no matter whose corns are trodden on; and during the five years that I served with Sedgwick on the frontier, on every occasion where we were threatened with great danger he plainly showed – a lamentable lack of nerve. My old comrades who were there know this to be so.

When we reached Colonel Sumner's command, at the Big Bend, we found that a few teams, loaded with plenty of rations and forage, but with a scant supply of clothing and blankets, had just reached him from Fort Leavenworth, instead of Fort Riley. The messenger (or express rider, as we called them then) who had been sent on this errand was big Nick Berry, one of P. G. Lowe's wagon-masters, who had been serving in the capacity of chief of packers for our command. On arriving at Fort Riley, Berry had found that the supplies we required were not to be had there; so procuring a fresh horse at Riley he rode on to Leavenworth, 130 miles, in twenty-four hours; but his horse dropped dead at Salt Creek, within three miles of Fort Leavenworth, and Nick "hiked" the three last miles, carrying his saddle and bridle. He then quickly loaded up those teams and hurried back to Sumner with the much-needed supplies. After reaching the buffalo range

Colonel Sumner's party had had an abundance of meat, but nothing else to eat till the arrival of Berry's teams.

A passing Santa Fe mail had brought the colonel an order from the war department to send his command across the country to Fort Kearney, there to join the forces of Bvt. Brig. Gen. Albert Sidney Johnston, *en route* to Utah to put down Brigham Young's rebellion, and for Sumner himself to report for other duty at Fort Leavenworth.

The evening after our arrival at Sumner's camp an "undress parade" was ordered, and it came about as near filling the bill in regard to the "undress" part as often occurs; for we had not yet received the little bit of clothing that had come with our other supplies, and many of the men were nearly as lightly clad as Indians. For instance, our dandy, Sergeant-Major Arlington, the dude of the regiment, who was usually most fastidious in dress – a fine-looking soldier and proud of it – now performed his duties forming the battalion attired in a pair of moccasins, Indian leggings over a pair of dirty drawers, no trousers, an old cut-off stable frock for shirt, no jacket, and a bandanna handkerchief tied about his head in lieu of a hat; and this had been his best and only suit since we burned the Cheyenne village. Many of our men were in as bad or worse fix for clothing.

On parade the adjutant read an order from the colonel, highly commending his men for their proven pluck, prompt and cheerful obedience and patient endurance of great hardships, and saying that, ragged though we were, he was proud of us. Then came the unwelcome order transferring the command to Major Sedgwick, and directing him to proceed with it across the country to Fort Kearney and there report to Gen. A. S. Johnston for the Utah expedition.

In the morning, when we were mounted in line, before making the start to Kearney, "Old Bull o' the Woods" rode out in front of us to have a parting word with his men. He never called us "boys," nor would he tolerate any one else addressing us by such a puerile title; for he always insisted that there were no boys in his regiment – they were all MEN, and manly men, too.

"My men," he said, in that stentorian voice that could be heard all along the line, "I am truly sorry to see you start on such a trip so unprepared, but like the true soldiers that you are, I know you will obey the order cheerfully and promptly, disagreeable as it is. The War Department is not aware of our worn-out condition, or, I am confident, this order never would have been issued. I think I can safely promise you, however, that you will not have to go farther than Fort Kearney, for I shall hurry in to Fort Leavenworth and acquaint the department with the true condition of my men and horses; and by the time you reach Kearney I am positive you will find an order there sending you back to Riley or Leavenworth to winter and recuperate. Till then, good-by, my men, and God bless you!" We felt like cheering the old colonel, but rigid military rules forbid all such hilarious demonstrations, and we knew he would not be pleased with anything that savored of lax discipline. Taking our Delawares with him, and a small mounted escort, he started down the Santa Fe road, while we moved out north across the trackless prairie for Fort Kearney.

Crossing the country here, from the Big Bend to Kearney, we found it a pleasing contrast to what it had been on the Cheyenne trail, about a hundred miles west of this route. There we had an arid desert, almost, with water and grass poor and scarce, no timber, no game. Here we find numerous streams of good water;

plenty of good grass; nearly all the watercourses timbered; and we are in the heart of the buffalo range, with an abundance of other game. Although the weather had turned somewhat rainy, we had no tents, and were still short of clothing and blankets – for the little we had received from Leavenworth was not enough to go half-way around – yet we enjoyed this trip, and, compared to the Cheyenne chase, it was a picnic. Some of the men had contracted scurvy, from our enforced protracted meat diet, but we found plenty of wild plums and grapes – excellent anti-scorbutics – at nearly every creek, and a free use of the fruit soon cured them.

We struck the old Salt Lake road two or three days' marches southeast of Kearney, at a place on the Little Blue called Fremont's Orchard, and there met Gen. Albert S. Johnston, with his staff and an escort of the Second dragoons, en route to Kearney, to overtake his command which had been rendezvousing there. General Johnston halted a little while, to talk with our officers, and then hurried on, while we followed on more leisurely.

When within a day's march of the fort we found that the "old Bull o' the Woods" had fulfilled his promise, for we were then met by our company teams, coming from Kearney, and the "sick, lame and lazy" of our command whom we had left with P. G. Lowe's train up on the South Platte, when we started with the pack-mules; and these men brought with them an order, which General Johnston had found awaiting him at Kearney, for us to return to Fort Leavenworth. General Johnston, however, appropriated the rest of Lowe's train and took it on to Utah.

We were not to go directly to Leavenworth, either, for the order was accompanied by another directing

Major Sedgwick, on arriving at Marysville, on the Big Blue, which was then the farthest town west on this road, to scatter his command, sending a single company here and there to several different points mentioned, for another election was about to be held in Kansas, and we were to umpire the game, and after the election all were to proceed to Fort Leavenworth. Right glad we were to take the back track for the settlements, every fellow promising himself all sorts of a good time, to make amends for our hardships, when we got back into "God's country," and had an interview with the pay-master, Major James Longstreet (afterwards a rebel general), for it was now the middle of October, and in a few days more we would have six months' pay coming to us.

After dispersing his command from Marysville, as ordered, Sedgwick, who had been messing with our company officers all summer, accompanied us (Captain Sturgis's company) to Atchison, where we lay several days, when, the election having passed off quietly, we moved on in to the fort. From our stragglers who joined us with the company teams near Fort Kearney, we heard, for the first time, from Captain Foote's little command, whom we had left in the sod corral on the Solomon taking care of the wounded after the fight with the Cheyennes.

Next day after we left Foote a party of about a hundred Cheyennes had returned and made an attack on his party, but finding them well protected behind their sod walls the Indians succeeded in doing no other damage but to drive off the garrison's beef cattle, and then withdrew and were seen no more. The loss of their beeves was a serious blow to the little command, however, and as they then had nothing left to eat but their pack-mules, and these would be needed for transporting the wounded, Foote was compelled to evacuate the works and strike out east for the buffalo range, which he did the next day after the loss of his cattle. Fortunately the Indians did not learn of the dilemma in which they had placed Foote, and probably immediately left the locality to try to rejoin their own much-scattered people.

Captain Foote now had a perplexing task to march to Fort Kearney and carry a dozen wounded men, with such poor facilities for transporting them; but he had an efficient assistant in Jeb Stuart, for, though the lieutenant was one of the wounded, having his left arm disabled from a bullet in the shoulder, he was still worth a half-dozen ordinary men; for Jeb was always prolific of expedients for working his way out of difficult, or embarrassing situations. Next to having no rations, the most serious problem confronting Foote was how to carry so many wounded men with only one small ambulance that would not hold half of them. Some of the men had found a few old lodge-poles along the river bank, and Stuart soon had some improvised stretchers made of them by fastening a piece of stout canvas – pack-covers – across the center of each two poles, then hitching a pack-mule – one before and one behind – between the ends of the poles, which were lashed to the pack-saddles – the front mule's tail to the wounded man and the rear one's head – with a man to walk alongside and lead each mule carefully, a very comfortable litter was formed.

For a couple of days the little command suffered some from the heat and want of water, as well as for rations, as they made their tedious way across the prairie in the supposed direction of Fort Kearney; but after they got into the buffalo range they all had plenty of meat, at least, and finally reached the fort without the loss of a man or mule; and also brought the Cheyenne prisoner along with them.

It will be remembered that Lowe, with our big train, had gone back to Fort Laramie after supplies, and then returned to the South Platte near the old Salt Lake crossing, to await some word from Sumner. Our men who had been with this train informed us – and a recent letter from Mr. Lowe corroborates their statement – that while camped on the Platte, on the evening of the next day after we had the fight on the Solomon (30th of July), they not having heard anything from us, did not of course know where we were, or that we had had a fight; on that evening about sunset three Cheyenne warriors rode into Lowe's camp to beg something to eat, mistaking the train for a citizens' freighting outfit. Two of these Indians were made prisoners by the trainmen, the third escaped.

The strange part of this incident is that these Cheyenne prisoners informed the trainmen, through an interpreter, that they had been in the fight with us at noon the day before (the 29th), and that the Cheyennes had been whipped and scattered in every direction; describing our command, and giving such other testimony as to leave no doubt in the minds of Lowe and others as to these Indians having been in the engagement.

Making a careful and conservative estimate of the average length of our day's marches for the sixteen days we had been on the trail, up to the time of the fight; of the general southeast course we had been traveling, and the estimated location of the battle – which, after a careful scanning of the latest maps of Kansas, I would place on the main or south fork of Solomon River, somewhere in the present county of Sheridan – we must have been, at the time of the engagement, at least 150 miles from Lowe's camp, on the South Platte.

It seems almost incredible that those three Cheyenne warriors had ridden their ponies that distance, without change, in thirty-six hours, but I think it is possible, for those Indian ponies have great powers of endurance, and we know that it was customary for a warrior to select his very best and fleetest horse to ride in battle, and we had evidence that the Cheyennes' horses were fresh and well-rested on going into the fight. The two Cheyenne prisoners captured by the trainmen, and the one taken in the fight, were all put in the guard-house at Kearney, but shortly afterward they succeeded in digging their way out of the old 'dobe one night, and made good their escape.

D: SUBSEQUENT DEPREDATIONS OF CHEYENNES

1. REPORT OF LIEUTENANT E. G. MARSHALL [1]

HEAD QUARTERS, FORT KEARNY N.T.

August 2nd, 1857

SIR: I have the honor to state that two Herds of Beef cattle destined for Salt Lake for Beef for the Utah Expedition passed this Post yesterday. The whole number of men all told was nineteen. When they arrived today about 28 miles west of this Garrison they were attacked by a Party of about 150 Cheyenne Indians, who run off all the cattle (824,) and horses and mules (20 in number) excepting two which the Drover succeeded in escaping with. The attack was made about 11 o'clock this morning, and the whites lost one man, who was killed on the ground, and one who was badly wounded in the thigh,[2] with a fracture of the bone, who is now under charge of the Surgeon of the Post. The whites arrived here about 9 o'clock this evening in a very destitute condition having lost every thing but the clothing they happened to have on and their arms. I shall send a party tomorrow with the Drovers, to bury the man who was killed and also to try to find some of the cattle. But the men report that they believe they will not be able to find any of them, as the last they saw of the cattle they were being driven off by the Indians,

---

[1] Found in the National Archives in Washington, A.G.O., Letters Received, 1857, 489 M.

[2] A Mr. Sanborn was killed and Mr. Robb wounded. For a fuller description see Morehead's account in Section D, 6.

who were all the time shooting them with arrows, and lancing them with their spears.

The whites report that without doubt they must have killed at least two Indians and wounded some four or five others.

Allow me again to state that an Infantry Post in this country is entirely useless, that depredations are continually perpetrated by hostile Indians near this Garrison without ever being able to even assist those who are so unfortunate as to be attacked by them.

I am, Sir: Very Respectfully   Your Obt. Servt.

E. G. MARSHALL

1st Lt 6th Inf   Comdg

COLONEL S. COOPER
Adjutant General   U.S. Army Washington (D.C.)

---

2. SECOND REPORT OF LIEUTENANT MARSHALL [3]

HEAD QUARTERS, FORT KEARNY, N.T.

August 4th, 1857

SIR: The detachment which started yesterday to pick up the Beef cattle, which were being driven to Salt Lake for Utah Expedition, has this moment returned. They have succeeded in recovering but *43* head out of the 824. I sent a few Pawnee Indians with the detachment, and they as well as my Party report that the Indians have driven the cattle directly south, in the direction of the Pawnee Republican Fork. They also rifled the wagons of every thing. My party buried the man, (Wm. Sandburn), who was killed. When found he was entirely stripped of his clothing, scalped and the Indians had cut open his privates. He was shot evidently through the heart, and after being dead, some Indians must have counted his "coup," as he was pierced by a

---

[3] A.G.O., Letters Received, 1857, 500 M.

spear. From the clothing, trappings, &c., which was brought in I have no hesitation in saying the Indians belong to the Cheyenne Nation. I have sent a message to all persons of this Post who may be on the road, warning them of the danger in travelling in this country. Also to pick up any stray cattle they may find and then bring them in to this Post or to Fort Leavenworth, when they will be properly remunerated.

The Pawnee nation, now encamped near this Post, will leave tomorrow to hunt Buffalo on the Headwaters of the Little Blue, south of the Garrison. I have directed them to scour the country for the lost cattle and if they should find any, to return them to this Post. There is a large amount of condemned Provisions now here, which are not saleable, which will remunerate them for their trouble. But my impression is, that there is a large village of the Cheyenne Indians not very far from this Garrison, in a south easterly direction, and they have driven the cattle to their village. From thence they can send Parties in all directions to watch the road, and commit depredations. Also are in a fine position to retreat in any direction.

I am, Sir   Very Respectfully   Your Obdt. Servt.

E. G. MARSHALL
1st Lt 6th Inf comdg

COLONEL S. COOPER
Adjutant General U.S. Army, Washington, (D.C.)

---

3.   GENERAL HARNEY'S RESPONSE [4]

HEAD QUARTERS, ARMY FOR UTAH
Fort Leavenworth, August 8, 1857

COLONEL: I have the honor to enclose a copy of a communication from Lieutenant Marshall, 6th Infan-

---

[4] Ibid., 85 H.

try, reporting the loss of (824) head of cattle, en route for Utah, for the use of the Army – This mischief was done by the Cheyenne Indians, and is but the commencement to a series of disasters which will take place upon that route, if a suitable cavalry force is not placed at both Forts Kearney & Laramie.

Infantry is useless against mounted Indians – I shall retain the two companies of the 2nd Dragoons at Fort Laramie, and have to request the General-in-chief will cause the two companies of the 1st Cavalry, ordered to this Post under Colonel Sumner, to be stopped at Fort Kearney, to furnish escorts from that place, as I have no disposable mounted force at my command for this service.

I am, Colonel, Very respectfully, Your Ob't Serv't
WM. S. HARNEY
Colonel 2n Dragoons, & Brt. Brig. General
Commanding
LIEUT. COLONEL S. THOMAS
Assistant Adjutant General   Head Quarters of the Army   West Point, N.Y.

[Entered in red ink, on back of letter, is the following by Gen. Winfield Scott, Commander of the Army.]

The loss of those herds of beef cattle seems the result of some grave blunder. They were in advance of all the troops; passing thro' a country infested with hostile Indians, & yet without any military guard for protection! It is hoped that the lost cattle were not deemed indispensable to the success of the expedition or that the general commanding may be able to supply the loss. The only measure he seems to have taken, consequent on the loss, is the *Circular* of the same date as the within – directing that commanders, *in future,* shall "give such protection as may be necessary, to the supply trains."

Respectfully submitted to the Sec. of War.
WINFIELD SCOTT,
August 18, 1857

4. GENERAL SCOTT'S ORDERS REGARDING BEEF CATTLE [5]

HEAD-QUARTERS OF THE ARMY

West Point, N.Y. August 19, 1857

SIR: In forwarding, yesterday, the communication of General Harney respecting the loss of a large number of beef cattle for the Utah Expedition – on which paper I endorsed my remarks – I omitted to refer you to my instructions issued June 29th, to the Commander of that Expedition.

I now beg your attention to the extract, given below, from my letter, of that date, to General Harney, from which it will be seen that the loss in question has resulted from a neglect of my orders in the case.

(EXTRACT) A small, but sufficient, force must, however, move separately from the main column, guarding the beef cattle and such other supplies as you may think would too much encumber the march of the main body. The cattle may require to be marched more slowly than the troops, so as to arrive in Salt Lake Valley in good condition, or they may not survive the inclemency or scanty sustenance of the winter.

This detachment, though afterwards to become the rear guard, may, it is hoped be put in route before the main body, to gain as much time as possible before the latter passes it.

I have the honor to be, With high respect, Your obt. servt.

WINFIELD SCOTT

HON. J. B. FLOYD,
Secretary of War.

---

[5] *Ibid.*, 253.

5.   HARNEY BLAMES SUMNER [6]

HEAD QUARTERS, ARMY FOR UTAH
Fort Leavenworth, August 22nd, 1857

COLONEL: I have the honor to enclose a copy of a communication from Colonel Sumner to the Commanding officer of Fort Kearney, reporting an affair with the Cheyenne Indians on the 29th ultimo near Solomon's Fork of the Kansas River.

Also, a copy of a communication from Lieutenant Marshall of the 6th Infantry Commanding Fort Kearney, reporting the loss, on the 2nd instant, of 824, head of beef cattle intended for the Army for Utah, in consequence of an attack of 150 Cheyenne Indians upon the party in charge.

Colonel Sumner's action took place some sixty or seventy miles south of Fort Kearney on the 29th of July – and the fact, that in four days after, 150 of these Indians attacked this cattle party within twenty-eight miles of Fort Kearney, shows they not only had no fear for their families from Colonel Sumner's Command, but that his action was not attended by any moral consequences. Colonel Sumner makes no mention of the number of killed & wounded of the Indians in his Engagement, which I judge to be small from the above facts & from private reports of the affair.

Colonel Sumner should have sent at least two companies of his mounted force, to Fort Kearney, immediately after his action, to protect the millions of both public and private property upon that road, which is without a single mounted soldier from this to Fort Laramie; as I have stated before, Infantry is useless to pursue mounted Indians.

---

[6] *Ibid.*, 343 H.

I am, Colonel, very respectfully,   Your Obt Sevt,
                                   WM S. HARNEY
Colonel 2nd Dragoons & Bvt. Brig. General,
                                   Commanding
LIEUT. COLONEL L. THOMAS,
Assistant Adjutant General   Hd. Quarters of
the Army,   West Point, New York

---

6.   C. R. MOREHEAD TELLS OF CHEYENNE DEPREDATIONS [7]

Early the next spring (1857) the Cheyenne Indians, a numerous and warlike tribe of the plains, went on the warpath, as did the Mormons. As shown by the report of the Secretary of War, for reasons given by him the Government determined to establish a military post in Salt Lake valley to protect emigration to California, which was on the increase, and the contractors for the transportation of army supplies were called upon for almost double the quantity of wagons and teams that had ever been necessary before. Consequently transportation had to be provided for – two regiments of infantry, six companies of cavalry and two batteries of artillery in addition to what had theretofore been required. So every available wagon, yoke of cattle and teamster was called for and were promptly provided by the transportation company.

Captain James Rupe, the most experienced plains-

---

[7] From "Personal Recollections of Charles R. Morehead," in W. E. Connelley, *Doniphan's Expedition and the Conquest of New Mexico and California* (Topeka, published by the author, 1907), 603-605. Mr. Morehead, born in Richmond, Missouri, in 1838, served for some years as a wagonmaster for the freighting firm of Russell, Majors, and Waddell. At Mr. Connelley's request, Mr. Morehead prepared a sketch of his career on the plains, which sketch Connelley printed in the appendix to his above-cited book.

man then to be had, was appointed general agent of the company, and myself as his assistant and clerk. Captain Rupe had been a soldier in Colonel Sterling Price's cavalry regiment of Missouri volunteers in the Mexican War, and since that time had been a conductor on the Santa Fe mail line, and also a wagonmaster from the time he left that service until the present. So his experience in the management of freight trains and Indian warfare was successful up to that time.

We left Fort Leavenworth about the first of May, 1857, in a two-mule spring wagon. Some of the trains and 800 head of loose beef cattle had preceded us, the company having contracted to furnish the army two thousand head of beef cattle in Utah, 800 head of which were driven on foot from the States and the balance after the work cattle were fattened after arrival in that territory.

We expected to overtake the beef cattle and travel with them through the Cheyenne country, or until we reached Fort Laramie, 640 miles out; but at Soldier Creek, this side of the Big Blue River, we overtook a train the teamsters of which had mutinied against the wagonmaster. We had to send back for another wagonmaster and settle the mutiny before we could go on, which required several days. We then resumed our journey, passing another train at Big Blue, and pressed on to overtake the beef cattle, when we heard the Cheyennes were infesting the country west of us.

At the point where we first struck the Little Blue our mules began to prick up their ears and act a little strange. Captain Rupe stopped to look around for the cause, when he discerned what appeared to be eight or ten Indians on the opposite side of the river among the

trees. He handed me the reins, took up his breech-
loading rifle and said:

"You turn around and drive as fast as you can; if
they pursue us I will hold them back."

As soon as we made this move the Indians broke for
a point up the river to find a crossing, the banks being
very steep opposite our position. By the time they got
over the river and on the road we were a considerable
distance ahead, and as soon as Rupe saw they were
gaining on us and that they were near enough for a
shot he opened fire on them. After five or six shots they
slackened up, returning the shots. We went on to the
train we had left behind us and remained with it that
night.

The next evening about dusk we left the train,
traveled all night and reached Fort Kearny about noon
the following day. The small band of Indians alluded
to were Cheyennes, scouting around to see what was on
the road.

At Fort Kearny we met a party of packers, ten in
number, from California, who told us they had met our
beef cattle between that post and Plum Creek; that
they had seen Indians popping their heads up from
behind the sandhills all the way down the Platte River,
and thought the cattle were in danger. So we waited
until dark and left to overtake the cattle. By the time
we got to the big bend of the Platte, where the road left
the river, it began to rain so hard that we had to stop.
It was not long before we discerned, by the vivid flashes
of lightning, a party of men and one mule with a rider
coming down the river-bank. We at once concluded that
it was our own men, which proved to be the case. They
told us the Indians had come down Plum Creek into

their camp, one at a time, and professed friendship and begged for something to eat, which was given them. After fifteen or twenty had assembled in camp, and while they were eating, a large band of Indians on horseback charged among the cattle and stampeded them. One of the Indians started to get into one of the wagons and a man named Sanborn resisted him, when the Indian stepped back and shot Sanborn dead. The Indians then retreated to a ravine close to the corral, from which they opened fire upon the other herders, numbering thirteen, who had by that time gathered about the wagons. The fight was kept up until the herders retreated to the river-bank. Sanborn was killed outright, and a man named Robb was shot through the thigh and severely wounded. The herders managed to get one mule, upon which they placed Robb, and he made the journey to a meeting with us. We then put Robb in the wagon with myself, and Captain Rupe got on the mule and led the way back to Fort Kearny, where we put Robb in the hospital under the care of the post surgeon. Robb afterward recovered and returned to Kentucky.

The following morning we applied to the captain commanding the post for an escort, to try to recover the lost cattle, as we had a right to do under the contract. We were informed that there were but fifty soldiers at the post, all infantry, and that the best he could do was to give us ten men and one six-mule team to carry them. We managed to get ten mules and ponies from the sutler and others about the post, and upon these mounted our men, who were provided with army muskets. We then started for the camp where the cattle were stampeded, under the direction of Captain Rupe. We found the body of poor Sanborn terribly mutilated, and we proceeded to bury it. While doing so Magraw's Pacific Wagon Road expedition passed us, and camped at or near Plum Creek. Some of his men stopped and viewed the remains and battle-ground, where were found evidences that several Indians had been wounded or killed. The wagons, minus the sheets, yokes, chains, medicine-chests and Bibles, were all that was left of the equipment.

We then started in the direction in which the cattle had been driven, their trail having been almost entirely obliterated by the previous night's rain-storm. After getting a short distance up in the sandhills we found, scattered about, sixty-five head of the cattle. The mounted men were ahead of the wagon carrying the soldiers and our wagon, in which were a young man named Doolittle and myself. When we were on a table-land, skirted by a long canon, suddenly there appeared coming down the canon, a band of mounted Indians, about one hundred and fifty in number, dashing toward us. The sergeant in charge ordered the men to dismount and tie the mules to the wheels, which was instantly done, myself and Doolittle following suit. A gun was fired to attract the attention of our mounted men, who soon came to us. Captain Rupe ordered all of us to repair to a side canon near by, and as soon as the Indians came within safe range all present (twenty-two in number) were ordered to fire at the line as we stood, our first man aiming at the head of the band, and so on down the line, which was done with good effect. The charge was checked, and by the time we were ready and delivered our second fire they were in flight. They did not locate us until after our first fire, and fired only a few shots in return. They left no

dead on the field, but it was believed that eight or ten of them were killed or mortally wounded.

We then gathered the cattle and returned to Fort Kearny. We left the men there to take care of the cattle until some company train should come along, and themselves to be returned to the States, unless they found other employment.

Captain Rupe and myself remained at the post that night and next day until nightfall, when we left for Fort Laramie. . .

---

7. LIEUTENANT MARSHALL REPORTS DEPREDATIONS ON PLATTE ROAD [8]

HEAD QUARTERS   FORT KEARNEY NT
September 12th, 1857

SIR: I have the honor to state that Mr. Russell a son of the Contractor for Government [9] has just arrived from Fort Laramie. He Reports, that one of the Contractors Trains was attacked near Ash Hollow by about 150 Cheyenne Indians: that (3) three whites (Teamsters) were Killed: and also the Indians took from one of the Wagons a lot of Government *Arms* and Ammunition. He also reports, that he being on his way to this Post was shot at by about 17 Cheyenne Indians near Plum Creek 36 miles west of this Garrison.

I am Sir   Very respectfully   Your obt. Sert.

E. G. MARSHALL

To   1st Lt 6th Inf   Comdg
COLONEL S. COOPER
Adjutant General   U.S.A.
Washington   D.C.

---

[8] A.G.O., Letters Received, 1857, 613 M.
[9] Son of William H. Russell, of Russell, Majors, and Waddell, freighters.

8. MARSHALL REPORTS CHEYENNE HOSTILITIES [10]

HEAD QUARTERS FORT KEARNEY   N.T.
September 15th 1857

SIR   I have the honor to state that the road west of this Post is lined with parties of Cheyenne Indians. They have become so bold as yesterday to come within one mile of this Garrison. The Report concerning the Attack upon one of the Government freight Trains, and the loss of three Teamsters, is confirmed. The Indians succeeded in running off about 50 head of cattle and seperating one wagon from the train: they rifled it of such Articles as they chose, including U.S. Arms and Ammunition. I am obliged to use the utmost vigilance in guarding the Herds, Hay, Parties &c at this Post. Allow me to state that it is my opinion that the *Cheyenne war* has only commenced, and the future will bring with it many depredations and murders committed by this hostile Tribe upon the Travellers on this route. This being a one Company Infantry Post, we can only remain on the defensive. There is no doubt the Indians are well aware of this, otherwise they would not be so bold as to make their appeerence so near. Two different Express men west of this, have been shot at and run by the Cheyenne Indians.

I am Sir   Very Respectfully   Your obt. Sert.

E. G. MARSHALL
1st Lt 6th Inft   Comdg

To ADJUTANT GENERAL   U.S.A.
Washington   D.C.

---

[10] A.G.O., Letters Received, 625 M.

II
Relations with the Plains Indians
1858 and 1859

Relations with the Plains Indians
1858 and 1859

INTRODUCTION

Colonel Sumner's disappointment at the breakup of his Cheyenne Expedition of 1857 was reported above. During the following winter he was back at Watertown, New York.[1] There he received orders for a General Court Martial trial, on charges transmitted by Gen. W. S. Harney.[2]

Apparently, he was cleared of the charges, for on March 26, 1858, at St. Louis he is under orders to join his regiment. At Fort Riley, on April 15, 1858, he reports that he has assumed command of the regiment.[3]

He set out on his campaign from the vicinity of Fort Kearny on July 23, 1858. His activities are described in the reports that follow, in Section A.

The discovery of gold in the Colorado region in 1858 led to the coming in of a considerable number of gold seekers and town founders in the fall of that year. The following spring saw a great gold rush, with the newcomers overrunning the country.[4] The Indians made no resistance at first, but their antipathies grew with the numbers in the emigrant tide.

---

[1] A.G.O., Letters Received, 1858, s 69, s 72.

[2] *Ibid.,* s 53 and s 76. Antipathy between Sumner and Harney had existed since Mexican War days. In 1855 Sumner had disobeyed orders from Harney, but he was upheld by the War Department.

[3] *Ibid.,* s 95, s 108, s 174.

[4] LeRoy R. and Ann W. Hafen, *The Colorado Story* (Denver, Old West Publishing Co., 1953).

There were no military campaigns against the Indians of the central high plains during 1859. Major Sedgwick and Lieutenant Stuart, who were to figure prominently in 1860, had extensive leaves of absence during 1859.[5]

During that year efforts were made toward negotiating treaties to induce the Indians to cede much of their land in return for annuities. The principal effort was that of Agent Twiss. His proposals are presented in documents below. But his suggested treaty, signed by the Indians, failed of acceptance in Washington.

Another peace effort was to be made the next year; also some military maneuvers. These will be discussed in Part III.

---

[5] Major Sedgwick obtained a leave of absence and was in Connecticut from May to Oct., 1859.– See A.G.O., Letters Received, 1859, S 202, S 248, S 319, S 351. Stuart also was given a leave, most of which he spent in Virginia and North Carolina, April to October.– A.G.O., Letters Received, 1859, S 53, S 166, S 201, S 232, S 237, S 317, S 319, S 345, S 393.

A: OPERATIONS OF 1858

1. SUMNER BEGINS HIS CAMPAIGN [6]

HEAD QUARTERS 1ST CAVALRY
Camp 9 miles from Fort Kearney,   July 22, 1858

SIR   In compliance with General Orders No. 17 from the Head Quarters of the Army, to which I have been referred by the Commanding Officer of the Utah Forces. I have the honor to report that I shall march from this Camp tomorrow. I shall leave the Platte river Seventeen miles above Fort Kearney; and proceed as directly as possible from that point to Old Fort Atkinson on the Arkansas, in which vicinity I hope to find the Kioways.[7] That tribe has been very troublesome for sometime past, and I hope to make such an impression upon them as to prevent them from Committing depredations in future.

I am Sir   Very Respectfully   Your Obt Servt:

E. V. SUMNER
Col 1 Cav. Comdg.

ASST: ADJT: GENERAL
Head Quarters of the Army   West Point   N.Y.

---

[6] A.G.O., Letters Received, 1858, s 326 and s 176.

[7] The Kiowas, usually associated with the Comanches at this time, ranged the country south of the Arkansas.

2. SUMNER REPORTS HIS OPERATIONS OF 1858 [8]

HEAD QUARTERS, 1ST CAVALRY
Saint Louis, Mo.   October 5, 1858

SIR: I have the honor to submit the following report. In compliance with General Orders No. 17, Head Quarters of the Army, and General Orders No. 7, Head Quarters, Utah Forces,– I left Fort Kearny with six companies of the 1st Cavalry on the 23rd of July, 1858, for an excursion through the Indian Country.– As my route was not pointed out, and the season was far advanced – I decided after due reflection, to open a wagon road from the Platte to the Arkansas, to remain some time on the latter river, in the heart of the Indian Country, and then to return to Fort Leavenworth by the Santa Fe road. I thought I should find those Indians on this route, that it was particularly desirable to meet, and it proved so. I met a party of Cheyennes, who were perfectly humble, and afterwards a considerable band of the Kiowas, with the principal chief of the nation (Little Mountain) at their head. I had several conferences with this man, and some of the sub chiefs and elders of this tribe, and they all assured me of their strong desire to remain at peace with the Whites, of which I have no doubt, as they are fully sensible of their own weakness. They have, however, a great deal of difficulty in restraining their turbulent young men. In all Indian towns, there is a set of vagabonds, as there is in our own towns, and these Indians having no moral restraint, or fear of the laws, it is next to impossible to keep them quiet – These restless men will go off in small parties under the pretext of hunting or the like, and commit depredations, not only without the sanction

---

[8] A.G.O., Letters Received, 1858, s 404.

of their Chiefs, but entirely without their Knowledge. These principal men pledged themselves to do all they could to keep these marauders in check.

I inclose a sketch of my route from the Platte to the Arkansas;[9] this road may be considered as the western limit of Kansas for all agricultural purposes, the country west of it, to the mountains, is only fit for pasturage, and hardly that – the country over which I passed is, by no means, an inviting one – the soil is not good, there is but little timber, and in common seasons, there would not be sufficient water – the grass is short, and mostly of the perennial kind.

I reached the Arkansas on the 14th of August, and left it on the 9th of September, arriving at Fort Riley on the 17th, and Fort Leavenworth on the 24th of September. I have the pleasure to report that my command, both men and horses returned in high order.

I would respectfully remark that the best position, and I believe the only one, to protect the Santa Fe road effectually, is the site of old Fort Atkinson.[10]– This point is above the two roads, and below the two crossings, and all travel to New Mexico must pass that point. – Besides this, the Indians congregate in large numbers, every summer in that vicinity, and if there are no troops there, travelers have no safety but in the forbearance of the Indians. The great objection to the site of this post, is the scarcity of wood, but this can hardly be considered insuperable, when wood can be got at the distance of twelve miles. I would respectfully and earnestly recommend the re-establishment of this post. I think it should be built of stone, which is found in

9 A map accompanies the document in the National Archives. It covers a route over plain country and is not especially important.

10 Near the present town of Fort Dodge, Kansas. For data on Fort Atkinson, see fn. 11, above, in I, A.

the vicinity, and for a garrison of four companies, two of horse and two of foot. This would seem to be one of the few points on the frontier, for a permanent post, for the country is so sterile on the Upper Arkansas, there will be no inducement to push settlements, in that direction for a long period.[11]

Very respectfully, Your obdt. servt.

E. V. SUMNER

Col 1 Cavlry   Comdg

THE ASSISTANT ADJUTANT GENERAL
Head Quarters of the Army   New York City.

---

3.   AGENT MILLER'S ANNUAL REPORT, 1858 [12]

BENT'S FORT, KANSAS TERRITORY

August 17, 1858

SIR: The following I respectfully submit as my annual report for the year 1858.

Leaving Leavenworth City on the 24th of June, I arrived at the Little Arkansas on the 10th of July, where I found Captain Bent,[13] with the train of Indian goods, water bound, who had only arrived a few hours previously, although he had preceded me from the States some ten or twelve days. At this point I found encamped a large body of Kansas Indians returning home from the villages of the Upper Arkansas Indians, which they informed me were at that time near the mouth of the Pawnee Fork. They had been on a visit to them for the purpose of exchanging presents and making peace – a yearly performance on their part;

---

[11] The gold discoveries beginning in 1858 and the subsequent settlement of the region discredited Sumner's appraisal.

[12] *Annual Report of the Commissioner of Indian Affairs, 1858,* pp. 96-100.

[13] William W. Bent of Bent's Fort. He had long been a trader on the upper Arkansas and had married into the Cheyenne tribe.

and the treaties entered into on these occasions (though provision is made for their continuance "as long as the waters flow and the grass grows upon the prairie") are violated as often. These Indians had been encamped at this point for several days, attracted to the spot by the loadstone of whiskey, dealt out to them by a creature bearing the face and form of man, who receives, in return for his vile stuff, the few ponies and robes they had obtained from the Indians of the Arkansas. Not being within the district of my agency I did not deem I had authority to interfere with him in his nefarious traffic. I however reported him to Agent Montgomery, at Council Grove, though doubtful whether he could act, as I am told that country belongs to the Pawnees. Since the settlement of Kansas Territory, many of these fellows may be found just upon the borders of the Indian country, cheating the Indians not only out of what little property they may possess, but life itself. There is no punishment too severe for such miscreants. Learning from the Kaws that the Comanches, Kiowas, and other Indians of my agency had been awaiting my coming for nearly a month, but being then in a starving condition would, no doubt, soon separate in search of buffalo; and being also informed that the five tribes, Comanches, Kiowas, Cheyennes, Arapahoes, and Apaches had assembled there for the purpose of proposing new treaties with the government, I was anxious to meet them all in full council. I therefore determined, so soon as the creek was passable, to hasten ahead of the trains for the purpose of detaining them until the arrival of their annuities. Securing the valuable services of Captain Bent, as interpreter, (my old interpreter, by reason of age and infirmities, was unable to accompany me on this visit to the Indians,) I proceeded two days in advance of the train. At Walnut creek, learning that the Cheyennes, Arapahoes, and Apaches, had several days previously parted with the others, awaiting myself the coming of the train, I despatched Captain Bent to overtake and bring them back to their recent camping ground. On my arrival at the mouth of Pawnee Fork, the morning of the 19th of July, I found all the Indians assembled, the captain having without difficulty succeeded in his mission. The Cheyennes and Arapahoes expressed much gratification on learning that they would not be compelled to return to Bent's Fort, the usual point of distribution to them for their presents. The village was situated on the green bank of the river, extending up and down as far as the eye could reach, numbering, perhaps, fifteen hundred lodges, whose snow white sides in giving back the light of the sun, together with the numerous horses grazing quietly upon hill and dale, covering the whole face of the prairie like "cattle upon a thousand hills," presented a sight well calculated to captivate the eye. The Indian in his simple ignorance, gazing upon such a scene, may well be pardoned his egotism in believing his people more than a match for the white man; for it is seldom you can find one who is not fully satisfied of their superiority. Having no adequate knowledge of the extent of our possessions, or the number of our people, and meeting only year after year the same faces of those trading with New Mexico, they naturally fall into the belief that we are few in number. Besides, the few forts that have been heretofore established in their midst, garrisoned as they generally have been by scarcely a full company of infantry, wholly unsuited to cope with the Indians, who coming down upon their fleet prairie horses depredate, in full view of the fort, upon the luckless traveller, escaping as swiftly to their distant home, defying pursuit, together with the impunity with which they have latterly been suffered to commit their numerous outrages, are not calculated to impress them with a very high appreciation of our power; but, on the contrary, to fill their minds with the most supreme contempt for the authority of the government, inflating them with this idea of superiority. Nothing short of a thorough chastisement, which they so richly deserve, will bring these people to their proper senses. The salutary effect of a good whipping will be seen as this paper progresses, exhibited by the Cheyennes during their "talk" with me in council. Colonel Sumner has worked a wondrous change in their dispositions towards the whites! These people are very rich in horses and mules, many individuals frequently possessing hundreds of these animals, swift footed and beautiful in form, which they love next to their children, parting with them only in case of absolute starvation or when they desire to pay some high compliment to a friend, and then, miser-like, the poorest of the herd is selected. While the goods were being prepared for distribution I had an opportunity, in frequent conversations with the Indians, of learning their disposition in regard to a new treaty, and found the information given me by the Kaws was correct. I, therefore, brought the subject up in council. The Arapahoes, Cheyennes, and Apaches were much pleased when told I was ready to listen to them, and if they desired to treat to make known their wishes. The Cheyennes were especially anxious. They said they had learned a lesson last summer in their fight with Colonel Sumner; that it was useless to contend against the white man, who would soon with his villages occupy the whole prairie. They had eyes and were not blind. They no longer listened to their young men who continually clamored for war. They wanted peace, and as the buffalo, their principal dependance for food and clothing, (which even now they were compelled to seek many miles from their home, where the Pawnee and Osage, their natural enemies roamed), would soon disappear entirely, they hoped their Great Father, the white chief at Washington, would listen to them, and give them a home where they might be provided for and protected against the encroachments of their white brothers until, at least, like them they had been taught to cultivate the soil and other arts of civilized life. They have often desired ploughs and hoes, and to be taught their use. The Comanches expressed an utter unwillingness to treat, manifesting a disposition to annul entirely the existing treaty. Truly have they forgotten the teachings and influence of their good old chief "Shave Head," as he sadly predicted they would so soon as he should "go under." I found among them many Comanches of the south, who, with "Buffalo Hump" at their head, had fled from before the Texans in their recent fight. "Buffalo Hump" was exerting a controlling influence over the Comanches of the north, and I doubt not was the instigator of an attack made by a party of Comanches and Kiowas in sight of my camp, while preparing to distribute presents to them, upon two Mexican trains which they robbed of all their provisions. He boldly boasted of his hostility towards the Texans, stating that they had surprised him and thereby obtained a temporary triumph; but so soon as the distribution was over, it was his determination to lead not only his own band, but a portion of the Comanches of the north, against the "white man of the south," and true to his boast he subsequently led off a large number.

The Kiowas, (from whom I anticipated the only opposition,) while they exhibited but little desire to treat, expressed a willingness to send with the others a delegation of their chiefs to Washington to hear what their Great Father had to say. Agreeably to your instructions I spoke to them all as plainly and forcibly as circumstances would admit, repeating what I had from year to year told them – that if they did not cease their depredations, their Great Father would not only withhold their presents, but would send his soldiers against them to burn their villages and take captive their women and children. Listening with the most marked respect and silence until I had concluded, To-Hosea, or "Little-mountain," a Kiowa chief, sprang to his feet, pointing to the Kiowa and Comanche lodges in the valley below, called my attention to their *vast* number, and said —"The white chief is a fool; he is a coward; his heart is small — not larger than a pebble stone; his men are not strong — too few to contend against my warriors; they are women. There are three chiefs — the white chief, the Spanish chief, and myself. The Spanish and myself are men; we do bad towards each other sometimes, stealing horses and taking scalps, but we do not get mad and act the fool. The white chief is a child, and like a child gets mad quick. When my young men, to keep their women and children from starving, take from the white man passing through our country, killing and driving away our buffalo, a cup of sugar or coffee, the 'white chief' is angry and threatens to send his soldiers. I have looked for them a long time, but they have not come; he is a coward; his heart is a woman's. I have spoken. Tell the 'great chief' what

I have said." The distribution being over, the Cheyennes and Arapahoes, accompanied by Shave Head's
band of Comanches, (who had joined the latter tribe),
together with the Apaches and a portion of the Kiowas,
immediately proceeded up the Pawnee fork in search
of buffalo, with the understanding that they were to
join me at Bent's Fort in sixty days for the purpose of
preparing for their visit to Washington. The balance
of the Kiowas, with the Comanches, separated in two
bodies; the one going eastward in search of the Osage;
the other, headed by Buffalo Hump, turned their faces
toward the frontier of Texas. The health of the tribes
of my agency has not been good during the past year,
sickness having prevailed to a considerable extent,
resulting in the death, among others, of five of the
principal chiefs. A few years ago the cholera and small-
pox breaking out in the village of the Arapahoes, swept
them off by hundreds, and at this time *veneral* is
gradually but surely thinning them out, and in a few
years this once powerful and warlike people will cease
to exist as a distinct tribe, for there is scarcely a family
which is not to a greater or less extent afflicted with
this terrible disease. A few nights previous to my
arrival at their villages a terrible thunder storm pros-
trated one of their lodges in which there were ten
persons sleeping, three of whom were instantly killed,
the others shocked and bruised.

The Cheyennes expressed a desire, in the event of a
new treaty, to be assigned the country about the headwaters of the South Platte, and it was my intention,
with a view of reporting on its eligibility, to have
visited this region, but being unable to obtain a suitable
guide I have been reluctantly compelled to abandon
the trip; but in lieu thereof I start in a few days to visit
Agent Carson, at Taos, from whom, I doubt not, all

necessary information can be obtained, as it is well known he is perfectly familar with the whole country from Santa Fe to Fort Laramie.

Should the Comanches be persuaded to reconsider their determination not to treat, they, with the Kiowas, will ask that a reserve be assigned them near the tributaries of the Red River. Satisfied that the department is fully impressed with the importance to the "commerce of the *plains*" of the removal of the several tribes of these Indians from off the Santa Fe trail, and thereby releasing it of its greatest drawback, and confident that in its wisdom every effort will be exerted to accomplish this desirable end, I do not deem it necessary to urge this matter further, but remain your obedient servant,

ROBT. C. MILLER

United States agent of the Upper Arkansas
COLONEL A. M. ROBINSON
Superintendent of Indian Affairs, St. Louis, Mo.

---

4. AGENT TWISS' ANNUAL REPORT OF 1858 [14]

INDIAN AGENCY OF THE UPPER PLATTE, N.T.

Deer Creek, September 23, 1858

SIR: In submitting my annual report in relation to the Indian affairs within the Upper Platte agency, I beg leave to state that the different bands of Indians are quiet and peaceable, and well disposed towards the government of the United States. It is true that during the latter part of the year 1857 the Indian mind was greatly disturbed and excited by certain evil disposed and designing men, which resulted, however, in no bad

---

[14] *Annual Report of the Commissioner of Indian Affairs, 1858*, pp. 94-96. Twiss had been Agent to the Indians of the Upper Platte since 1855. The Northern Arapahoes, Northern Cheyennes, and the Sioux were his wards.

consequences, and was happily allayed by the prompt measures adopted by the department and contained in instructions sent to this office early in November last.

It may not be considered out of place, I trust, that I should state that, among these wild tribes of the prairies and the mountains, it requires but a small matter to disturb and excite them. They are widely scattered, and constantly moving in search of game for subsistence. When they meet with white men they are most eager to hear news, and it not unfrequently happens that news is made up for the occasion, either false or greatly exaggerated, and this, as it passes from party to party, increases in the marvellous, and often, by interpolations and additions to the original, becomes of grave and serious import to the Indians, who, with untutored minds, are incapable of sifting the true from the false; or, in other words, from their isolated position and habits, and slight intercourse with the civilized race, they have not sufficient experience to form just opinions or a correct judgment of passing events.

In regard to the internal state of affairs as existing between the various tribes, I would state that the different bands of this agency observe strictly the conditions and stipulations of the treaty of 1851,[15] in abstaining from sending out war parties against neighboring tribes, but it is with much difficulty that I am able to restrain them; for both the Crow and Blackfeet tribes are constantly sending war parties against the Sioux, Arapahoes, and Cheyennes, of this agency. A war party of the Blackfeet tribe killed a party of Sioux on the headwaters of the Cheyenne, in June, 1857, and robbed the Arapahoes of horses, near the Platte Bridge, in April last.

---

[15] The famous Fort Laramie Treaty of that year, negotiated by Supt. Mitchell and Agent Thomas Fitzpatrick.

A war party of the Crow tribe stole from the Sioux horses, in January last, on the Cheyenne River; and another war party of the same tribe stole a larger band of horses from the Sioux, in August last, at the Indian agency. I sent a messenger to the chiefs of the Crow tribe, and three of the principal men came in and held a "talk" with me, and promised to restore the horses, but have failed to comply with my demands or to fulfil their promises. I feel it incumbent upon me to put a stop to these war parties, if possible, but I am powerless to prevent them, if they refuse to listen to me. Whenever these war parties fall in with small parties of whites travelling along the Platte they rob them of some of their property, or force them to give them whatsoever they demand. They are insolent, audacious, and lawless.

In order to check these war parties, and put a stop to these constantly recurring outrages, I would earnestly and urgently recommend that the proper department of the government be requested to establish a permanent military post in the vicinity of this agency, to be garrisoned by at least four companies, two of which shall be mounted men; and also another military post on the Sweet Water, near Independence Rock. Detachments from either of these posts marching into the country of the Crow tribe when occasion requires will overawe and effectually put down these war parties, and render this great road along the Platte safe for weak parties of emigrants, which is very far from being the case at the present time.

In view of the probable settlement for agricultural purposes of some portion of this Indian country, which is exceedingly fertile and enjoys the most salubrious climate under the sun, I would respectfully press upon the attention of the department the positive necessity of adopting at once and without delay, and carrying into effect, with all the means and force at its command, the colonization of these wild tribes on military reservations.

It is, in my judgment, formed from careful observation, the best if not the only method by which the government can advantageously and successfully ameliorate the condition and change the roving habits and dispositions of these wild tribes of the prairies.

In regard to economy, it would certainly save the United States treasury millions in expense which it has been necessary to advance in the outfit and contingencies of military expeditions over the prairies. Aside from this question of economy, as we are not a great military government, it seems to me that it would be a sound and wise polity to husband the personnel and materiel of war for external enemies, and not permit the nucleus of a small army to be wasted away, and be continually at war with the Indian tribes; but rather adopt the milder arts of peace to subdue, soften, and render harmless these latter, fierce, and warlike barbarians it is true, yet nevertheless not altogether untamable, judging from past history and experience. The Indian tribes are not in a condition to contend with disciplined troops. They are sensible of this, and fight only because they are brave men, and believe it is decreed that the white race shall supplant them. It is the Aztec superstition "that when the white man shall come from towards the rising sun their power and greatness must cease."

With the earnest hope that the honorable the Commissioner of Indian Affairs will duly weigh and consider these matters in relation to the civilization of the wild tribes of the prairies, and adopt and recommend to be carried into effect at an early day such measures as in his wisdom shall seem best and proper,

I have the honor to be, sir, very respectfully, your obedient servant,

THOMAS S. TWISS
Indian Agent, Upper Platte

HON. CHARLES E. MIX,
Commissioner of Indian Affairs.

---

5. REPORT OF WILLIAM W. BENT [16]

BENT'S FORT   KANSAS TERRITORY
Big Timbers, Arkansas River   December 17th 1858
MR. ROBINSON
Super. Indian Affairs   Saint Louis Mo.

DEAR SIR: The Cheyenne Arappahoe and other Indians of this river are now very uneasy and restless about their country, the whites coming into it, making large and extensive settlements and laying off and building Towns all over the best part of their country, on this river also on the South Fork of the Platt & Cherry Creek.[17] This is their principle Hunting Grounds. This movement they do not understand, as they have never been treated with for it. Nothing has ever been said about it. They have been talking very hard against the whites, and I been doing all in my power to keep them reconciled and will still continue. I have told them that I thought there would be a treaty made with them early in the summer. The Indians have appointed me to go on and see what I can do for them, and try to settle the matter for them, and if you can possible do anything for them I would be glad you would do so, as I will leave here about the first of March for your City which

---

[16] Found in the Indian Department files, National Archives.

[17] The towns of Montana City, Auraria, and Denver had been started near the junction of Cherry Creek and the South Platte by recent gold-prospecting parties. Other towns had been started on Fountain Creek, the Arkansas, Clear Creek, Boulder Creek, and the Cache la Poudre.– See L. R. and A. W. Hafen, *The Colorado Story, op. cit.*

I will reach about the first of April if I do not meet with any bad luck. They wish their goods or presents to be taken to the South Platte so that all of the two Tribes may meet, those of the North Platte Laramie & this river, to make a treaty. Some commissioners should be sent out if possible as this matter ought not to be overlooked and layed aside for the sooner it is arranged the better, and should it be put off too long they will cause a great deal of trouble to the Whites and Mexican traders traveling through and on this country.

The emigration to the Gold Diggins this fall has been very large and they still continue to come. They have all passed unmolested by the Indians, although they have stolen several horses from them allready, this they do not think much of, but loosing the favorite Hunting Grounds & their only place to get their summer and fall provisions, that goes rather hard with them, although I hope it may turn out well and food for them.

They will now have to go to farming for a living, and that is something they do not know anything about they have not a single idea about what to commence at first. They are anxious to get at it if you will only give them a start they will go ahead.

I hope you will be so kind as to do something for them, this winter and when I get in I will explain all to you thougherly and satisfactory.

I remain   Very respectfully   Yours truly

WM W. BENT

Pr Jno W. Prowers Clk.[18]

---

[18] Prowers married a Cheyenne girl, as did Bent. Prowers became one of the outstanding pioneers of southeastern Colorado, and a leading cattleman.

B. RELATIONS WITH THE INDIANS, 1859

1. AGENT TWISS TO COMMISSIONER DENVER [1]

DEPARTMENT OF THE INTERIOR
Office of Indian Affairs   February 2d 1859
TO THE HONBL. J. W. DENVER
Comms. Indian Affairs

SIR: In consequence of the excitement about the discovery of Gold on the fork of the South Platte, it is reasonable to suppose that there will be a large emigration to that region early in the ensuing spring, various parties of which will seek for Gold deposits in all of the country situated between the forks of the Upper Plattes.

The Arapahoe & Cheyennes claim these hunting grounds & from the fact that so large a number of whites being there, as to destroy the game, the only means of support of the Indians, I would earnestly recommend that immediate steps be taken to quiet any apprehensions that may arise in the mind of the Indians & to obtain their consent to the cession of these lands to the United States, by payment of a stipulated annuity in Indian Goods, support of farmers, blacksmith, physician & missionaries of the Gospel. Should you

[1] Upper Platte Agency files, National Archives. James W. Denver, currently Commissioner, had been governor of Kansas when the town of Denver was founded, and named in his honor.

deem it advisable, I will submit a plan of a Treaty &c. &c.[2]

Very Respectfully   Your Obt. Servt
THOMAS S. TWISS, Indian Agent

---

2. PROCEEDINGS OF A TREATY COUNCIL SEPTEMBER 18, 1859[3]

U.S. INDIAN AGENCY OF THE UPPER PLATTE
Deer Creek, N.T.   Sept. 18, 1859

PROCEEDINGS of a Council held this day, with the following Sioux, Arapahoe & Cheyenne Chiefs, viz.:

Sioux Chiefs –"Man Afraid of his Horses," "Bold Bear," "Sitting Bear," "Stabber," "Standing Elk," with twenty of the principal men, Ogalalah, Yokpah, Brulés & Wasagahas Bands.

Arapahoe Chiefs –"Little Owl," "Friday," "Cut Nose," "Medicine man," "Black Bear," with thirty of the principal men.

Cheyenne Chiefs –"White Cow," "Big Wolf," "White Crow," with fifteen of the principal men of the Cheyennes.

Major Twiss, U.S. Indian Agent, had Mr. Edw. Clandes (?) for U.S. Interpreter on this occasion, & opened the Council by addressing the chiefs & principal men in the following short speech:

My Children: Your Great Father has seen proper to send me back to you, after my visit to his Council Lodge last winter. He gave me a large present of Annuity Goods, this year, which He promised you at the Treaty of Fort Laramie – These, I have distributed to your old people & little Children, all along the

---

[2] This communication was written while Twiss was in Washington. Apparently, he was authorized to proceed to negotiate a treaty, as the following document indicates.

[3] Indian Bureau records, National Archives.

great road, from Fallon's Bluff to this place, wherever & when ever I found a camp of your lodges. Your people have been clothed & fed & their hearts thereby made glad, by the bounty & foresight of your Great Father.

My Children: Your Great Father is pleased with you because you listen to my words, & keep away, & not mingle with the white people who are hunting for Gold on the South fork of the Platte & in the Parks, far away in the Mountains. You have done well. The white men are settling in every part of your country.

Your Great Father has ordered this year, Topographical parties through the Yellow Stone Country,[4] & wills that you treat them well wherever you may meet them. He will send his white families to build houses & settle on farms in these vallies. He wishes that the whites shall plant corn & raise herds of cattle, where once, you had plenty of Buffalo. These are now all destroyed.

My Children, your Great Father directs me to say to you that as the Buffalo, & small game also, are rapidly diminishing what do you propose to do to gain subsistence, when there is no longer any game for food, & prevent your old people & little children from dying by starvation? Will you labor like the White man, plant, hoe & raise corn for food? or will you die with hunger? Reflect & counsel well together, & give me the result of your deliberations, which I will write down, & send by mail to your Great Father.

After deliberating among themselves, the Chiefs & principal men of each Tribe, present, signified to the U.S. Interpreter, that the Chief, "Medicine Man" of the Arapahoes, was authorized to speak for all the Indians present in Council. The "Medicine Man" spoke briefly:

Father – The words which you have given us from our Great Father are good. We listen to his voice. Our country for hunt-

---

[4] Capt. W. F. Raynolds was sent out from St. Louis in May, 1859. See his "Report . . . on the Exploration of the Yellowstone and Missouri Rivers in 1859-1860," in *Sen. Ex. Doc.* 77, 40 Cong., 2 sess. (1867-68).

ing game has become very small. We see the white men everywhere; their Rifles kill some of the game, & the smoke of their
Camp fires scares the rest away, & we are no longer able to find
any game; our little children are crying for food. We are
obliged to travel many days before we can find Buffalo; & this
too, when the snow is deep, & the weather cold. It is but a few
years ago, where we encamped here, in this valley of Deer
Creek, & remained many moons, for the Buffalo were plenty, &
made the Prairie look black all around us. Now, none are to be
seen, & we are obliged to go to the Yellow Stone, ten days
travel, & then find only a few, for the Crow Tribe of Indians
show hostil feelings towards us when we hunt there; oftentimes
scaring away the game & stealing our horses. Our old people &
little Children are hungry for many days, & some die; for our
hunters caught no meat. Our sufferings are increasing every
winter. Our horses, too, are dying, because we ride them so far
to get a little game for our Lodges. We wish to live.

Our Great Father, & you, too, our Father for these five
winters, think for our good, & speak always kind & encouraging
words which make our hearts glad.

We are willing that our people should plant & raise corn for
food, & settle on small farms & live in Cabins. We ask our
Great Father to help us until we can learn to labor like the
white people. The Arapahoe Tribe wish to settle on a reservation on the Cache la Poudre. The Cheyenne Tribe will settle on
Laramie River above Fort Laramie. The Ogalalahs will settle
on Horse Creek, in part; & another part on Deer Creek, the
present Agency.

The Brulés & Wasagahas will settle on White river. We
request that our Great Father will supply us for a few years
with a Blacksmith, Carpenter, farmers, physicians, Missionaries
of the gospel, & teachers; seeds, agricultural impliments & stock;
& such annuity goods as our necessities may require.

With this assistance & a good disposition on our part, we shall
in a few years be able to raise corn & live like the White man,
without any further aid from our Great Father.

Father, we give all the rest of our Country to our Great
Father, except the reservations above named. It is no longer of
any use to us, as nearly all the game has disappeared. We would

ask our Great Father to permit us to hunt where the White man has not settled.

Father – We wish our Great Father would order away these White Traders; for they do no good to our people. Father, we ask you to write out what we desire, in the form in which our Great Father does business of this nature, & when it has been read & agreed to by us, we wish you to take it & lay it before our Great Father & his Councillors in the great Lodge at Washington. We know that you, who feel so much for us, will speak such strong words to the Great Council that our Great Father & his Chiefs will take pity upon us, & grant us the request which we now ask, & which we believe to be the only one that will preserve us from extinction, & permit us to dwell for a long time on these beautiful Prairie lands.

The following draft of a Treaty was then submitted & read by sections, & interpreted slowly & with great care to the Chiefs, who assented to all of the propositions contained therein, viz:

ARTICLES OF AGREEMENT, stipulations & promises made in Convention by the United States of the first part, with the Sioux, Arapahoe & Cheyenne Tribes of the Upper Platte Agency of the Second part. Witnesseth –

ARTICLE FIRST.   That for, & in Consideration of the several agreements, stipulations & promises hereinafter mentioned, duly performed, on the part of the United States, the Chiefs, Head men, & Braves of the above mentioned Tribes of Indians, agree to cede to the United States all of their lands, within the following boundaries, except certain reservations herein after described; viz: Beginning at the mouth of White River in the Missouri, thence up the said White River to Cache Butte, & thence in a Northwesterly direction to Bear Butte, on the north bank of the Cheyenne River, thence up said north fork of the Cheyenne to Pumpkin

Butte; from thence to the Red Buttes on the North Platte, & thence up the same to its source; thence easterly along the dividing ridge that separates the waters of the Arkansas from the Platte, to the 100th Meridian, or the line drawn from Old Fort Atkinson on the Arkansas River to the Forks of the Platte; thence to the mouth of White River, the place of beginning & excepting as follows: viz:

1st A Reservation on White River for the Brulé & Wasagadas Bands of Sioux, not exceeding forty-five miles in length by ten miles in breadth, to be occupied & improved for agricultural purposes by the said Brulé & Wasagahas Sioux Indians.

2d A Reservation on Horse Creek near its junction with Bear Creek, twenty-five miles in length by ten miles in breadth, to be occupied & improved for agricultural purposes by the Ogalalah Band of Sioux Indians.

3d A Reservation on Deer Creek, the present U.S. Indian Agency, beginning at a point two miles above its mouth in the North Platte, & extending thence to its source in the Black Hills to the south, & embracing all land on each side of said Deer Creek from the Muddy on the West to Box Elder on the East, to be occupied & improved for Agricultural purposes by the Ogalalah Band of Sioux Indians.

4th A Reservation on the Laramie River, beginning at a point on said river five miles above Fort Laramie & extending to its source, & embracing all lands on each bank of said river to the distance of five miles to be occupied & improved for agricultural purposes, by the Cheyenne Tribe of Indians.

5th A Reservation on Cache la Poudre, a tributary of the South Fork of the Platte, beginning at its mouth

& extending to its source in the Black Hills, & extending five miles on each bank of said Cache la Poudre, to be occupied & improved for agricultural purposes by the Arapahoe Tribe of Indians.

ARTICLE SECOND.   In consideration of the foregoing cession, the United States agree to pay to the Chiefs of the said above named Tribes of Indians for the use of said Tribes parties to this Convention, an annuity of one hundred thousand dollars, to be expended in the purchase of Indian Goods, provisions, clothing, & articles of prime necessity, for a period of time at the discretion of the President of the U.S. to be delivered on the reservations of each Tribe respectively – and commencing in one year after the ratification of this Convention.

ARTICLE THIRD. The United States also further agree to pay annually for a period of time at the discretion of the President of the U.S. the sum of fifteen thousand dollars for each of the above named Tribes of Indians, to be expended solely under the direction of the President, for the support of farmers, purchase of farm stock, agricultural implements & seeds; for support Blacksmith & Carpenter & purchase of iron & tools; building work shops, & dwelling houses; fencing the lands under cultivation; for salary of a Physician; for Missionaries & teachers, for the benefit of the above several Tribes of Indians, on each of their respective above mentioned reservations.

ARTICLE FOURTH.   The United States further agree to pay ten thousand dollars, or so much as may be necessary, for the survey, & marking the boundaries of the above named reservations within two years; also to pay for the transportation & incidental expenses of the Annuity Goods as stipulated in the 2d Article, the sum of thirty thousand dollars, annually if so much be necessary.

ARTICLE FIFTH. In the distribution of the annuities as specified in the 2d article of this Convention, it is agreed that the following proportions shall be observed, being as near the ratio of the population of each Tribe as can be determined, viz:

1st   To the Arapahoe Tribe, the sum of twenty thousand dollars.

2d   To the Cheyenne Tribe, the sum of sixteen thousand dollars.

3d   To the Ogalalah Tribe of Sioux, the sum of forty thousand dollars.

4th   To the Brulé & Wasagahas Tribe of Sioux the sum of twenty-four thousand dollars.

ARTICLE SIXTH. The aforesaid Indian Tribes, parties to this Convention, do hereby agree & bind themselves to make restitution or satisfaction, out of their annuities for any depredations or wrongs committed after the ratification of their Convention, by any band or individual of their people, on the citizens of the United States whilst lawfully residing in, or travelling through the above ceded country.

ARTICLE SEVENTH. It is stipulated that the country hereby ceded shall be held by the United States as Indian land, until otherwise ordered by the President of the United States: and it is also further agreed that the law regulating trade & intercourse with the Indian Tribes shall remain in full force on the reservations, above mentioned.

ARTICLE EIGHTH. These articles of agreement & convention shall be binding & obligatory upon the contracting parties; when ratified by the President & Senate of the United States.

A true copy of the proceedings of the Council, held this 18th day of September, 1859.

THOMAS S. TWISS

U.S. Indian Agent, Upper Platte [5]

---

3. WILLIAM W. BENT'S REPORT OF 1859 [6]

ST. LOUIS, October 5, 1859

At the moment of my return from an official visit to the Indian tribes within the agency under my control, I submit my report to the department. The limits of territory assigned by the treaty of Laramie to the Cheyenne and Arapahoe tribes, is defined by a meridian line passing from the Santa Fe crossing of the Arkansas, running north to Laramie; thence ascending by the channel of the North Platte to the Red Buttes; thence south along the mountain foot in which Chugwater, Cache a la Poudre, and the western affluents of the South Platte have their sources, and including the streams descending from Pike's Peak to the Arkansas River, and by the channel of said Arkansas to the beginning point. [7]

This country is very equally divided into halves by the South Platte. A confederate band of Cheyennes and Arapahoes, who are intermarried, occupy and claim exclusively the half included between the South Platte and the North Platte.

A similar confederated band of the same people

---

[5] As indicated in the Introduction to Part II, this agreement was not ratified by the U.S. Senate. It was probably too liberal to suit the white settlers and the officials in Washington.

[6] Found in the *Annual Report of the Commissioner of Indian Affairs, 1859*, pp. 137-39. W. W. Bent, the trader and owner of Bent's Fort, had been appointed Indian Agent for the Indians of the Upper Arkansas Agency.

[7] This is an inaccurate description; the official one is in the Fort Laramie Treaty of 1851.

distinctly occupy the southern half, included between
the South Platte and Arkansas rivers.

These latter also frequent and claim the region south
of the Arkansas River, between it and the Raton mountain, which last territory, formerly a part of New
Mexico, is not occupied or claimed by any other tribe.
I had a full and satisfactory interview with the Cheyenne and Arapahoe Indians on the 16th of August;
and, on the 15th of September last, I submitted to them
the wish of the department that they should assume a
fixed residence, and occupy themselves in agriculture.
This they at once received with favor, and declared
with great unanimity to be acceptable to them. They
expected and ask, that the department shall supply
them with what is necessary to establish themselves
permanently.

Being Buffalo Indians, they require dwelling-houses
to be constructed for them, where they may elect to fix
their reserved districts. They desire to have a treaty
with the government without delay at a very early day
of the coming spring season. They ask for pay for the
large district known to contain gold, and which is
already occupied by the whites, who have established
the county of Arapahoe and many towns. They further
ask annuities in the future for such lands as they may
cede and relinquish to the government.

They ask to select their reserved lands where the
choice of their people may designate, expressing a
preference for the region between the Arkansas River
and the Raton mountain, embracing the Fontaine qui
Bouille and Purgatory creeks.

The Cheyenne and Arapahoe tribes scrupulously
maintain peaceful relations with the whites and with
other Indian tribes, notwithstanding the many causes

of irritation growing out of the occupation of the gold region, and the emigration to it through their hunting grounds, which are no longer reliable as a certain source of food to them.

These causes precipitate the necessity of immediate and sufficient negotiations for the safety of the whites, the emigrant roads, and the Indians. Regulations, strictly enforced, are essential in the granting of licenses to trade with the Indians. All trade, excepting by licensed traders, ought to be prevented. No agent should have power to grant any license outside of his specific jurisdiction. Full power to prevent violations of the United States laws, and promptly punish such as may occur, should be given to the agents.

In case that these Indians should elect to remain, as at present, separated into two distinct bands, a favorable country, at present most frequented by them, exists between the Cache a la Poudre and Chugwater.[8]

The Kiowa and Comanche Indians have, for two years, appeared in full numbers and for long periods upon the Arkansas, and now permanently occupy the country between the Canadian and Arkansas rivers. This is in consequence of the hostile front opposed to them in Texas, by which they are forced towards the north, and is likely to continue perpetual.

These I encountered, on my return at the mouth of Walnut creek, on September 16, to the number of 2,500 warriors. They signified to me their desire for peace, which up to that time they have continued to preserve in the presence of the United States troops.

So soon, however, as the latter withdrew to Fort Riley, the Comanches assumed a threatening attitude, which resembles the prelude of predatory attacks upon

[8] This would be for the Northern bands of Arapahoes and Cheyennes.

the unprotected whites, now at all seasons passing and repassing by the Santa Fe roads in great numbers. I consider it essential to have two permanent stations for troops, one at the mouth of Pawnee Fork, and one at the Big Timbers,[9] both upon the Arkansas River. A smothered passion for revenge agitates these Indians, perpetually fomented by the failure of food, the encircling encroachments of the white population, and the exasperating sense of decay and impending extinction with which they are surrounded.

To control them, it is essential to have among them the perpetual presence of the controlling military force. The Comanches have acquainted me with their intention to remain during the winter upon the Arkansas River, and ask that their annual supplies may be hereafter delivered to them in this direction. I recommend that immediate and prompt negotiations be entered upon with them, as the present time is propitious, their condition especially favorable, and their temper tractable.

There are in each of these tribes a few half-breeds, the children of white men intermarried with the Cheyennes and Arapahoes, for whom these tribes desire to make suitable reservations and provisions. The prominent feature of this region is the recent discovery and development of *gold* upon the flanks of the Great Cordillera and its spurs protruding out over the great plains. I estimate the number of whites traversing the plains across the center belt to have exceeded 60,000 during the present season. The trains of vehicles and cattle are frequent and valuable in proportion; post lines and private expresses are in constant motion. The

9 The Big Timbers, a grove of cottonwood trees, extended along the Arkansas for many miles east of Bent's New Fort.

explorations of this season have established the existence
of the precious metals in absolutely infinite abundance
and convenience of position.

The concourse of whites is therefore constantly
swelling, and incapable of control or restraint by the
government. This suggests the policy of promptly
rescuing the Indians, and withdrawing them from con-
tact with the whites, as the element capable of such
immediate management as may anticipate and prevent
difficulties and massacre. I repeat, then, as the sugges-
tion of my best judgment, that immediate and sufficient
steps be taken to assemble and finally dispose of these
particular tribes of Indians, viz:

The Kiowa and Comanches, the Cheyennes, and the
Arapahoes, by reducing them, under treaties and
arrangements, to become agricultural and pastoral
people, located within specific districts, judiciously
selected and liberally endowed, to which they shall be
restricted, and the white men excluded from among
them. These numerous and warlike Indians, pressed
upon all around by the Texans, by the settlers of the
gold region, by the advancing people of Kansas, and
from the Platte, are already compressed into a small
circle of territory, destitute of food, and itself bisected
athwart by the constantly marching line of emigrants.
A desperate war of starvation and extinction is therefore imminent and inevitable, unless prompt measures
shall prevent it.

W. W. BENT,   U.S. Indian Agent

THE SUPERINTENDENT OF INDIAN AFFAIRS

III
Campaigns and Negotiations
1860

Campaigns and Negotiations, 1860

INTRODUCTION

The Comanches and Kiowas were the chief disturbers of the peace on the southern plains in 1860. Their raids on the Santa Fe Trail had been recurring dangers from the time wagon caravans first traveled to New Mexico. Then in 1853 Thomas Fitzpatrick, first United States Agent to the Indians of the high plains, had succeeded in negotiating the first treaty with the Kiowas and Comanches. It pledged the Indians to peace, granted the government the right to lay out roads and establish military posts, and provided an annuity of $18,000 in goods. The treaty was to run ten years, subject to an extension of five years.[1] The Indians agreed not to molest the whites, but if such violations of the treaty occurred, annuities might be withheld.

It was ever difficult for the Comanches and Kiowas, raiders for generations, to comply with their promises. Alfred Cumming, Superintendent of Indian Affairs, wrote in his annual report of September 25, 1856:

> The Comanches, who spend the winter months in the country below the Arkansas, committing depredations along the frontiers of Texas as far as the Rio Grande, are a wild and intractable race; well supplied with horses, they enrich themselves by rapine in the south, and in the spring proceed northwardly in pursuit of

---

[1] L. R. Hafen and W. J. Ghent, *Broken Hand, the Life Story of Thomas Fitzpatrick, Chief of the Mountain Men* (Denver, Old West Pub. Co., 1931), 251-55; and C. J. Kappler, *Indian Affairs, Laws, and Treaties* (Wash., U.S. Govt. print. off., 1903), II, pp. 600-602.

buffaloes. They pitch their lodges on the banks of the Arkansas, and there await the annual arrival of their agent with the goods for destribution among them. The annuities they receive from the government they regard as a compensation for permitting travellers to pass unmolested along the Santa Fe road. They, like the Kioways, are audacious and insolent, and always exhibit to the Indian agent evidences of their power, and their utter contempt for the officers of the government.[2]

Agent Robert Miller met the Comanches and Kiowas at Pawnee Fork of the Arkansas in July, 1858, and found the Comanches hostile, and threatening to annul the treaty of 1853. They and the Kiowas had recently robbed two Mexican trains nearby; and were confident of their superiority over United States troops. Miller concluded that "Nothing short of a thorough chastisement, which they so richly deserve, will bring these people to their proper senses." [3]

One of the Kiowa chiefs, pointing to numerous lodges in the valley, said:

> The white chief is a fool; he is a coward; his heart is small — not larger than a pebble stone; his men are not strong — too few to contend against my warriors; they are women. . . [The white chief] threatens to send his soldiers. I have looked for them a long time, but they have not come; he is a coward; his heart is a woman's.[4]

Indian Agent William Bent encountered some 2500 Comanches and Kiowas on Walnut Creek in September, 1859. They exhibited a degree of friendship, he reports, when troops were near; but when the soldiers were withdrawn "assumed a threatening attitude. . . A smothered passion for revenge agitates these Indians,

[2] *Annual Report of the Commissioner of Indian Affairs, 1856*, pp. 71-72.
[3] Miller's report above, doc. 3, Part II, A.
[4] *Ibid.*

perpetually fomented by the failure of food, the encircling encroachments of the white population, and the exasperating sense of decay and impending extinction with which they are surrounded." [5]

The attitudes and actions of the Comanches and Kiowas, and their depredations on the Texas frontiers and along the Santa Fe Trail, led to the organization of a campaign against them in the spring and summer of 1860. The orders from Headquarters directed "active operations against the hostile Comanches and Kiowas" and left no room for holding any intercourse with them until after they had been punished.[6]

One column of troops, under Major John Sedgwick, was to operate from Fort Riley and a base on the Arkansas River; another, under Captain S. D. Sturgis, was to advance from Texas. Reports of the operations follow.

---

[5] Bent's report, doc. 3, Part II, B.

[6] See Col. Sumner's Instructions below, in doc. 3.

A: LETTERS AND REPORTS

1. EXPEDITION ORDERED AGAINST KIOWAS AND COMANCHES [1]

SAINT LOUIS, MO., April 3d, 1860

The four companies of the 1st Cavalry, at Fort Riley, under Major Sedgwick, and two companies of the 2nd Dragoons, at Fort Kearny, to be designated by the commanding officer of that post, will compose an expedition to operate against the hostile Kiowas and Comanches. The Cavalry will march from Fort Riley on the 15th and the Dragoons from Fort Kearny on the 8th of May, for Paunee Fork. They will march well armed and carry with them an abundant supply of ammunition, a few necessary articles of clothing, and the equipments for the additional horses they will require. Besides two wagons to each company (including the company wagons) each command will be furnished with transportation for 30 days provisions – five-sevenths (5/7) of the meat rations to be fresh beef on the hoof.

Instructions for the conduct of the Expeditions beyond the Arkansas, will be furnished hereafter.

By order of COLONEL E. V. SUMNER

(Signd) D. R. JONES   Asst Adjt Genl.

---

[1] Adjutant General's Office, Special Order no. 34, Department of the West, 1860; in the National Archives, Washington.

2. COLONEL SUMNER ASKS FOR
DELAWARE SCOUTS [2]

HEAD QUARTERS DEPARTMENT OF THE WEST
Saint Louis, Mo.   April 16, 1860

SIR: I would respectfully ask for authority to employ twelve Delaware Indians for the expedition against the Kiowas. These men will be very useful as scouts and guides. They have a perfect knowledge of the Country, and Know exactly where the Kiowas must go, to subsist themselves and families. I think the success of the expedition may depend very much upon having a small select party of these braves attached to the command.

I have offered the command to Bvt. Colonel May,[3] as the senior cavalry officer for detail in the Department. If he should prefer to remain in command of his post – Major Sedgwick will command the expedition unless I receive orders to the contrary.

Very respectfully   Your obdt. servt

E. V. SUMNER
Col 1 Cav. Com'g.

THE ASSISTANT ADJUTANT GENERAL
Head Qrs. of the Army,   New York City.

---

[2] A.G.O., Letters Received, 1860, W 54. The employment of six Delaware scouts was authorized. Fall Leaf was the most famous of these. The others were: Sarcoxie, John Williams, Bascom, Wilson, and Bullit –"The Kiowa and Comanche Campaign of 1860, as Recorded in the Personal Diary of Lt. J. E. B. Stuart," in the *Kansas Historical Quarterly,* XXIII, p. 395.

[3] Charles A. May was born in Washington, D.C. He became a 1st Lt. in the 2nd Dragoons in 1837; a captain in 1841; a major in 1855. He won a colonelcy in the Mexican War. He resigned in April, 1861, and died Dec. 24, 1864.– Heitman, p. 698.

[On cover of letter]:   HD. QR. OF THE ARMY
                                   New York, Apr. 19, 1860
The General in chief approves of employing the Delaware
Indians as suggested by Colonel Sumner.
    Respectfully forwarded to the Adjutant General
                        L. THOMAS   Sub. Adj. Genl.
        Apri 21-1860
        Respectfully laid before the Secretary of War.
                        E. D. TOWNSEND   Asst. Ag. Genl.
        WAR DEPT.   25 Apl 1860
        Approved for six Delaware Indians.
                        J. B. FLOYD   Secy of War

---

3.   COLONEL SUMNER'S INSTRUCTIONS
TO MAJOR SEDGWICK [4]

HEAD QUARTERS, DEPARTMENT OF THE WEST
                    Saint Louis Mo.   May 9, 1860
    MAJOR: In framing instructions for the expedition
against the Indians, of the Plains, I would in the first
place refer to the inclosed letter from Army Head
Quarters of March 10, 1860. This letter directs "active
operations against the hostile Comanches and Kiowas"
and leaves no room for holding any intercourse with
them, till after they are punished, this makes your duty
perfectly plain. You have only to make a fierce pursuit
– overtake them, and attack them. In this pursuit, it will
be necessary to divest your command of nearly all their
baggage. It is utterly in vain to attempt to catch Indians
with a wagon train, for they will, of course, lead over
ground that will be impracticable for wheels. You
should therefore leave all your wagons at Pawnee Fork

---

[4] A.G.O., Letters Received, 1860, 178 w.

and cross the Arkansas with Pack mules, and a sufficient number of beef cattle. If all your other rations should fail before you accomplish your object, you can subsist your command on fresh beef alone, for a long time, and keep your men in vigorous health. In pursuing Indians a steady determined march will always overtake them when they are traveling with their families, and when you press them closely, the warriors will separate themselves from their families, and draw up to protect them. This is the moment to attack them, for you have then only men to deal with. If the Comanches and Kiowas should unite, they might be very strong, requiring great prudence and judicious management in approaching them. In attacking a superior force I would suggest to you, the great advantage of turning their flank, Indians can never stand that. As the three columns that are to move upon the plains have been made independent, no instructions can be given for any cooperation, but the government would undoubtedly expect, and rightly too, that the Commanders would act in concert, if it should be necessary to do so, to attain the objects of the campaign. As you advance into the Indian country, you will be met by messengers, with proffers of peace and disclaimers of all connection with the hostiles, but it is impossible for us to make distinctions, wherever Comanches or Kiowas are found they must give the character to the whole party.

You will please report as often as possible during the Campaign.

Very respectfully,   Your obedt. Servant:

(Sgd)   E. V. SUMNER
Colonel 1st Cavalry,   Commanding

MAJOR JOHN SEDGWICK
1st Cavalry, Fort Riley, Ks.
Hd. Qrs., Dept. of the West

[Papers accompanying the above]:

HEAD QUARTERS,   DEPARTMENT OF THE WEST
Saint Louis Mo.   May 10, 1860

SIR: As I have received no orders for the conduct of the Expedition upon the plains, and as the Command is to march on the 15th instant, I have thought it necessary and proper to issue the inclosed instructions. Will you please inform me immediately, if they are not approved.

Very respectfully,   Your obedient Servant:

E. V. SUMNER
Col 1 Cav   Comdg

THE ADJUTANT GENERAL OF THE ARMY
Washington City D.C.

Respectfully submitted to the Secretary of War. If any modification is required to be made in the instructions given by Colonel Sumner to Major Sedgwick, it should be done immediately, as the expedition under the latter officer is to march this day, and cannot be conveniently reached, even by telegraph after this.[5] [Written in red ink].

A. G. OFFICE
May 15/60.

E. D. TOWNSEND
A. A. Genl.

---

4.   MAJOR SEDGWICK'S LETTER TO HIS SISTER REPORTING CAMPAIGN PREPARATIONS [6]

FORT RILEY,   May 12, 1860

MY DEAR SISTER: I am very busy in making preparations, which is no small matter. To think of everything necessary for five hundred men to take the field for the whole summer requires some thought as well as labour. We go two hundred miles, to Pawnee Fork,

---

[5] Apparently the instructions were approved; or at least were not overruled.

[6] In the two-volume work, *Correspondence of John Sedgwick, Major-General* (Printed for Carl and Ellen Battelle Stoeckel, 1902-1903) are published letters from Sedgwick to his sister. Sedgwick never married; and his relations with his sister were close. These letters give such important supplemental data that a number of them are reprinted. This one is in vol. II, pp. 12-13. For a biographical sketch of Sedgwick, see above, in Part I, c, fn. 2.

with wagons, from there with pack-mules, where we can carry nothing but the absolute necessaries: two blankets, two shirts, socks, etc., with just enough to eat to keep your bones together. If the expedition should be a fortunate one we may be in in September, or October at the latest. The orders have not yet arrived, and it is not certain that I am to have the command, but it is most probable. I shall write you from Pawnee. We shall have a weekly mail at that post, and it is likely we shall be in there as often as once a month during the summer. But with this to relieve us, I cannot anticipate a pleasant summer's work. The spring has been very dry; no rain for four or more months, and everything looks dry and parched up. If rain does not come soon it will be a disastrous summer, not only for our horses but for all the farmers in this part of the country.

I hope everything goes on well. I am daily looking for a letter from you, and if it does not come before leaving I shall leave an express for a day or two to bring all letters. Your last letter was only seven days coming, and the Litchfield paper comes in seven or eight days. I see that John E. has come back to the Democratic ranks. Tell him (if you ever see him) that on entering the fold again his past sins will be forgiven. But he must sin no more. I hope to welcome you back on the same conditions.

Major Wessells [7] and myself have been on very friendly terms the past winter. He has now gone to establish the new post at Pawnee.[8] His wife is a very

---

[7] H. W. Wessells, of Connecticut, graduated from West Point in 1833 and became a captain in 1847. He won distinction in the Mexican War and the Civil War. His death occurred on Jan. 12, 1889.–Heitman, p. 1019.

[8] The Pawnee River enters the Arkansas near the town of Larned, Kansas. Maj. Wessells was to establish on the Pawnee, about six miles above its mouth, Fort Alert, afterwards to become Fort Larned. See below.

agreeable woman. They have three boys, and the Major a daughter by his first wife.

I shall try and make you a visit next winter or spring, but not a long one.

I am your affectionate brother,   J.S.

---

5. SEDGWICK'S LETTER FROM THE CIMARRON [9]

CAMP ON CIMARRON,   June 23, 1860

MY DEAR SISTER: We are going to cross the New Mexico road to-morrow, and I write a line hoping to meet some train going into the States which will take it. We left Pawnee on the 2nd instant, taking only pack-mules; of course carrying only such articles as were absolutely essential for our subsistence. Up to this time we have not seen an Indian or signs of one later than three or four months date. Our supplies will run out on the 31st, and we are making our way to the Arkansas River to send for more. I do not mean to be caught as we were in 1837 [1857]. Of game we have had an endless variety. One Sunday, whilst lying over a day about two hundred miles south of this, we had bear, wild turkey, deer, antelope, ducks, pigeons, and fish – unluckily, we had no condiments to cook them with and season them properly. Our table daily consists of four or five kinds of meat, sugar, and coffee and flour, and when our supplies reach us we hope to add several little luxuries to them. It is the worst country that ever was run; not a stick of wood or green bark in the whole of it, and add to this there has not been a drop of rain for eight months – of course no grass, no water in the small streams and pools where water is usually found – and you can imagine some of the sufferings that our

---

[9] Sedgwick's *Correspondence, op. cit.,* pp. 14-15.

animals, in common with us, have had to undergo. We have several times marched upwards of forty miles without a drop of water, and when found it was so brackish that nothing but thirst could have induced any one to drink it. We are now getting nearer the mountains, and the water grows better. I expect a mail on the 3rd of July, and I shall then have an opportunity of sending you a letter, provided you do not receive this precious one. Write me how the house, stable, and grounds look. I have wished often that I was there this summer. I am growing tired of the war, but suppose I shall feel better when it is over. I hope to go in early in October, but may not till November – at all events, in time to get the election news.

With love to all at home, believe me, as ever,

Your affectionate brother,   J.S.

6. MAJOR SEDGWICK'S OFFICIAL REPORT OF JULY 2 [10]

CAMP ON ARKANSAS, NEAR AUBREY'S CROSSING [11]

July 2d 1860

CAPTAIN : I regret exceedingly that I am compelled to report to you our want of success in finding any Trail of the hostile Kiowas or Comanches. We marched from Pawnee Fork on the 1st ulto; [12] crossed the Arkansas at Jackson's Island, and took a South Easterly direction, intending to go down Crooked Creek to its mouth, but found we had gone too far East to strike it. We crossed Salt River forty miles East of the great "Salt Plain,"

---

[10] A.G.O., Letters Received, 1860, s 263.

[11] This crossing point of the Arkansas was at the place where the command reached the river on its return from the tour into Oklahoma and Texas. See J. E. B. Stuart's diary below, entry of June 29th.

[12] The route will be traced below, in connection with Stuart's official, detailed diary.

when taking a more Southerly course, after crossing the "N. Fork of the Canadian," we struck "Middle River" a large clear and well timbered stream. Our guide Sarcoxie said it was the N. Fork, that he had traded on it with the Comanches, and with the other guides was certain we would find the Indians on it. After proceeding up it forty miles, until within sight of the "Antelope Hills" we met a surveying party direct from Fort Cobb, who informed us that they had seen no signs of the Indians, and that the South Fork of the Canadian was entirely dry. We followed up Middle River (incorrectly supposed by us to be the N Fork) to its head, eighty miles, when turning north we returned to the N. Fork of the Canadian, following it as long as we could find water. Middle River (not laid down on any map which I have seen) is a stream evidently much resorted to by the Indians: there are signs of their having wintered on it for many years, but none of them having been on it for several months. After leaving the N. Fork of the Canadian, we crossed to the Cimaron, from it to Bear River, and thence to the Arkansas. We have marched five hundred miles since leaving Pawnee Fork, passing through the heart of the Kiowa Range, and over the worst country I have ever seen. There had been no rain on it since last Fall, and consequently all the small streams and pools where water is generally found, were dry. Our animals have suffered excessively for want of water and grass, and we have been obliged to abandon several of our beeves from utter exhaustion. We have made five marches of over forty-three miles each without water, the water when reached being in small pools and of the worst description. This severe service has used up our horses to such an extent as to render it necessary to remain here several days to recruit them, as well as to obtain supplies, our own having been exhausted on 30th ulto – these I expect tomorrow.[13] When I have received them, I shall again cross the Arkansas and proceed up towards the Mountains.

Respy your ob svt,   JOHN SEDGWICK
                                        Major 2d Cavalry
CAPT. D. R. JONES   A. A. GEN., U.S.A.
Hd. Qrs. Dept of the West   Saint Louis, Mo.

---

7. SEDGWICK'S LETTER TO HIS SISTER[14]

CAMP ON ARKANSAS,   July 5, 1860

MY DEAR SISTER: I wrote you a letter about ten days since, expecting to find an opportunity to send it after striking the Santa Fe road. I have heard of its arrival at Pawnee Fork, where I suppose it was mailed, and you may stand a chance of getting it. Our supplies reached us on the 3rd, bringing a very large mail, with your letter of the 29th of May.

I have just received an express from Major Wessells[15] that the Indians that we are in pursuit of are probably in the vicinity of Denver City. It is so authentic that I shall act upon it, and will start on the 7th for that place, so that the next letter you receive from me may be from Pike's Peak. Our scout has been unsuccessful so far. If we could meet the Indians, and give them a flogging, I should feel that our summer's work was over. It becomes very tiresome, this marching day after day, without any change of country. That we have marched over is the worst I have ever seen, and

---

13 Supplies were obtained from the fort on Pawnee Fork.
14 From Sedgwick's Correspondence, pp. 15-17.
15 Who was at Fort Larned.

that we are going over not much better. Game is very abundant, and of the greatest variety, but we have not the facilities for cooking to make it the daintiest for the table. I intend to be back near Pawnee Fork by the 20th of August, as our supplies will run out by that time; but probably I will have an opportunity to write you before.

Major Wessells is sadly distressed by the loss of his youngest boy, some four or five years old, and other sickness in his family. With much love, I am your affectionate brother,   J.S.

---

8. OFFICIAL ORDERS
REGARDING INDIAN CONFLICT, OF JULY 11 [16]

DEPARTMENT OF THE WEST
Commanded by Colonel *Edwin V. Sumner,* 1st Cavalry
I. . . . July 11, 1860.– Major *John Sedgwick,* of the 1st Cavalry, commanding Companies C and K 2nd Dragoons, F, G, H and K 1st Cavalry, while examining the Upper Arkansas region, despatched two detachments in pursuit of a party of hostile Kioways, some twenty-five miles from Bent's Fort. One was under Captain *William Steele,*[17] 2nd Dragoons, consisting of 1st Lieutenant *Francis C. Armstrong,*[18] 2d Dragoons, 2d Lieutenants *George O. Bayard*[19] and *Joseph H.*

---

[16] General Orders, Headquarters of the U.S. Army, Book 178, General Orders no. 11 (National Archives). For additional data see Stuart's diary, below.

[17] William Steele graduated from West Point in 1840. He became a 1st Lt. in 1846, a captain in 1851. He fought in the Mexican War and served the Confederacy in the Civil War. He died Jan. 12, 1885.– Heitman, p. 919.

[18] Francis C. Armstrong, native of Arkansas, became a 1st Lt. in the 2nd Dragoons in 1859. He reached the rank of brigadier general in the Confederate army.– Heitman, p. 169.

[19] See fn. 26, Part I, B, above.

Taylor,[20] 1st Cavalry, and eighty-six men; the other under 1st Lieutenant *James E. B. Stuart,* 1st Cavalry, with twenty men. The two, in rapid pursuit, joined, and killing two warriors, captured sixteen women and children of the party.

Lieutenant *Bayard* was severely wounded (in the face), also Private *John Smith* (1st) of Company G, & *Ferdinand Schwartz,* of Company F, 1st Cavalry.

The personal daring of Lieutenant *Bayard,* and the gallant conduct of Sergeant *William Occleston,* of Company G, 1st Cavalry, who killed one of the warriors, and of Corporal *George S. Newman,* of Company K, 1st Cavalry, are especially noted.

Officers and men are commended for eagerness in the pursuit and cheerfulness in enduring hunger, drenching rains and hard riding.

---

9. SEDGWICK'S LETTER OF JULY 19[21]

CAMP ON ARKANSAS, IN SIGHT OF
PIKE'S PEAK,   July 19, 1860[22]

MY DEAR SISTER: An opportunity will occur tomorrow of sending in to Pawnee, and I thought I would write a line. We have had no mail since I last wrote, and do not expect one till about the 10th of August. By that time I hope the hardest part of our summer's campaign will be over, although nothing has

---

20 Joseph H. Taylor, native of Kentucky, graduated from the U.S. Military Academy in 1856. He became a 2nd Lt., 1st Cavalry in 1857. He served the Union in the Civil War, and reached the rank of colonel. He died March 13, 1885.– Heitman, p. 947.

21 Sedgwick's *Correspondence,* pp. 17-18.

22 They camped on the Arkansas, 22 miles east of Bent's Old Fort. See Stuart's diary, below.

been done worthy of so large and fine a command. We routed a small band of Kiowas a few days since, killing two, taking sixteen prisoners, and destroying their plunder, and taking forty horses. We have one officer and two soldiers wounded, none badly. In a day or two we start again, working in the direction of Pawnee, which is about three hundred miles from here. We shall probably make five hundred before reaching there. The friendly Indians about here [23] report that several skirmishes have taken place with the other troops, in one of which one hundred and fourteen Indians were killed. This is probably exaggerated, but if anything like the truth, they have been so much punished that we shall hear no more from them. The road is filled with emigrants going and returning from Pike's Peak;[24] so far no one has been molested. The mountains of the Peak are visible from our camp, although from eighty to one hundred miles distant. What a change since I was there in '37 ['57]. Then there was not a person to be met with except, occasionally, a trader; now there are sixty thousand inhabitants, with towns containing large and handsome houses, and stores well filled with the most fashionable goods, and everything denotes an old settled country. The mines are proving very rich, from all accounts, and every one is looking forward to a fortune.

I shall not, probably, write again till I reach Pawnee. There is a report that a post is to be established here.

Your affectionate brother,   J.S.

---

[23] The friendly Cheyennes and Arapahoes, gathered at Bent's New Fort, received their annuities from Agent William Bent the next day (July 20).

[24] The whole gold mining region of Colorado was then referred to as Pike's Peak.

10.   SEDGWICK'S OFFICIAL REPORT OF JULY 24 [25]

CAMP ON THE ARKANSAS RIVER   July 24, 1860

SIR: I have the honor to report that I left camp
near Aubrey's Crossing of the Arkansas, on the 6th
instant, intending, guided by information I had received from Major Wessels, second infantry, to proceed to Denver City, or its vicinity, in pursuit of the
Kiowas. Reaching Bent's Fort on the evening of the
8th, it was reported to me that a small band of Kiowas
was some twenty-five miles north of that place. I
immediately detached Captain Steele, second dragoons,
with eighty-six men to ascertain if the report was
correct. On resuming my march the next morning, I
learned whilst passing Bent's Fort, that Litarki, the
principal chief of the Kiowas, with his family and a
few warriors, had been about an hour previously in
that neighborhood, and had gone off in a northerly
direction. Lieutenant Stuart, first cavalry, immediately
started in pursuit with twenty men, and after a chase
of twenty-seven miles, just as he was about to overhaul
the Indians, was met by Captain Steele, returning to
the command. Unitedly they killed two warriors and
captured sixteen women and children, with more than
forty mules and ponies. Only two (both women) of the
party escaped, it having been ascertained afterwards
that Litarki was not present when the affair occurred.
I regret to report that Lieutenant Bayard was severely,
and two privates slightly wounded. Captain Steele's
and Lieutenant Stuart's reports are herewith inclosed.
Insomuch as they would have much embarrassed my
future movements, and as I believed that no object

25 "Report of the Secretary of War," in *Sen. Ex. Doc.* 1, 36 Cong., 2 sess.
(ser. no. 1079), pp. 14-17.

would be accomplished by keeping them, at the urgent request of Colonel Bent, Indian agent, I turned over the women and children taken prisoners to him, to be held as hostages for the safety of emigrants on the road. Having learned from Colonel Bent and others directly from Denver City that there were no hostile Indians in that vicinity, I detached Captain DeSaussure,[26] first cavalry, with a command of 100 men, to cross the river and proceed up Purgatory creek, said to be a place of resort for the Kiowas and Camanches, until satisfied there were no Indians on it. After a scout of five days he returned, reporting that there were no signs of Indians having been on the creek since March or April. I then determined to proceed down the river until I could cross to the Smoky Hill, and thence down it and Walnut creek to the buffalo range.

Respectfully, your obedient servant,

JOHN SEDGWICK
Major First Cavalry

CAPT. D. R. JONES A.A.G.,   U.S.A.
Headquarters Department of the West,
St. Louis, Mo.

(a) CAPTAIN STEELE'S REPORT

CAMP, NEAR BENT'S FORT,   July 14, 1860

SIR: I have the honor to report, that having been detailed on the night of the 9th instant, with four officers and eighty-six enlisted men to seek a party of Kiowa Indians, under the chief Litarki, reported as being about twenty miles distant. I left camp at midnight, and after a rapid ride of five hours and three quarters arrived at the point where the Kiowas were supposed to be, and found neither Indians nor fresh signs; after grazing the horses one hour, I proceeded to

---

[26] William D. De Saussure, of South Carolina, became a captain in the 1st Cavalry in 1855. He was killed at the Battle of Gettysburg as a Confederate colonel.– Heitman, p. 369.

another water-hole fifteen miles distant, still without success; then to a watering-place fifteen miles, where I arrived at three o'clock p.m., having passed over in fifteen hours from fifty-five to sixty miles, and been disappointed in getting any trace of the band we were in pursuit of. After remaining all night at the last mentioned water-hole, and encountering one of the most violent thunder storms I have ever seen, I started back by a different route; after traveling eighteen miles, two Indians were seen in the distance running off; the guide having informed me that the only water near was a spring just in front of us, I disregarded the running Indians and pushed forward, sending forward rapidly two platoons under Lieutenant Armstrong, second dragoons, and Lieutenant Taylor, first cavalry, who, coming upon the women and children, captured the whole party, sixteen in number. At this time what appeared to be a large party was obscurely seen through the clouds of dust passing to our left, and the whole force except a guard for the prisoners, directed towards it; it proved to be Lieutenant J. E. B. Stuart, with a platoon, and a number of friendly Indians in pursuit of the braves who had been with the families already captured. Lieutenant Stuart having pursued the whole party from the vicinity of Bents' Fort, all joined in pursuit and killed two Kiowa Indians, all (as we are credibly informed) of the party. The party captured proves to have been the family of Litarki, that chief having been absent at the time; the men killed are said to be his brother and son; these Indians fought desperately, wounding Lieutenant Bayard severely in the face, and two men of Lieutenant Stuart's party slightly.

As soon as possible I started Lieutenant Otis,[27] with the larger portion of my command for camp, remaining at the spring with a guard, to take care of the wounded, until the doctor and an ambulance could be sent to bring them in.

I finally arrived with them on the evening of the 12th instant. I am glad to be able to bear testimony to eagerness displayed both by officers and men to engage the enemy, where he was supposed to be in large force, and to the cheerfulness with which they endured hard riding, drenching rains and hunger, for not expecting to be under

---

[27] Elmer Otis went to the Military Academy from Ohio in 1849. After graduation he served in the 1st Infantry and then became 1st Lt. in the 1st Cavalry, in 1856. He continued in the army to 1891 and died Aug. 18, 1897.– Heitman, p. 762.

the necessity of going more than twenty miles, very little to eat was carried along in pockets, &c., no packs being taken.

Very respectfully, your obedient servant,

WM. STEELE
Captain, second Dragoons

LIEUTENANT J. A. THOMPSON,
Adgt. Kiowa Expedition

(b) LIEUTENANT STUART'S REPORT

CAMP, SEVEN MILES ABOVE BENT'S FORT
On Arkansas River,   July 12, 1860

SIR: I have the honor to make the following report of a scout made by a detachment of twenty United States cavalry, under my command, in compliance with instructions from the major commanding, on the morning of 11th instant. The detachment formed from the column at a moment's notice, marched directly north from Bent's Fort, the direction in which the "Kiowa war-chief *Litarki*" was reported to have just fled with his family, in all two lodges. I soon found the trail and commenced a rapid pursuit. In a short time I came in sight of them several miles ahead, just as they, having abandoned their lodge poles and other weighty articles of baggage, were prepared for more rapid flight. I saw that my pursuit, to be successful, must be rapid, and followed at full gallop. I gained very perceptibly on them, and after two hours and a half from Bent's Fort, during which I had traversed twenty-six miles, I was just about overhauling the body of Indians, when I recognized Captain Steele's detachment, who were returning to Bent's Fort, from a two-days' scout, and were approaching me, directly in front of the Indians. Perceiving that my capture of the main body would be thus anticipated by the unexpected presence of Captain Steele's detachment, I turned to the right, in order to catch some scattered warriors, who having separated from the main body, were likely to escape in that direction. I had not proceeded far, however, till I saw that part of Captain Steele's command, having mistaken my detachment for Kiowas, were coming after us at a charge. To avoid this, I had already had several calls sounded, but they were not heard. They recognized us on nearer approach, and coming up, the two columns saluted each other with a shout, and joined in pursuit of the common foe.

My horses, though much jaded by the hard run, did well, and the last warrior killed was mortally wounded by Sergeant Occleston, of my detachment, who, after both he and the Indian, having left their horses exhausted, kept up the chase on foot. Two warriors were killed, and one squaw taken prisoner; in this pursuit two squaws mounted on the fleetest ponies escaped.

Privates John Smith, first company G, and Ferdinand Schentz [or Schwartz], company F, first cavalry, of my detachment, received severe but not dangerous wounds.

Finding further pursuit fruitless, and that Lieutenant Bayard had received a severe arrow wound in the face, I rallied the men in advance and conducted him safely back a distance of six miles, to Captain Steele's camp, as he belonged to that detachment. Though not of my command, I deem it proper to add my testimony to the gallant bearing and personal daring he displayed.

Sergeant William Occleston, company G, and Corporal George S. Newman, company K, first cavalry, deserve special commendation for their gallantry and good conduct throughout. Every man in my detachment proved himself every inch a soldier.

The sixteen women and children, and twenty or thirty ponies captured by Captain Steele's detachment, would have been inevitably captured by my party. I have since learned that Litarki was not with this band at the time, but that the two warriors killed were his brother and son, and the squaws were his.

As I joined Captain Steele at Black Water, the remainder of my scout is embraced in his report.

I reached this camp at 8 p.m., without the loss of a man or a horse.[28]

Most respectfully, your obedient servant,

J. E. B. STUART

First Lieut.   First Cav. Com'g Detachment

LIEUTENANT J. A. THOMPSON,
Adj't of Major Sedgwick's Column

---

11.   MAJOR SEDGWICK'S REPORT OF AUGUST 11 [29]

CAMP   NEAR FORT LARNED, K.T.,   August 11, 1860

SIR: I have the honor to report that I left the

---

[28] See Stuart's Journal in the following section, for another account of the action.

[29] *Sen. Ex. Doc.* 1 (ser. 1079), *op. cit.*, p. 18.

Arkansas on the 25th ultimo, forty miles below Aubrey's Crossing, marching northward, with the intention of ascertaining if there were any hostile Indians on the Smoky Hill, its tributaries, or in their vicinity.[30] Before reaching the Smoky Hill, I found water only in three places, once at a spring, and twice in pools. The Smoky Hill I found perfectly dry. I sent a command up the stream, which returned, reporting neither water nor late Indian signs for seventeen miles. The main command then moved down the river, a detachment crossing to the Saline, (striking near where Colonel Sumner destroyed the Cheyenne village in 1857,) proceeding down the stream a portion of two days, and rejoining on the Smoky Hill. Captain Steele, with his squadron second dragoons and Captain Walker's company first cavalry, proceeded down the river to the old bridge, crossed to Cow Creek, and thence to this camp, which he reached this day. With the remaining three companies of the command, I recrossed to Walnut Creek, followed it down to within a few miles of its mouth, and then leaving it, reached this camp on the 9th instant, having been out seventy days, and having marched upwards of twelve hundred and fifty miles, in all the scout discovering no Indian signs. On arriving here, I learned that Captain Sturgis, upon the information of certain Kaw Indians, (twenty of whom have accompanied him, promising to lead his command to a camp of about a hundred Indians on Solomon's Fork,) marched from this post on the 28th ultimo.[31] I trust he may be more successful than we have been. My opinion is that the Kiowas and Camanches have scattered; a few roving about in small bands, the others, with the women and children, being mixed with the

---

[30] A fuller account is given in Stuart's Journal, which follows.

[31] The Sturgis report is given below, as Section c.

Cheyennes, Arrapahoes, and Apaches. Late accounts from Major Ruff say he has been unable to find them. I have discharged and sent to their homes the Delaware guides, and shall proceed to obey General Orders, No. 8, (which I found waiting me here), as soon as practicable.

Very respectfully, your obedient servant,

JOHN SEDGWICK
Major First Cavalry

CAPTAIN D. R. JONES, A.A.G.,
Headquarters Department of the West,
Saint Louis, Mo.

B: LIEUTENANT J. E. B. STUART'S JOURNAL, MAY 15 TO AUGUST 11

INTRODUCTION

James Ewell Brown Stuart, in command of Company G of the expedition of 1860, was a native of Virginia, having been born at "Laurel Hill" plantation, in Patrick County. He graduated from the United States Military Academy in 1854, and served first with the Mounted Rifles in Texas. Transferred to the 1st Cavalry in 1855, he spent most of the next six years in Kansas. There he married Flora, a daughter of Colonel Philip St. George Cooke. With the outbreak of the Civil War, Stuart joined the Confederate forces. His distinguished service as a dashing cavalry officer is so celebrated that it need not be recounted here.[1]

In the campaign of 1860, Lieutenant Stuart was the official journalist of the expedition. At the end of the document it is stated that the journal was kept "very accurately" "from notes taken during the day, and copied every evening." The record was kept in conformity with the following official instructions:

The journal should be kept in a pocket note book; or, if one cannot be obtained, in a book made of sheets of paper folded to half the letter size.

The record is to run from the bottom to the top of each page.

The horizontal divisions in the column headed *"Route"* repre-

---

[1] *Dictionary of American Biography*, XVIII, pp. 270-72; H. B. McClellan, *The Life and Campaigns of Major-General J. E. B. Stuart* (1885); J. W. Thomason, *Jeb Stuart* (New York, 1930).

sent portions of a day's march. The distance, in miles, between each of the horizontal divisions, will be noted in the column headed "*Distance,*" which will be summed up at the top of each column, and the sum carried to the bottom of the next column.

The notes within each horizontal division are to show the general direction of the march, and every object of interest observed in passing over the distance represented thereby; and all remarkable features, such as hills, streams with their names, fords, springs, houses, villages, forests, marshes, &c., and the places of encampment, will be sketched in their relative positions.

The "*Remarks*" corresponding to each division will be upon the soil, productions, quantity and quality of timber, grass, water, fords, nature of the roads, &c., and important incidents. They should show where provisions, forage, fuel, and water can be obtained; whether the streams to be crossed are fordable, miry, have quicksands or steep banks, and whether they over-flow their banks in wet seasons; also the quality of the water; and, in brief, everything of practical importance. [From General Orders, no. 12, Adjutant General's Office, Washington, April 16, 1860, attached to the Journal].

The original journal is in Yale University Library, and is published here by the kind permission of that distinguished institution. On the left-hand page of the open journal are five columns, headed: Date, Hour, Weather, Distance, Route. A small sketch map of the day's travel is generally drawn under the "Route" heading, and the direction of travel is given. The right-hand page carries the diary, with a paragraph for each day or part of a day, and beginning at the bottom of the page.

In transcribing the journal we have transposed the paragraphs on each page to put them in chronological order. At the beginning of each day's entry we have added, from the opposite page of the manuscript, the date and hour; and at the end, the number of the camp, the record of the weather, the distance traveled, and the direction of travel.

J. E. B. STUART'S OFFICIAL JOURNAL

JOURNAL OF THE MARCH
OF COMPANIES F, G, H, & K, 1ST CAVALRY,
COMMANDED BY MAJOR JOHN SEDGWICK, 1ST CAVALRY,
FROM FORT RILEY, K.T., ON AN EXPEDITION
AGAINST THE HOSTILE KIOWAS AND COMANCHES;
PURSUANT TO SPECIAL ORDERS NO. 34,
HEAD QUARTERS, DEPARTMENT OF THE WEST,
SAINT LOUIS, MO., APRIL 3D, 1860.

MAY 15, 9 a.m.[2] Cross Clark's bridge over Repub. Fork, ¼ miles above post, thence traverse prairie bottom 2¾ miles, passing Junction City, thriving town, 500 inhabitants, road excellent, grass good, timber on banks of Smoky Hill.[3] S.W.

11:50 a.m. Road rolling, grass good quality. Halted 10 m. [minutes] road good up Smoky Hill, left bank, bluffs to right. Cross big bend of river. Soil rich, farm houses and cultivated fields to left, timber skirting stream. Crossing a small stream, road leaves river bottom, turning westward over high rolling prairie. Good soil and grass. After several miles, turn S.W. to river bottom, passing 7 Springs. Fine water and grass. Wood ½ mile off on Smoky Hill F. S.W. & W.

2:15 p.m. 10 m. halt at the 7 springs, Kansas Falls City, with saw mill, a small town 1 mile to left. Farm houses and cultivated fields, soil remarkably rich. Grass generally good, road generally excellent. Continued up bottom from ½ to 1½ miles fm river, banks of latter

---

[2] Stuart's personal diary, which covers most of the expedition, is in the Alderman Library of the University of Virginia. It was edited by W. Stitt. Robinson and was published in the *Kansas Historical Quarterly* (Winter, 1957), XXIII, pp. 389-99. Hereafter it will be cited as Stuart's Personal Diary. In its first entry Stuart writes: "We expect a 5 mos arduous campaign principally with packmules having our grand depot at Pawnee Fork."

[3] From Junction City they are to follow the Smoky Hill Trail, present U.S. Highway 40, to the vicinity of Ellsworth, which place they reach May 20th. This country was well known and so need not be identified in detail.

skirted with timber ½ miles from 7 springs, pass Rock Spr. at farm house, left of road. Good camp gr. near road. Expr. to Pike's Peak fork took left hand. Ascend high rolling prairies for sev. miles, then descend to crossing of Chapman's Creek, deep ford, boggy and steep on west bank. halt 15 m. and then go into camp on Smoky H. 1 mile beyond. Camp no. 1. Clear and warm, cloudy in afternoon. Distance, 16 miles. S.W.

MAY 16, 6½ a.m.   Crossed bluff. Ascent heavy sand, then bottom of River, traversing immense bottom, road level and hard, grass very fine. At 3½ miles halted 10 m. 8½ miles further water at bend of river near road, then walked ½ hour, reaching Lamb's farm, well cultivated, (new port 2 miles back, almost deserted) fine well at Lamb's. Grass continues fine. River bottom very rich & capacious. Farms at intervals. Bluffs to right of road. Halt 10 m. and mount. W.S.W.

8:45 a.m.   Grass continues fine, road good. Cross two ravines. Crossing good in dry season; traverse long river bottom of very fine grass & soil, formed by big bend of river. At 6 m. cross Muddy Creek; imperfect bridge; crossing tolerable; water & grass good; thriving farm & well; timber on creek and river. Halt ½ hour to see first wagons over. W.S.W.

At 11 continued march up Sandy Hill bottom. At 3½ miles touch bank of Smoky Hill, at mouth of Sand Creek. Small stream; good water. Cross it. Good crossing in dry season *above*. Cross Sand bluffs and pass farm house to left. At Sand Springs fine water rounding about bend. Camp in Smoky Hill bottom, ½ mile fr. spring. Grass good; banks of river boggy. Camp 2. Clear and pleasant. 34 miles.

MAY 17, 6:20 a.m.   Continued up Smoky Hill bottom; bluff to right; road level and very good. At 2 m.

cross; small stream and farm house; crossing good. 3 miles beyond reach Solomon's Fork ferry, passing a small settlement on left bank, called White Cloud. River fordable, but quick-sand at farther bank. Much delay in ferrying. Stream well timbered. Good camp on each bank. Advance at 9:40 a.m. and traversing immense bottom, turn off at 8 miles to Camp on Saline. Camp 3. Rainy forenoon, clear & bright p.m. 13 miles.

MAY 18, 6:25 a.m.   Continued up Saline Fork, on same immense bottom as yesterday. Waters of Saline salt; banks narrow; steep and skirted with good timber; boggy near water's edge, soil exceedingly rich, grass excellent. Pass quite a settlement, with cultivated fields near ferry. 2 miles, crossed at ferry, halting for that purpose till 9:20. Resumed march, turning S.W.

11:15 a.m.   Pass through a magnificent bottom in junction of Saline and Smoky Hill Forks. At 4 miles pass a thriving town called Salina, on Smoky Hill.– Houses built principally of clap-boards. 1 doz. houses. A ferry here across Smoky Hill, on a road leading to Lawrence. Fine crops of corn raised in vicinity. 2 miles farther pass Dry Creek. Banks high; water rather stagnant. Crops good. S.W.

1:10 p.m.   Leaving dry creek after halting 15 minutes, ascend gradually. Soil & grass not so good. Pass pond to right, at 1½ miles; good water. Near this point we leave Bryant's Trail, turning to left to make a cut-off recommended, & leave Mulberry Creek entirely to right. Pass slight ravine 1½ miles farther and descending gradually, again camp on Powell Creek (Spring Creek). Good water, wood & grass, six miles from Dry Creek. Delaware guides[4] join us to-day. Camp 4. Clear & very pleasant. 14 miles. S.S.W.

---

[4] Fall Leaf and others, referred to previously.

MAY 19, 6:17 a.m.   Cross Spring Creek immediately
at camp. Trail led up its left bank a short distance, then
turned to right over bluff. Soil sandy; grass not very
good, except patches; pass land-mark on right hand, on
ridge, 3½ miles. Halt 10 min. March afoot ½ hour,
and halt 10 m. Reach at 3 miles a point on W. Fork of
Spring Creek. Good wood, water & grass. Halt 15 m.
Came on old trail 1 mile back. Settlers guide us.
Advance at 8:45 up W. Fork; cross several bad ravines,
more or less water in their beds, rocky bluffs on right,
– road uneven, but good. S.W.

9:15.   At 1½ miles farther pass land mark to right.
As we advance the country becomes more broken &
abrupt; though very winding the road continues good
in spite of a number of bad ravines intersecting it north
& south. Spring Creek forks near this point again;
rocky bluffs. Halt 20 m. Advance at 10:15 – mile
farther timber to our left in fine quantity on fork of
Spr. Cr. two prominent peaks on farther side of creek;
timber at base. 1 hour's march finds us on a ridge over-
looking creek in front; cross it at 2 miles and cross over
ridge – miles; reach clear creek. camp. Wood, water &
grass excellent. Tributary to Smoky Hill. Camp 5.
Clear, warm. Windy in afternoon. 18 miles. W. & S.W.

MAY 20, 8:10 a.m.   Crossed Clear Creek at Camp,
and going W.S.W. over broken country, about ½ miles,
pass spring in ravine near road on left; cross ravine,
and pass by a buffalo-lick on left, mound to right.
Descend gradually to Smoky Hill fork, full view. Cross
ravine. Spring to right and lone tree. Cross Smoky Hill
Fork (excellent ford) & camp on south bank. Grass
tolerable. Camp 6. Clear & pleasant. Slight rain at
night. 5 miles. W.S.W.

MAY 21, 6:22 a.m.   The route led over a barren and

uninteresting prairie, very uneven, intersected constantly by ravines.– buffalo grass the only vegetation, the prairie covered with myriads of buffalo.[5] At 12 miles cross what is supposed to be Cow Creek, here a dry bed with timber and grass. 13 miles farther brought us to what was supposed to be Walnut Creek [6]– very recently dried up – timber and grass. Column moved on at 2:40 p.m. for water – said to be 16 miles off. S.W. & S.

At 8 miles passed a few miles to our left a lake resembling mirage, probably 34 miles from Camp No. 6, continued our course to a creek in sight, 2 m. farther, well timbered, which proved to be dry. Halted here some time and grased. Continued march at 6:20, and after 7 miles march, almost due south, came to Walnut Creek. Plenty of wood, water and grass. Day's march, 42 miles. Camp 7. Weather clear and pleasant. Southerly breeze. 42 miles. W.S.W. last 7 mi. S.

MAY 22d.   Remained at Camp No. 7 to-day.

MAY 23, 6:30 a.m.   Crossed Walnut Creek over bridge at camp. At 2½ miles cross ravine. Road generally level and through Prairie-dog *cities;* soil barren – Strike Santa Fe route 12 m. from Camp No. 8, at Pawnee Rock; continue it to Ash Cr. 5½ m.– dry but timbered. Ranch here. Leave old road here and cross at bridge, 7½ m. over Pawnee Fork, near Camp Alert [7] and camp below. Poor grass. Camp 8. Clear and windy. Very warm at noon. 25 miles. S.W.

MAY 24, 9 a.m.   Co's C & K 2d Dragoons joined to

---

[5] They are crossing from the Smoky Hill Trail to the Santa Fe Trail, which they will reach on May 25, at Pawnee Rock.

[6] Cow Creek and Walnut Creek are both branches of the Arkansas.

[7] Camp Alert was on the Santa Fe Trail, about six miles up the Pawnee Fork, west of the site of Larned. Camp Alert was afterwards re-named Fort Larned, in honor of Col. B. F. Larned.

day from Fort Kearney.[8] Moved down Pawnee Fork
to Arkansas R. for better grass. Good water and grass.
Wood on Pawnee Fork, 1½ miles off. Camp 9. 5½
miles. E.

Remain in Camp No. 9, recruiting animals and
organizing the pack mule expedition. On the 26th Lt.
J. E. B. Stuart, 1st Cav. detached with 32 rank and file
to reconnoitre to the south. Rejoined Camp on 28th.[9]
Storms of wind and dust from 28th to 29th. On 31st
thunder storm in the afternoon. Preparations are making to march tomorrow with 30 days' rations, and pack
mules into the Kiowa Country south of the Arkansas.
Clear and bright.

JUNE 1st, 8:20 a.m.   The six companies of the command marched on pack mule expedition, continuing
the Santa Fe road (river route).[10] 2d Lt. Merrill,[11] 2d
Drags, and Bayard, 1st Cavalry, joined by the mail late
last night. At 10 miles cross coon creek, (no wood).
5.33 miles farther, Camp on bed of river. Water and
grass. No wood. Camp 10. Clear and pleasant. S.W.
wind blowing. 15.33 miles. S.W.

8 They are under Captain Steele, whom we shall mention later. In his
Personal Diary, Stuart says the command got an odometer here; hence the
more accurate mileage readings hereafter.

9 In his Personal Diary, Stuart gives a record of this expedition. He went
25 miles southeast, to Otter (Rattlesnake) Creek; up the stream northeast
for 32 miles; 20 miles north to the Arkansas; and up the river 25 miles to
camp. "Whole march 102 miles in 48 hours. Men & horses in fine condition."
— Kansas Historical Quarterly, XXIII, p. 392.

10 This was the route along the Arkansas River. Another variant of the
Santa Fe Trail roughly paralleled the river, but was farther from it. See
the large, detailed map prepared and published by the Kansas State His-
torical Society and accompanying its "Report of Committee Appointed to
Prepare a Correct Map of the Old Santa Fe Trail across the State of
Kansas."

11 Lewis Merrill, of Pennsylvania, graduated from the U.S. Military
Academy in 1855. He served in the Civil War and later against the Indians.
He died Feb. 27, 1896.– Heitman, p. 705.

JUNE 2d, 6:20 a.m.   Continued up River bottom,– at 10 miles road touches river bank, and again 8 miles farther. Camp in bend of river. Good grass and water, – no wood. Camp 11.   20.20 miles. S.W.

JUNE 3d, 6:20 a.m.   Advanced up Arkansas, a level road, for ten miles, touching here river bank, then turning over long ridge for 8 miles turn off to camp on Arkansas River, in bottom. Camp 12. Weather good. 18.43 miles. S.S.W.

JUNE 4th, 6:30 a.m.   Crossed Arkansas River, fording it without difficulty, & marched from south bank at 7:30 a.m., due south 3½ miles, touch Mulberry creek, high banks.[12] Good wood and water, Tributary to Arkansas. Crossed ½ mile above there. Dry bed. Continuing southward over barren and monotonous prairie, intersected by many ravines, reach tributary to crooked creek.[13] Water milky hue, but good. Well timbered. Grass scarce and poor. Camp 13. Clear and warm. 17.45 miles. S. & 10° E. of S.

JUNE 5th, 6:20 a.m.   Followed down dry bed of stream, now and then passing water in holes; soil sandy & barren, banks of stream skirted with trees and under growth. Grass very scarce. Camp at poor water and worse grass, on same stream as last night. Water sinks

---

[12] This would make their point of departure from the Arkansas a little above the mouth of Mulberry Creek and west of the present town of Ford, in Ford County. The distance of 53.96 miles traveled from the mouth of Pawnee Fork, June 1 to 3, indicates the same position, which is about 12 miles down the river from Dodge City. In tracing the route through Kansas and Oklahoma we are using the large U.S. Geological Survey Maps of the two states compiled in 1921.

In his Personal Diary, Stuart says they sent back "all the wagons but a Light ammunition wagon & sick ambulance." The odometer was attached to one of these.

[13] Crooked Creek merits its name. It enters the Cimarron a little south of the Kansas-Oklahoma line. But the stream they encountered was not Crooked Creek of today, but Bluff Creek, another branch of the Cimarron.

in sand below this point. Camp 14. Clear and warm. 15 miles. S.E.

JUNE 6th, 6:30 a.m.   March east over rolling prairie 3 m., then S.E. for remainder of day's march. At 5 m. from last camp another stream running S.W. joins the one which we follow; bed sandy and generally dry, running thence nearly south. Camp on the stream. Doubtless tributary to Crooked Creek. Grass very scarce; also water. Good by digging. Wood plenty. Camp 15.[14] Clear and windy. 14.68 miles. E. & S.E.

JUNE 7th, 6:15 a.m.   Left course of stream & crossing a divide S.W. 8 miles, came to dry bed of stream running S.E. supposed to be Crooked Creek. Water in ponds; fresh, and full of fish;– good grass and wood. March thence S. for about 12 miles, over very broken prairie and high ridges. Thence S.E. to dry bed of Cimaron.[15] Camp on small tributary. Grass and water scarce and bad. Little wood. Soil barren and reddish. Camp 16. Clear & pleasant. 25.42 miles. S.W., S. & S.E.

JUNE 8th, 6:20 a.m.   Crossed the dry bed of this stream, and going South over very barren and desolate region, 1½ miles, crossed a very distinct wagon trail, E & W, apparently a year or two old; probably Col. Johnston's 1857 route.[16] Continuing S. about 8 miles, reach dry bed of stream, with water scattered in holes, strongly impregnated with salts; bad taste; probably red fork of Cimaron.[17] A few trees. Grass poor. Soil barren – red. Camp 17. Cloudy. 10.17 miles. S. & S.W.

---

14 This would be in the vicinity of Coldwater, Kansas.

15 They reach the Cimarron about two miles above where it crosses from Kansas into Oklahoma.

16 J. E. Johnston's route in surveying the southern boundary of Kansas. Johnston's journal is found in the *Kansas Historical Quarterly* I, (Feb., 1932), pp. 104-39; other journals in *ibid.*, VI, pp. 339-77, and in R. P. Bieber (ed.), *Frontier Life in the Army* (Glendale, Arthur H. Clark Co., 1932), 121-211.

17 Probably Buffalo or Salt Creek fork of the Cimarron.

JUNE 9th, 6:15 a.m.   Cross directly south for about
7 miles & gradually ascending a rugged and barren
country, intersected by deep ravines, in which are
clumps of timber (cedar and cottonwood). At this
point two streams, well timbered are in full view in
front, near their junction.[18] Cross the first and camp
after 3 miles descent S.E. The main stream guides pro-
nounce N. Fork of Canadian. Good wood and grass.
Water slightly saline. Camp 18. Clear and warm. 9.91
miles. S. & S.E.

JUNE 10th.   Remain in Camp. Col. Johnston's return route, 1857, discovered. Clear.

JUNE 11th, 1860, 6:15 a.m.   Marched up N. bank
of N. Fork of Canadian,[19] over sand bluffs, falling into,
and continuing for a few miles, Col. Johnston's return
route 1857, now quite indistinct. Stream well timbered,
water very good. Entered, at about ten miles, a very
extensive bottom of fine grass and fertile soil, intersected by narrow belt of timber. At 16 miles crossed to
S. bank of stream, and continued up south bank, passing
over barren sand bluffs, and remains of several old
Indian Camps. Camped in bend of stream. Wood,
water and grass. Camp 19. Cloudy & foggy before 7
a.m. Clear thereafter. 26.81 miles. S.S.W.

JUNE 12, 6:05 a.m.   Continued up the N. Fork of
Canadian, the country preserving the same characteristics as already noted; the timbered portion abounding
in bear, deer and turkey. At 5 miles cross to N. bank; a
few miles farther recross, and about 2 miles farther
still, cross tributary running due north, another entering from north 1 mile above. Crossing again to the

---

[18] Junction of the North Canadian and Wolf Creek, near Supply, Oklahoma.

[19] They ascend Wolf Creek, not the North Canadian; see correction in
entry of June 13th.

north side, marched about 6 miles to camp on North
Fork. Grass poor; water and wood good.

In the afternoon we were joined by a party of the
United States and Texas boundary Commission under
Mr. Clark.[20] From them we learned that they had recently left Fort Cobb,– that there was no water in the
main Canadian south of us. No trace of the Kiowas &
Comanches of a recent date on their route. They are
forty strong and well armed. The Commission is now
following the 100° of longitude. Observations made
show we are in long. 100°, lat. 36° 16'. Camp 20.[21] Clear
and warm. 17 miles. W.S.W.

JUNE 13th, 6:05 a.m.   Continued up same stream,
which from a map furnished by Weiss of the Boundary
Commission,[22] we find is middle river, instead of N.
Fork of Canadian, and that camp No. 18 was on the N.
Fork proper, now about 30 miles north of this. Streams
& Country preserve same characteristics as already
noted, except that timber is scarcer to-day. Camped in
good grass. Road, to-day, much cut up by ravines.–
Several small tributaries crossed en route, now dry.
Camp 21. Fair. Slight hail storm p.m. 21.70 miles.
West.

JUNE 14th, 6:05 a.m.   Marched up Middle River,
now skirted with less timber. Abrupt cedar bluffs on
either side, outcropping rock near their summits.
Camped on last appearance of water in stream. Grass
very scarce and poor. Wood and water. Country becomes more broken and abrupt. Passed Indian Camp

---

20 A map of the survey and an account of it are found in Marcus Baker,
The Northwest Boundary of Texas (Bulletin of the United States Geological
Survey, no. 194, Wash., 1902).– Cited in W. S. Robinson, *op. cit.,* p. 395.

21 This camp is where Wolf Creek crosses the Oklahoma line.

22 John E. Weyss was surveyor of the southern Kansas boundary of 1857
also.– Stuart's Personal Diary, and its editor.

remains, about 2 months old. Camp 22. Clear a.m., Rain p.m. 13.50 miles. West.

JUNE 15th, 6 a.m.   Having left Middle River, a direction of 5° W. of North brought us to Camp on N. Fork of Canadian. Country traversed, a level tract of prairie dog settlements. About 10 a.m., a herd of wild horses, at first believed to be Indians, were seen in the distance. The N. Fork has no timber at this point. Grass not sufficient for the Command. Camp 23. Clear & warm. 34.75 miles. 5° W. of N.

JUNE 16, 7 a.m.   Followed up banks of stream, crossing it several times. Small bottoms of good grass in the bends. Sand hills to right. Little or no timber. Camped on grass very limited. Great scarcity of fuel.– The country traversed to-day, though quite broken, was monotonous,– no game, no buffalo. A good deal of quick sand in the stream. It receives, 4 or 5 miles back, a tributary from S.W.[23] Camp 24. Clear, warm & hot wind. 19.35 miles. W.S.W. 5 mis., W. 3 m., then N.N.W.

JUNE 17, 6:10 a.m.   Marched up north Fork 3½ miles and crossed to south bank. 1½ miles farther we came into Col. Johnston's 1857 trail. Quite distinct, followed it remainder of day's march. Passed, early in the day, a point where the Indians were encamped in 1857. Several bottoms of fine grass during march. Camp on bank of stream. No wood. Grass and water. Game scarce. Camp 25. Fine. 14.06 miles. W.

JUNE 18th, 6:10 a.m.   Marched up the river 6½ miles along Col. Johnston's route. Cross stream at 6½ miles. Game continues very scarce. The stream is dry on to-day's route, except in holes. Crossed tributary a mile or two from crossing, and then over a flat, barren prairie. For the remainder of the march the route

---

[23] Coldwater Creek.

descends gradually to a grassy bottom. Good water. No wood. Greasewood used for fuel. Camp 26. Clear & pleasant. 19.10 miles. W.S.W.

JUNE 19th. Lay bye to-day. Lt. J. H. Taylor sent forward 18 miles to ascertain if ponds on Col. Johnston's trail contain water. Lt. G. D. Bayard sent on reconnaissance up the river, 10 or 12 miles, water being reported very scarce ahead. Clear & pleasant.

JUNE 20th. The commander finding that there was no water up the stream, beyond 12 miles farther, and no water at the ponds visited by Lt. Taylor, on Col. Johnston's route, concluded to make farther reconnaissance. Accordingly Lt. Stuart went forward, with a small party, to a point 40 miles distant on the route, and Lts. Bayard & Taylor to a point on stream 27 miles off. Clear and warm.

JUNE 21st, 4:50 a.m. Lts. Bayard & Taylor returned at 9 p.m. on the 20th, reporting no water. Lt. Stuart returned at 1 a.m. on the 21st,[24] reporting water at the 40 miles point of Col. J.'s route. The command marched almost due west over a barren journada. Dry ponds at different points. Col. J.'s Camp at ponds 25 miles. The road very good. Camped at water in holes, being in dry bed of the north fork of Canadian. Water good by digging a few feet. Grass scarce. No fuel.– Antelope the only game. Camp 27. Clear and hot. West wind. 40.25 miles. W.

JUNE 22d, 6 a.m. [and 23d]. Marched N.N.W., crossing the Santa Fe road about 20 miles, passing over a level barren tract. A few miles farther came into Aubrey's trail.[25] Followed it to Cimaron. Co. H, 1st

---

[24] Stuart wrote in his Personal Diary, June 21: "I have marched 120 miles in 35 hours during all which time I have slept but 1½ hours." *op. cit.,* p. 396.

[25] Named for Francis X. Aubrey (Aubry), famous Santa Fe Trail trader, who pioneered a new trail in 1851 and '52. It left the main Santa Fe Trail

Cav. was detached at camp this morning to bring up the beef cattle, 3 having been abandoned en route yesterday, and many footsore. On the 23rd Co. H. joined with the cattle, and the command moved upstream to better grass.[26] On 22nd 3 horses abandoned from exhaustion, of Co. C. 2d Drags. Water good. Grass scarce. Scattered trees. An express was sent this morning to Pawnee Fork, for 30 day's provisions. Camp 28. Clear and pleasant. 32.90 miles. N.N.W.

JUNE 24, 4:20 p.m.   Early to-day, Lt. Otis,[27] with 10 men, sent forward to Bear (two butte river)[28] to reconnoitre for water. At 4:20 p.m. the command marched down to Aubrey's trail and followed it till 10½ p.m. Halted, stripped the animals, and picketed out to grass,— the men sleeping by their saddles till morning. Lt. Otis not having returned, it was concluded that there was water at Bear Riv. Camp 29. Cloudy. 18.75 miles. N.N.E.

JUNE 25, 4 a.m.   Saddling up at daylight, we pursued Aubrey's trail till 11½ a.m., when we arrived at Bear R. Water good, but very little grass. Lt. Otis' party joined here. A few trees. Camped. Cattle came up in afternoon. Camp 30.[29] Clear a.m., cloudy p.m. 26.25 miles. N.N.E.

JUNE 26, 4:15 p.m.   We lay by till afternoon, preparatory to another long march without water. A trail of small party of Indians discovered near camp, leading

---

near Cold Spring, in present Cimarron County, Oklahoma, and took a generally northeast course to Bear River, and thence to the Arkansas east of Syracuse, Kansas. See R. P. Bieber (ed.), *Frontier Life in the Army, op. cit.,* p. 189.

[26] The Personal Diary says they moved up stream four miles.

[27] See above, III, A, fn. 27.

[28] Two Buttes Creek was farther to the northwest.

[29] This camp would be on Bear River, near the site of Bartlett, Colorado, about 25 miles east of Springfield.

towards Bent's Ft. About 5 hrs march brought us unexpectedly to water on Bear R. Camp. Trees. Camp 31. Pleasant. 18.62 miles. N.E.

JUNE 27, 4:20 p.m. [and 28th]. We lay by as usual, preparatory to a long march, till the afternoon, when the command saddled & continued the march on Aubrey's trail till about 10 p.m. Having marched about 21 miles, the command was halted and animals picketed out on the roadside. At daybreak the command was again under way, and about 1½ past 8 a.m. reached the Arkansas River.[30] Grass good. Rain at night. Two of Bent's trains passin[g] on opposite side. Camp 32. Cloudy. Thunderstorm at night. 36.29 miles. N.E.

JUNE 29. About 8 a.m. we crossed the Arkansas to better grass, camping exactly opposite our former camp. Crossing good. Route to Bents Fort and Pike's Peak leads up the river. Camp 33.

JUNE 30 to JULY 2d.[31] Remain in camp 33, awaiting supplies from Pawnee Fork & resting animals. Clear.

JULY 3d, 8 a.m. Lts. Bayard & Taylor left yesterday for Capt. Sturgis' Camp,[32] which is said to be 60 m. off. Went down the river 7 miles to camp in bottom. Met supply train with mail. Grass good. Wood at clump of trees 1½ miles from camp. Camp 34. Clear & hot. 7.00 miles. E.

JULY 4. An express arrived early today from Com. Officer at Ft. Larned, informing Major Sedgwick of a rumor that the Kiowas & Comanches, in all 330 lodges, were camped 20 miles N.E. of Denver City. His dis-

---

30 They reached the Arkansas at Aubry's Crossing (see Sedgwick's letter of July 2nd). This was at a point about 8 miles east of Syracuse, Kansas.

31 In his Personal Diary of July 1st Stuart says that Col. [Ceran] St. Vrain passed in an ambulance and said that the command's supply train should arrive next day.

32 For Capt. Sturgis' campaign, see section c, below.

patch was dated July 2d. Lts. Bayard & Taylor returned. Capt. S.'s [Sturgis'] column contemplates crossing over to Pawnee Fork; thence by Cow Creek back to Cimaron.

JULY 6th.   Supply train sent back with disch'd men & extra animals to Pawnee Fork.

JULY 7th, 6:15 a.m.   Marched up the Arkansas along the route to Bent's Fort and Denver City. Road generally level.– Scattered trees on islands, but none on either bank. Grass very scarce towards latter part of march. Camped at lower end of "Big Timbers," [33] in bend of River. Camp 35. Clear & strong north wind. 20.00 miles. West.

JULY 8th, 5½ a.m. [34]   Marched up Arkansas. Scattered timber along either bank, constituting the grove called "Big Timbers," which extends to Bent's Fort. The grass is good in the bottoms, which are from ¼ to 1½ miles wide. The road winds near the low range of bluffs to right. Crossed, to-day, two dry beds. Scattered trees. Heavy sand about half way. Camp 36. Clear & pleasant. 22.40 miles. West.

JULY 9th, 5:45 a.m.   Marched up the Arkansas and camped 3 miles below Bent's Fort. Large Cottonwoods in the bend of River. Capt. Steele, with a portion of the command, leaving weak horses and packs, left at 12 o'clock at night, to surprise and attack a party of Kiowas reported 20 miles off. Det. supplied with two days rations. Camp 37. Clear & warm. 24.00 miles.

JULY 10th.   The command lay by, awaiting tidings from Capt. Steele, and getting supplies of Bent. The Fort is an enclosure of stone & clay, about 20 feet high,

---

[33] This large grove of cottonwood trees extended for miles along the Arkansas. It was heavier farther up, near Bent's New Fort.

[34] The Personal Diary skips from this date to August 1st.

with rooms arranged like Case-mates [?]. Foundation solid rock. 12 rooms 16′ by 18′ & 1.40′ long & 1.30′ long. Fire places.[35]

JULY 10th Contd. 5:45 a.m. The Command under Capt. Steele, after 4 miles march, struck the large Indian trail from Bent's Fort, running N.N.E., and at a brisk gait followed it about 22 miles,– reaching, at that point, two water holes where Indians were supposed to be, but found no sign of them. Water in dry bed; poor grass, water brackish. Clear. 26.00 miles.

3 p.m.–Leaving the water holes after an hour's rest, the command followed the valley of dry bed of that stream,[36] a little E. of N. for 7 or 8 miles; then a little W. of N., 15 miles from last water, reaching here another water hole. Good water; little grass. Thence N.W. 12 miles. Thence W. 3 miles to a slough in same valley, where the Kiowas were reported to have been, but found no trace of them. Camped.[37] Course of str. W. Terrific storm at night. 30 miles.

JULY 11th, 5:40 a.m. Hill 15 or 20 miles off, said to be Republican Fork bluffs. About 17 miles march due south to return to Bent's Fort, brought the command to a spring called Black Water Spring. Just as the command neared it, a few Indians, pronounced Kiowas, appeared directly in front, and a larger party, afterwards found to be Lt. J. E. B. Stuart's, who had pursued the Indians from Bent's Fort. The two commands

35 This was Bent's New Fort, built by William W. Bent in 1853, after he had abandoned his original and more famous fort about 35 miles farther up the river. Bent's New Fort was on the north bank of the Arkansas, nearly opposite the railroad station of Prowers, and about ten miles west of Lamar, Colorado. The ruins are clearly discernable, and a historical plaque marks the site.

36 Sand Creek, upon which later occurred the notorious Sand Creek Massacre (1864).

37 This would be a little below the site of the town of Kit Carson, Colorado.

joined in the pursuit, and 2 wariors were killed, 16 women and children captured, with 40 ponies, mules & baggage. Lieut. G. D. Bayard, 1st Cav. severely wounded in the face. Pursued 6 or 7 miles. 24 miles. s.

JULY 11th (contd) 7 a.m.   The remainder of the command, with the supplies, moved 10.47 miles up the river to fresh grass. As it passed Bent's Fort, Lieut. J. E. B. Stuart with 20 men was detached to give chase to Sotanke & family (2 lodges) who had just fled. After rapid pursuit of 26 miles traversed in 2½ hours over-hauld them in conjunction with Capt. Steele. Two privates wounded. Enemy's loss, (see previous page) [above, this page]. Pursuit of 7 miles farther. Distance traversed by Lt. S. 40 miles. Route almost level & hard soil. Cloudy & pleasant.

About 4 p.m. Lt. Otis, with large part of com'd of Capt. Steele & prisoners &c. started for Bent's Fort, arriving, at Major Sedgwick's camp about 6 p.m. Capt. Steele, with remainder, & Lieut Stuart, with his detachment, awaited at Blackwater, the arrival of Surgeon & ambulance for Lieut. Bayard. No rations in camp. Water good. But little grass. Camp 38. Cloudy & pleasant. 10.47 miles.

JULY 12th, 12 m.   The Surgeon arriving at 11 a.m., the party left at 12 m. and proceeding a little W. of S., struck road above Bent's Fort, and reached supply Camp at 8 p.m., 5 miles above.

JULY 13th, 8 a.m.   The command started for better grass, and in half hour camped in large bottom. Good grass; scattered trees. Bluff in front. Road leaves the river and passes over bluff a mile or two from camp. Kiowa prisoners put in charge of Agent Bent.[38] Camp 39. Good. 2.00 miles.

---

[38] William W. Bent had been appointed Indian Agent.

JULY 14th, 7 a.m.   A portion of command, under Capt. De Saussure,[39] 1st Cav., leaving weak horses and provisions;– taking five days rations, marched for a scout in that part of country on S. bank of river N.W. [S.W.] of camp. Lieuts. Merrill, Long [40] & Williams [41] with the command. Marched up river 11 miles.

The command forded the river at that point. Ford deep and impracticable. Guide reports better ford at mouth of Dry creek, below. Struck well beaten Indian trail up right bank of Purgatoire river.[42] Followed it 8 miles S.S.W., and camped. Good wood and water, but no grass at this season, but probably good after fall rains. Clear and very warm. Slight rain p.m. 8 miles. W. & S.S.W.

JULY 15th, 6 a.m.   Marched up right bank of Purgatoire 5½ miles and crossed at good ford. At 1½ miles farther, passed dry creek; a little timber on it. Left the bank of stream here some miles, and after 5 miles crossed dry creek. 1½ miles farther mounted the bluffs. A mountain visible to S.W.– supposed to be Spanish Peaks.[43] At 1½ miles crossed deep ravine bed of stream. Holes of brackish water. Banks rocky and steep.

Crossed very rocky bluff, and 2 miles brought us a granite valley of stream. Valley 2 miles wide, included between high & steep rocky bluffs, covered with cedar near their tops. 4 miles farther camped opposite the

---

[39] See above, III, A, fn. 26.

[40] Eli Long, of Kentucky, became a 2nd Lt. in the 1st Cavalry in 1856. He fought for the Union through the Civil War and lived until Jan. 5, 1903.– Heitman, p. 639.

[41] Solomon Williams, of North Carolina, graduated from West Point in 1858. He served as a Confederate colonel in the Civil War and was killed in battle, June 9, 1863.– Heitman, p. 1042.

[42] The Purgatoire, a main southern branch, enters the Arkansas about two miles below the town of Las Animas.

[43] The Spanish Peaks, or Huajatolla (Breasts of the World) were famous landmarks and are about 20 miles southwest of Walsenburg.

mouth of a dry creek – timber heavy and abundant near river. Water good. No grass. Bear and deer plenty. Remains of Indian camps, but none recent. Clear and warm. Cloudy p.m. 21 miles.

JULY 16th.   Marched up left bank of Purgatoire 11 miles, and returned by same road, 12 miles & camped. Valley narrow as we ascended. Good grass at the highest point reached. At camp no grass this season. Guide says Cheyennes and Arapahoes winter here. Remains of old Camps. Clear & warm. 23 miles.

JULY 17th. 6 a.m.   Marched back on our trail 4 miles, and marched thence N.W. to the Arkansas, 16 miles. Crossed river at Bents Old Fort,[44] and marched down one mile to camp. Good wood, water and grass. The ford at Bent's old Fort is excellent, and the footing for animals good. Clear and warm. 21.00 miles. N.W.

JULY 18th.   Marched down the river 10 miles and struck our outward. Continued 11 miles farther to the camp of supplies in bend of river, having moved up the river two or three miles to fresh grass. Clear & warm. Rainy p.m. 21 miles. East.

JULY 19th.   Lay by, recruiting animals. Camp 40.

JULY 20th, 7:15 a.m.   Marched down the river, past Bent's Fort, and camped 3 miles below, in Camp 37. The Cheyennes, Apaches and Arapahoes were assembled at Bent's Fort, to receive from him, their agent, their annuities to-day. The presents consisted of blankets, cloth, calico, provisions, hoop-iron, axes, rifles. Camp 41. Weather very fine. 15.81 miles. East.

JULY 21, 6½ a.m.   Marched down the Arkansas and camped near Camp 36. Crossed Dry creek, about 13

---

44 This was the original Bent's Fort, founded by Bent and St. Vrain in 1833, and famous in the history of the Southwest. For the fullest account of this early trading post, see David Lavender, *Bent's Fort* (Garden City, New York, Doubleday and Co., 1954). It was abandoned and partially destroyed in 1849.

miles. Grass greatly improved. No good camp for first 20 miles. Road sandy, but generally level. Camp 42. Clear & pleasant. 25.09 miles. E.

JULY 22, 6 a.m. Continued the march down the river, passing 2 dry creeks, and camped at Camp 35. Grass excellent. A large bottom of very fine grass about 7 miles above, in a large bend of the river. Camp 43. Cloudy a.m. 22.88 miles. E.

JULY 23, 6 a.m. Marched down the river over a level and good road, winding along the base of low bluffs, at from ¼ to 2 miles from river bank. Camped at Camp No. 34. Grass scarce; wood also. Camp 44. Cloudy. 21.30 miles. E.

JULY 24, 6 a.m. Continued the march down the Ark. At 10½ m. passed bend of river good for watering, and soon after mounted a mesa of 8 or 10 miles. Country broken. Crossed dry bed of 2 streams, one at beginning of mesa, the other after about 17 miles march. Camped in river bottom, some distance from the road. Camp 45. Clear & windy. 19.40 miles. N.E.

JULY 25, 6 a.m. Marched down the river. Leaving bottom passed over high level prairie. At 12¾ miles road came to bend of river. Good for watering. Several islands. Passed over similar high prairie, and gradually, descended. Camping several miles from road on bank of river. Camp 46. Very hot. Shower p.m. 21.76 miles. N.E.

JULY 26, 6:15 a.m. Marched down river 6 miles, then left road, bearing eastward. Lt. Bayard sent in ambulance direct to Pawnee Fork, with escort of Lt. McIntyre [45] & Detachment. After 2¼ miles' march over

---

[45] James B. McIntyre, native of Tennessee, graduated from the Military Academy in 1853. He became a 1st Lt. in the 1st Cavalry in 1857, and regimental quartermaster in 1858. He served the Union in the Civil War and died May 10, 1867.– Heitman, p. 669.

GENERAL "JEB" STUART
From a photograph made during the Civil War.
Courtesy of The National Archives, Washington.

a rolling prairie, we struck Lt. Bryan's 1855 trail, running N.E. Following it over a level prairie and excellent road, we struck Heck's [or Heth's] branch of Pawnee Fork & Camped. No timber. Grass good. The water here is in fine springs and detached pools. Camp 47. Clear and pleasant. Slight rain at night. 21.35 miles. E. & N.E.

JULY 27, 6 a.m. March down the bed of stream. Cross it dry at 3 or 4 miles. And soon after bear eastward. Route, to-day, continues on Bryan's trail, and is intersected by many ravines,– deep, and with abrupt banks. Camp on large pools of water.– Grass poor and scarce. Extensive deposits of sulphate of lime on to-day's march; chiefly of the variety *selenite*. Camp 48.[46] Clear & warm. 21.70 miles. N.E. 5 m., & E.

JULY 28, 6 a.m. Marched due north. Crossed a stream with water in pools, at 9 or 10 miles, supposed tributary to Pawnee Fork. About 3 miles farther crossed another, but dry. An extensive ledge of limestone rock on its bank to our left. Scattered Trees on both these streams. (cottonwood). At 19 miles from our last camp crossed another stream, with no water at present; bottom covered with good grass. A mile or two farther, turn N.E., descending gradually to Walnut Creek, which we crossed at about 23 miles from last camp. Finding no water, followed it down a few miles, and found water in its bed in pools. Little or no grass. Camped. Camp 49. Clear and pleasant. 26.33 miles. N.E. 4 m. E.

JULY 29th, 6 a.m. Marched over an extensive divide, bet. waters of Walnut Cr. & Smoky Hill Fork. Quite a grove of timber several miles to our right along the bed of Walnut Cr. Reach, in 1½ hours' march, a tributary to Smoky Hill Fork, with running water,

---

[46] This would be near the town of Ravena, in Finney Co., Kansas.

which I name Limestone Creek, from the great quantity of limestone in the vicinity. Grass limited, but better than yesterday. Camp 50. Clear and pleasant. Thunderstorm at night. 7.40 miles. 15° E. of N.

JULY 30th, 6½ a.m. Marched due north, passing a tributary to limestone Cr. at 2 miles. Running water, boggy banks; grass scarce. Ascended gradually, for several miles, a long slope thickly matted with buffalo-grass. Reaching the summit, the abrupt cliffs, blue & gray, of the Smoky Hill are in view, which we approach by a narrow, high, neck, between 2 tributaries for several miles. Camped a mile below. Camp 51.[47] Clear & pleasant. 18.88 miles. North.

JULY 31st, 7 a.m. A portion of the command followed up the Smoky Hill 17 miles, but finding no water at that point, returned across the bend of River 10 miles. The stream tends considerably northward, as high up as followed. Returned to camp of the remaining portion, 2 miles below the former. Camp 52. Good. 29.00 miles. N.W. ret. S.E.

AUG. 1st, 6 a.m. A portion of the command marched 20° W. of N. for 9 miles, reaching a tributary to Smoky Hill. Water in pools in bed of stream. Patches of fine grass; and wood plenty.– On the north bank a well travelled wagon road leads E. & W.,– same as course of stream. Proceeded thence E. of N. 10°, and at 8 miles reached another tributary to Smoky Hill, running East, Water in pools. Patches of fine grass. No wood. Pleasant a.m. p.m. hot. S. wind. 17.00 miles.

AUG. 1st, 12:30 p.m. After an hour's grazing we proceeded east down the course of this stream, which Fall Leaf said was tributary to Smoky Hill, 9 or 10

---

47 They are on the Smoky Hill River, near the boundary between Gove and Trego counties.

miles. Banks, at intervals, very abrupt; water becoming scarcer as we advance down it. Smoky Hill bluffs being in sight, strike due South, and at 4 miles reach 1st stream. Follow it down South 4 miles farther & Camp. Good grass, water and wood. Camp 53. Very sultry p.m. 18.00 miles.

AUG. 2d, 7 a.m.   Marched E.S.E., so as to join the remainder of Command on route down the Smoky Hill;– soon came in view of it & march parallel to it to camp (54). The column moving down the Smoky Hill having travelled Eastward for the 2 days, (see sketch on previous page) accomplishing therein 29.91 miles. Camped on rain water in pools. Buffalo seen. Camp 54. Good. 18.00 miles.

AUG. 3d, 7 a.m.   Travelled down the emigrant road which intersected our route yesterday near Camp, and, after 4 miles, crossed Smoky Hill Fork. The emigrant road here leads due South.– Leaving it, we continued due East about six miles, crossing again the river, and camp on a tributary about a mile from the river. Grass scarce, but good on the stream. Camp 55. Cloudy. 10.85 miles. East.

AUG. 4th, 6:40 a.m.   Continued East along the Smoky Hill Fork, over rolling prairie, frequently intersected by abrupt ravines. A wagon route, little travelled, but distinctly marked with pyramids of sod, coincided generally with our route to-day. being a branch of the emigrant road left yesterday. Pass small creek. Water in pools at 8 miles, with a few trees. At 9 & 13 miles, dry creeks. At 14 a tributary enters from S.W., well timbered. At 17, water in holes. Myriads of buffalo in sight. No grass to be found. Camp on Smoky Hill. Water, as usual, bad. Camp 56.[48] 22.28 miles. East.

---

[48] This would be near the town of Pfeifer, at the southern border of Ellis County.

AUG. 5, 6½ a.m. The command here separated, on account of the great scarcity of grass. 3 Cos. moving down the Smoky Hill, the remaining 3 Co's. crossing over to the Walnut Cr. to follow down it.[49] General course of the Smoky Hill east. Our route, to-day, coincides generally with emigrant road, and intersected by ravines every few miles. The banks of river are very abrupt and difficult of approach. No grass.– Camp on Smoky Hill. Feed horses on boughs of trees. Camp 57. Very hot & sultry. 24.50 miles. East.

AUG. 6, 6½ a.m. Route continued down Smoky Hill. Country gradually more timbered along the numerous ravines & tributaries. From the sides of these ravines springs of most delicious water ooze out, but sink almost immediately. Route coincides with emigrant route. Great numbers of buffalo. No grass on to-day's march. Camp on Smoky Hill, and feed horses on boughs of trees. Camp 58. Good. 20.93 miles. East.

AUG. 7, 6½ a.m. Continued generally east down the left bank of river, which now appears to have more water; though not yet running, many tributaries, now dry, put in from South side, and one at 7 miles, from north side. At about 16 miles halted till just at 4 p.m., and then resuming the march for a mile or two below, reach where the command from Riley crossed the Smoky Hill Fork, May 20th.[50] Citizens found here, hunting buffalo. Crossed over to tolerable grass, and camped on north bank. Camp 59. Good. 20.70 miles. East.

AUG. 8th. We lay by.

AUG. 9th, 6:20 a.m. Re-crossed Smoky Hill and

[49] Major Sedgwick led the 3 companies that took the more direct route to Fort Larned, and arrived there several days ahead of the companies with Stuart. See Stuart's Personal Diary, *op. cit.,* p. 398.

[50] A little east of Ellsworth.

followed Sedgwick's route [51] past Little Cow Cr. in which we found not water sufficient, and leaving the route a few miles beyond, proceeded 13 miles S.W., to a clump of trees and Sand Hills, where, as the guides told us, we found delicious springs, apparently perennial, and tolerable grass. In wet weather there are holes along to-day's march, *No* doubt abundantly supplied with water. Buffalo still abundant. Camp 60. Very pleasant. Heavy storm of sleet & rain p.m. 28.13 miles. W.S.W. & S.W.

Aug. 10th, 7 a.m.   Marched over a ridge 10° W. of S.W., crossing an immense basin 8 or 10 miles wide. Crossing another ridge brought us to Walnut Creek, (12½ mi), a mile or two below where Maj. Sedgwick crossed it going out in May, and 3 or 4 miles above Alison's Ranche,[52] on Santa Fe road. Striking thence 10° S. of S.W., crossed Santa Fe road at about 7 miles, and crossing it, proceeded 3 miles farther to Camp on Arkansas river.[53] No wood. Camp 61. 21.90 miles. S.W.

Aug. 11th, 6½ a.m.   Marched this morning westward, joining the remainder of the command in Camp near the Camp we left on the morning of June 1st.[54] Horses much worn, and lean from scarcity of grass. Fair. Storm p.m. 18.00 miles. W. Total distance, 1404.16 miles.

In compliance with General Orders, No. 8, from the Head Quarters of the Army, Companies F G H and K,

---

[51] They are now to retrace approximately the outward route of the command in the preceding May.

[52] Near Great Bend. Regarding Allison's Ranch, see fn. 8, in Part I, c, above.

[53] At the junction of Pawnee and Arkansas rivers.

[54] Here, according to Stuart's Personal Diary, they met Sedgwick's guides and learned that the expedition had been broken up and that four companies of cavalry had been ordered to Bent's Fort to winter and to build a military post. Wrote Stuart: "Everybody is blue and disgusted."

1st Cavalry, marched for Fort Wise, the new post in the vicinity of the big timbers, on the 18th of August, and arrived on the 29th. The distance is two hundred and thirty-seven miles; but the route was so well known it was not deemed necessary to record the days' marches.

This Journal has been very accurately kept by Lieut. J. E. B. Stuart, 1st Cavalry, from notes taken during the day, and copied every evening.

The season has been excessively dry. No water to be found in creeks and pools, where, in ordinary seasons, there is an abundance. In the Smoky Hill, where, in 1857, there was several inches of running water, there was none, and for an hundred miles below. Grass has been equally scarce; at this time there has been no rain for several months.

FORT WISE, BIG TIMBERS,
Sept. 12, 1860

C: STURGIS' CAMPAIGN

INTRODUCTION

Early in June, 1860, six companies of the 1st Cavalry (A, B, C, D, E, and I) were detached from Forts Washita, Arbuckle, and Cobb on a campaign against the hostile Kiowas and Comanches. Eleven officers and 419 enlisted men comprised the expedition, the whole under command of Captain Samuel D. Sturgis.[1]

The troops marched from the Canadian to the Arkansas River, and then followed a hot trail northward. The subsequent story is given in the Sturgis reports that follow.

---

[1] Samuel Davis Sturgis was born and reared in Pennsylvania, and graduated from West Point in 1846. He became a 1st Lt. in 1853, a captain in the 1st Cavalry in 1855. He served with distinction through the Civil War and reached the rank of major general. He retired in 1886 and died Sept. 28, 1889.– Heitman, p. 934.

A brief account of the campaign is given in "Adjutant General's Report of Nov. 20, 1860, accompanying Report of the Secretary of War," Sen. Ex. Doc. 1, 36 Cong., 2 sess. (ser. 1079), 197. In this report the other officers of the command are listed as: Ass't Surgeon Charles T. Alexander, Capts. W. N. R. Beall, James McIntosh, and Eugene A. Carr; 1st Lt. Alfred [Philip] Stockton, Jr.; 2nd Lts. Richard H. Riddick, John R. Church, Edward Ingraham, Lumford L. Lomas, Oliver H. Fish, and Andrew Jackson, Jr.

1. STURGIS' FIRST REPORT OF INDIAN BATTLE [2]

HEAD QRS. SOUTHERN COLUMN
COMANCHE & KIOWAY EXPEDITION
Fort Kearney   N.T.   August 9 1860

CAPT.   I avail myself of the opportunity afforded by the passing mail to report that we came up with a large band of Kioways, Comanches and (I think) Cheyennes, numbering from six hundred to eight hundred, on the 7th inst – on the "Republican," about sixty miles southwest of this place. They had evidently prepared to make a stand, but as we approached them they gave way so that we had a running fight for about fifteen miles, when they scattered into small parties, all taking different directions, and rendering further pursuit impossible. Twenty-nine Indians were killed and I think a large number wounded – on our side we had three men wounded – one missing – three horses killed and two friendly Indians killed. I will make a more minute report of the operations of the Column, since leaving the Arkansas, by the next mail –

I have the honor to be Sir   Most Respectfully Your obt servt.

S. D. STURGIS
Capt. 1 Cav   Comdg.

TO CAPT. JNO. WITHERS
Asst. Adjt. Genl.   Hd Qrs. Dept. of Texas
San Antonio Texas.[3]

[On cover of letter]:   HD. QRS. DEPT. OF TEXAS, San

---

[2] A.G.O., Letters Received, 1860, s 76, National Archives.

[3] On cover of this document is this note: "Hd. Qrs. Dept. of Texas, San Antonio, Sept. 4/ 60. Respectfully forwarded to the Adjutant General through the Head Quarters of the Army R[obert] E. Lee, Bvt. Col. U.S.A. Commdg. Dept."

Antonio, Sept. 4/60. Respectfully forwarded to the Adjutant General, through the Head Quarters of the Army.

R. E. LEE Bvt. Col. U.S.A. Commdg Dept.

Respectfully forwarded to the Adjutant General. J. THOMAS, Asst. Adj General

Respectfully submitted to the Secretary of War, S. COOPER, Adj. General, Sept 19, 1860

SEEN

---

2. OFFICIAL REPORT OF ENGAGEMENT [4]

HD. QRS. SOUTHERN COLUMN
KIOWAY & CAMANCHE EXPEDITION
Fort Kearney N.T. August 12th, 1860

SIR, I have the honor to submit the following more detailed report of the Engagement between the troops under my command and the hostile Kioways & Camanches, near the "Republican Fork" on the 6th inst. and of the Skirmishes which preceded the engagement.

On account of the haste in which my report of the 9th Inst., was prepared, several inaccuracies occurred, both as to dates and facts, which you will find here corrected.

On the 28th ult: we marched from the Arkansas River toward the North, leaving our Tents and heavy baggage behind under a proper guard, and by a series of rapid marches (several of them made at night) we succeeded in arriving so close upon the rear of the Enemy at "Solomons Fork" on the morning of the 2nd as to get possession of their camp, which they had abandoned during the previous night. Here we found large quantities of Buffalo meat and hides and a considerable number of lodge poles, all of which had been

---

[4] A.G.O., Letters Received, 1860, s 84.

left on account of the rapidity of their flight and which was distributed among our friendly Indians or destroyed.

As we had marched fifty miles within the last twenty-four hours and as there was little hope of coming up with them by an open daylight chase, we remained in camp during the day and marched again in a violent storm as soon as it was dark – striking directly for the North, by the Compass.

During the next day five of our Indian Scouts fell in with a large party of the enemy and two of them were killed and the others wounded – one fatally and has since died – three of the enemy were also killed and several wounded.

On the morning of the 3d inst, and just before daybreak, they made an attack upon our camp – in what numbers it would be difficult to say – some think they numbered fifty or sixty, others are of opinion that they did not exceed twenty, which I think is the more probable number; for, like the Coyote or Prairie wolf – half a dozen of them can make as much noise as one would expect to hear from a hundred throats. However they did us little injury and withdrew before it was light enough to pursue them – it is presumed that two of them, at least, were badly wounded as they went off howling piteously.

As soon as there was sufficient light to enable us to follow the trail, we marched again, when Capt. McIntosh [5] was sent, at his own request, with sixteen men to reconnoitre a ravine at a short distance on the right of the Column. As this ravine appeared to lead

[5] James M. McIntosh, a native of Florida, graduated from the Military Academy in 1849. He became a captain in the 1st Cavalry in 1857. He was killed at the Battle of Pea Ridge as a Confederate brigadier general on Mar. 7, 1862.–Heitman, p. 669.

in the direction of the trail, the column moved on, and, on reaching the high ground about a mile from camp, beheld this gallant officer and his handful of brave men furiously driving before them some fifty or sixty stalwart warriors – At this time a messenger arrived from the Capt. informing me that he (Capt. McIntosh) thought from indications he had seen, that a large force was ahead in waiting for us, and that he intended keeping up the chase. Lieut. Fish [6] was then detached with the advanced guard (thirty-six men) to the support of Captain McIntosh and the whole command followed at a good pace. Thus the pursuit was kept up for Eighteen miles, when I determined to abandon it and resume the trail knowing that sooner or later it must lead to their principal stronghold – In this affair two of the enemy were killed – one of whom, judging from the gaudiness of his decorations, was probably a chief, or at least an important personage among his people.

Soon after leaving Camp on Whelans (Beaver) Creek [7] on the morning of the 6th a party of the enemy, amounting probably to thirty or forty, again appeared in our front distant perhaps a mile; to overtake this party, Lieut. Fish was detached with twenty men on picked horses, with orders to catch them if possible, and not to spare the horses – Lieut. Ingraham, [8] with the advanced guard, followed in rear of Lieut. Fish with orders to keep in sight of that officer and hasten to his support if necessary. This pursuit, though conducted with great energy on the part of those zealous young

---

[6] Oliver Hazzard Fish of Kentucky, graduated from West Point in 1857, and became a 2nd Lt. in 1858. He became a military instructor in the Southern army and died Feb. 18, 1865.– Heitman, p. 420.

[7] Beaver Creek is the first major branch south of the Republican.

[8] Edward Ingraham, a native of Pennsylvania, became a 2nd Lt. in the 1st Cavalry in 1856. He served the Confederacy in the war.– Heitman, p. 563.

officers, was, nevertheless unsuccessful; and after keeping it up over hills and ravines for eight miles they found themselves no nearer the enemy than when they started. This last effort demonstrates, beyond a doubt, that our horses after marching a thousand miles over a country for the most part a desert, cannot compete with the fresh & fat horses of the Indians.

About 11 O'clock a.m. we crossed a boggy branch of the stream along which we had been marching and halted in order to see the wagons safely over. The difficulty of the crossing taken in connection with the increasing density of the timbers on the creek, and the presence of a good many Indians still hovering in our front, rendered it necessary to adopt precautionary measures against a surprise. Accordingly the troops were required to "stand to horse" while Lt. Ingraham with the advanced guard, was directed to reconnoitre the timber in the vicinity of the crossing, and Lieut. Stockton [9] was directed to deploy his company ("B") to the front as Skirmishers. Shortly after this arrangement was made, I received word, by one of the guides, that several of our own Indians had become entangled with the enemy; Lieut. Stockton was then ordered to move forward rapidly and, if such was the case, to afford them protection. The number of hostile Indians in our front was now evidently increasing, and Capt. Beall was sent with his Company ("A") to join Lieut. Stockton & take command of the Squadron. A few moments more, however, left no doubt of our being in the vicinity of the entire force of the enemy; and the

9 Philip Stockton, of New Jersey, graduated from West Point in 1852 and became a 1st Lt. in the 1st Cavalry in 1855. He served the Confederacy, and died Mar. 25, 1879.– Heitman, p. 927.

remainder of the command was, therefore, at once moved forward at a gallop. In our front lay a level plain, say a mile in width, intersected by numerous ravines and contained between a low ridge of hills on the north and a heavily-wooded stream on the south. As we advanced, the enemy poured in from every conceivable hiding place, until the plain & hill sides contained probably from six hundred to eight hundred warriors, apparently determined to make a bold stand. Capt. McIntosh who commanded the Squadron on the left, was now directed to move diagonally up the hill side and take the enemy in flank, while Capt. Carr's [10] Squadron moved on the centre with a view to charge or fight on foot as circumstances might render necessary. In this order the command moved up at a round gallop and in good order, but unfortunately, the enemy now began to give way and though our horses were put to the top of their speed, yet on account of the freshness of the Indian Horses and the jaded condition of our own, the distance between us gradually increased, thus rendering their own arms, to a great extent useless while our long range arms told with great effect upon them. The whole scene now became one of flight and pursuit for fifteen miles, when they scattered on the North Side of the Republican Fork, rendering all further pursuit impossible. So we returned to the wagons and encamped a little after night fall.

In this affair (and the Skirmishes which preceded it) Twenty-nine of the enemy were Killed – how many

[10] Eugene A. Carr, of New York, graduated from the Military Academy in 1850. He became a captain in the 1st Cavalry in 1858. He fought in the Civil War and in the Indian wars of the West, reaching the rank of brigadier general. He retired in 1893.– Heitman, p. 285.

were wounded it is impossible to say with any degree of accuracy – probably a great many.

Our loss is as follows:

KILLED,   Two friendly Indians – early in the action
WOUNDED
    1st Sergt. John O'Connell   Co. "B"   Slightly;
    Private Michael Wheelan   Co. "B"   Severely;
    "   Gerald M. Beech   Co. "B"   Severely
MISSING
    Private Matthew Green   Co. "D"
Number of Horses Killed, Wounded & otherwise disabled
    Six

From the nature of this engagement, it will appear that but little opportunity was afforded for individual prowess, as we were unable to bring matters to a hand to hand conflict – it remains therefore only for me to record here the companies and their officers engaged and thank them in general terms for the gallantry & zeal which characterized their conduct not only in the final struggle, but through all the long and weary marches they endured from the time we first struck the trail on the Grand Saline, to the present time.

Co. "A"   Capt. W. N. R. Beall & Lieut. Crittenden [11]
Co. "B"   Lieuts. Phil Stockton & O. H. Fish
Co. "C"   Lieut. Jno. R. Church [12]
Co. "D"   Capt. McIntosh
Co. "E"   Lieut. A. Jackson [13]
Co. "I"   Capt. E. A. Carr

[11] E. W. Crittenden, of Kentucky, became a 1st Lt. of the 1st Cavalry in 1859. He served the Union in the Civil War and died Aug. 1, 1874.– Heitman, p. 338.

[12] John R. Church, of Georgia, graduated from West Point in 1855. He served in the Confederate army and died Jan. 8, 1863.– Heitman, p. 301.

[13] Andrew Jackson, Jr., of Tennessee, graduated from the Military Academy in 1858. He resigned in May, 1861, and served the Confederacy in the war.– Heitman, p. 566.

To Lieut. & Adjt. L. L. Lomax my thanks are especially due for the energy with which he conveyed my orders to various parts of the field as well as for the cool foresight he evinced in furnishing details from time to time during the pursuit, for the protection of disabled & unhorsed men who were constantly falling behind.

To Lieutenants R. H. Riddick & E. Ingraham high praise is also due not only for the handsome & effective manner in which they protected the wagon train from repeated attacks of the enemy, but from the energy they displayed in driving them altogether away & Killing and wounding many of them.

To Asst. Surg. C. T. Alexander [14] I also return my thanks for volunteering his services to carry orders on various occasions.

Before closing this lengthy report, I would respectfully call attention to the handsome manner in which several private soldiers acquitted themselves after having fallen to the rear, on account of their horses becoming disabled.

Private Michael Wheelan Co. "B" was surrounded & attacked by nine Indians and though wounded in both legs – yet he killed two – wounded one & broke with his sabre, the heads from three lances, when he was rescued from further injury by three gallant fellows from the train who saw his desperate situation & hurried to his assistance.

Private Warren Hastings Co. "I" also left behind on account of his horse becoming disabled was attacked by some ten or twelve Indians, one of whom he killed, & three of whom he wounded, when he was rescued by

[14] C. T. Alexander, a native of Indiana, became an ass't surgeon in the army in 1856. He served in the Civil War and in Indian campaigns, and retired in 1897.

three or four of his comrades who had also fallen to the rear, by their horses becoming disabled.

Private Ballard of Co "A" [and] Private T. I. Simpson Co. "I" are reported by their respective Company Commanders for gallant conduct during the engagement – each killing an Indian in a hand to hand conflict – under circumstances similar to those mentioned above.

I am Sir   Very Respectfully   Your obt. Servt.

S. D. STURGIS

Capt. 1 Cav.   Commdg.

TO CAPT. JNO. WITHERS   Asst. Adjt. Genl.
Dept. of Texas [15]   San Antonio   Texas

---

[15] On the cover of the document it is noted that the report was sent by Col. Robert E. Lee to the Adjt. Gen's. Off. and thence to the Sec. of War.

FORT WISE, ON THE ARKANSAS

Bent's New Fort on the hill in the distance, left. Courtesy of The State Historical Society of Colorado.

D: THE ESTABLISHMENT OF FORT WISE

INTRODUCTION

While the campaigns were in progress against the Comanches and Kiowas it was decided by the military authorities to erect a fort on the Arkansas River in the vicinity of Bent's New Fort. Major Sedgwick did not learn of the plan until his return to the Pawnee Fork camp on August 8th. There he found orders, of June 30th, directing him to lead the expedition and undertake the construction of the post – Fort Wise.[1]

He and his men were disappointed and disgusted,[2] but they had no choice. They journeyed up the Arkansas and arrived at the site of the post on August 30th. The letters and reports that follow tell the story of the founding of Fort Wise (later known as Fort Lyon), Colorado.

I. SUMNER'S INSTRUCTION TO SEDGWICK [3]

HEAD QUARTERS, DEPARTMENT OF THE WEST
St. Louis, Mo.   July 6, 1860

MAJOR: Inclosed you have General Order No. 8. You perceive it leaves a great deal to the discretion of those who have to execute it. With regard to the position of the post upon the Big timbers I have supposed that Bent's fort would be purchased, for that is much the best site, but it has not been bought yet, and I don't

---

[1] Fort Wise was named for Gov. Henry A. Wise of Virginia.
[2] Sedgwick's letter to his sister, doc. 3, below. Also Stuart's reaction.
[3] A.G.O., Letters Received, 1860, W 274.

know that it will be. I think the next best site is a mile and a half above Bent's fort, at the upper end of the bottom. There may be some better places still higher. I am told that Lieut. Colonel Backus reported that there were two good places above Bent's fort, one at 4 miles and the other at 16. It will be necessary for you to examine those places and select the best one, if the particular place is not previously designated by higher authority.

With regard to abandoning the expedition against the Indians, it is difficult to judge what should be done. If you come in too soon, it will be thought that the pursuit should have been continued longer, and until the Indians were punished, if on the other hand, you stay out too late, you will not have time to shelter your command before winter,– of the two, it is better to err on this side. If you should be so fortunate as to give the Indians a blow you had better come in immediately for it is not likely you would get another chance at them this season. But if you have not yet come up with them and have any prospect of reaching them continue the pursuit till the middle of August.

If you come in for supplies, take the river road back so as to determine where the post will be, that the Infantry Companies may be sent to it at once.

Colonel May reports to me that a large body of Kiowas are on Solomon's Fork, near where we met the Cheyennes in '57.

Very Respectfully,   Your obedt Servant

(Sgd) E. V. SUMNER
Colonel   1st Cavalry, Commanding
MAJOR JOHN SEDGWICK,   1st Cavalry,
Comdg. Kiowa Expedition
Hdqrs. Dept. of the West, St. Louis, Mo.
July 9, 1860.   OFFICIAL: D. R. JONES, A.A.G.

2. GENERAL ORDERS NO. 8[4]

HEAD QUARTERS OF THE ARMY

New York,   June 30, 1860

GENERAL ORDERS NO. 8

I: . . . The following instructions have been received from the War Department: A military post will be established at, or in the vicinity of, the Big Timbers, Upper Arkansas, to be known as Fort Wise, and garrisoned by four companies of mounted troops, and two companies of Infantry, one of them Captain Tracy's company "H" of the 10th Infantry, now under orders for Fort Garland; also, the garrison of Fort Larned will be increased by the mounted companies.

The mounted force for these posts to be taken from the two companies of the 2d Dragoons, and the four companies of the 1st Cavalry, now on an expedition from the Department of the West, against the hostile Kiowas and Comanches.

The necessary buildings at Fort Larned and Wise will, if possible, be erected during the present season by the troops, and the most vigorous means will be adopted to this end.

Fort Fillmore will be re-occupied and garrisoned by Brevet Major Sprague's Company "E" 8th Infantry.

II: . . . Companies "F", "G", "H" and "K", of the 1st Cavalry, are assigned to Fort Wise, and companies "C" and "K" of the 2d Dragoons, to Fort Larned. The other company of Infantry for Fort Wise will be designated by the Commander of the Department of the West, and immediately put in route for the post.

The mounted troops will repair to their respective stations with the least practicable delay, after they have

---

[4] W. D. Hqrs., Army, G. O. 8, June 30, 1860 (photostat kindly supplied by the National Archives).

made the expedition against the hostile Kioways and Comanches.

The Head Quarters of the 2d Regiment of Infantry are established at Fort Kearny. The Senior Major of the 2d Regiment of Dragoons will take post at Fort Larned. The Junior Major of 1st Regiment of Cavalry will take post at Fort Wise.

III: . . . The Commanding Officer of the Department of the West will give such additional orders as may be necessary to promptly carry out the foregoing instructions.

By command of Bvt. Lieutenant General Scott

(Sigd) L. THOMAS
Asst. Adjt. General

---

3. SEDGWICK TELLS OF ORDERS TO FOUND FORT WISE[5]

CAMP NEAR PAWNEE FORK, August 8, 1860

MY DEAR SISTER: I arrived at this camp to-day, and have received your two letters of June 13th and July 7th. This was the first mail we have had since the 3rd of July, and it only brought sad news, which I am sure you will be sorry to hear. I am ordered to return to a spot two hundred and thirty miles west of this, and to select and establish a military post to be called Fort Wise. This is very hard on all of us, to be out all summer, and no sooner come in with a prospect of returning to our post and spending a comfortable winter, when we receive an order to build quarters or live in tents (late in the season), and with nothing to do it with. I have not been so much disgusted since the fall of '37 ['57] when, at this very place, I received

---

[5] Sedgwick's *Correspondence, op. cit.,* pp. 18-20.

orders to go to Utah. That order was countermanded, and this may be, but there is very little prospect of it. If we could have gone there in the spring, and had material, we could have made ourselves very comfortable before winter, and none of us could have objected to going; but we all left Fort Riley expecting to be absent for four or five months, and return finding our quarters and furniture ready at our hands; but now all our furniture has to be sacrificed, as there is no way of getting it out, and even if there was it would be of little use to us. I am so disgusted that I cannot write anything pleasant.

I shall be here several days yet, and will write again before leaving. I do not know how to tell you about directing my letters. This is the nearest office, but probably we shall have one there with a weekly mail from here, so for the present direct, "Fort Larned, Pawnee Fork, Kansas." I think I must have received all of your letters due. In my next I will send you a small check; but it is a part of my principal, and to be used only in case of urgent necessity.

Your affectionate brother,   J.S.

---

4. SEDGWICK PLANS TO MOVE WESTWARD [6]

CAMP NEAR FORT LARNED, K.T.
August 11, 1860

SIR,   I have the honor to acknowledge the receipt of General Orders, No. 8, with the letter of instruction from the Colonel commanding the Department, dated July 6th. The four companies of Cavalry are now at this camp, ready to proceed to the point indicated, as soon as implements are forwarded to commence the

---

[6] A.G.O., Letters Received, 1860, s 303.

work. The Colonel is aware that we left Fort Riley, in May, last, for the purpose of making a pack-mule scout against the hostile Indians, and that, of necessity, we took as little baggage as possible – not more than two axes and two spades are in possession of each company; barely sufficient for the daily use of the companies.

If these articles could be procured in this vicinity I would move at once, and commence therewith;– but nothing can be had, and it is useless to go without them.

I regret that we are ordered to build so late in the season. Our animals are very thin, and the men have but little clothing,– having left all their private effects at Fort Riley. I cannot see how we are to procure any hay for our animals. I do not think forty tons can be cut within as many miles of Bent's Fort.

You can have no conception of the drouth that has prevailed throughout this entire country this summer.

My present intention is to erect stables and huts near Bent's Fort,– I think from a half, to a mile this side,– perhaps there may be found a more suitable site on the Western side. Nothing more than this can be done this winter to be able to erect such quarters and stables as will make the command comfortable.

I hear that a supply of corn has been consigned to Col. Bent, for our use. If so, we will probably store it in his Fort, and I desire your approval of the renting the same for the purpose of storing our Commissary stores and Quarter Master's Property, and also for a Hospital.

I would strongly urge that it be purchased,[7]– both for convenience and economy. It is offered at sale for twelve thousand dollars, and I do not think the government can put up such a work for that money. My impression

---

[7] It was later purchased.

is that the Fort should be located near Bent's Fort, as, in that vicinity, there is more grass that can be used for garrison purposes, and I believe a larger amount of timber than can be found at any point on the river. A proper military reservation will cover much the greater portion of desirable ground, and will prevent the building of small towns around the Post.

A yearly estimate for clothing, camp and garrison equipage, and Quartermaster's stores have been forwarded. They are very large,– perhaps the Colonel will think too large,– but taking into consideration the impossibility of obtaining such articles as we might be short of, I thought it might be best not to cut it down.

I regret that the Commissary stores were not ordered earlier, as I cannot, with my train, carry more than forty days' supplies, (with the ammunition that must necessarily be taken,) barely sufficient to last the command until the arrival of the stores,– provided they should be lucky in reaching there at the proper time.

I am, sir, Very Respectfully   Your obt. Servt.
JOHN SEDGWICK
Maj of Cavalry

TO THE ASSISTANT ADJUTANT GENERAL,
Head Quarters, Dept. West.

5. SEDGWICK ASKS FOR MAIL SERVICE [8]

CAMP ON ARKANSAS,   August 11th, 1860
TO THE ASST. ADJUTANT GENERAL,
Head Quarters, Dept. West.

SIR,   I have the honor to request that the Colonel commanding the Department will take such measures as he may think best, to secure proper mail facilities at

---

[8] A.G.O., Letters Received, 1860, 295 S.

the new Post about to be established at the Big Timbers. I would suggest that the mail now running to Santa Fe could go by that post, without very materially adding to the distance or expense. In the event of an office being established there, I would recommend Mr. A. B. Miller as a suitable person for Post Master. I make this recommendation without Mr. Miller's knowledge, and do not know that it would be acceptable to him, but have acted upon the presumption that it would.

I am, sir, Very respectfully Your Obt. Servt,

JOHN SEDGWICK

[Enclosure] Maj 1 Cavalry

[Entries on Cover page of letter]
Recd. AGO August 27, 1860
Submitted to Col. Sumner, Sept. 4, 1860.

HD ARMY DEPT WEST, ST. LOUIS Aug. 20 1860
I would respectfully ask the favorable indorsement of the Gen in Chief on this application.– If the mail contractors were told that they could only be protected, if they went by Fort Wise, they would probably be willing to change the route.

E. V. SUMNER Col 1 Cav Comdg

WAR DEPT. Approved by the Comdg General
See letter to Postmaster Genl. & respectfully forwarded
1 Sept. 1860 E. D. KEYES Lt. Col. U.S. Army
HD QR OF THE ARMY, N.Y. Mil. Sec. to Gen. Scott
Aug. 24, 1860.
(etc. etc.)

[Enclosed with above document]
WAR DEPARTMENT September 1, 1860
SIR I have the honor to inclose to you a copy of a letter from Major Sedgwick, 1st Cavalry in which he requests that measures be taken to secure mail facilities at Fort Wise, and respectfully to invite your favorable consideration of the subject.

Very respectfully, Your obt. Servt. SECRETARY OF WAR

JOSEPH HOLT Post master General
[outside entry] POST MR GENL 1860
MSS GR, p 400

6. SUMNER'S LETTER
REGARDING FORTS LARNED AND WISE[9]

HEAD QUARTERS, DEPARTMENT OF THE WEST
Saint Louis Mo. August 17, 1860

SIR: I regret that the measures I have taken for the building of Forts Larned and Wise, have been disapproved and countermanded. When General Order No. 8, of June 30, 1860, was published I supposed that it was thereby intended to put this matter into my hands, and my orders were given with great deliberation, and a firm belief, that I was acting for the best interests of the service. The order above referred to required that "the necessary buildings at Forts Larned and Wise will, if possible, be erected during the present Season by the troops, and the most vigorous measures will be adopted to this end." The last paragraph of this order charges the Commander of the Department of the West "with giving such additional orders as may be necessary to promptly carry out the foregoing instructions."

Under this order it appeared to me an imperative duty to act promptly. I took it for granted that the quarters at the new posts were to be built in the same manner as they had been at all the frontier posts in this department. I am aware that troops can be quartered in Mexican huts, in a mild climate, and have done it myself repeatedly in New Mexico, but I did not anticipate that such quarters would be thought sufficient for the Military post on the Arkansas.

The buildings at Fort Larned must be made of adobes and with roofs and floors they will be good permanent buildings. There is timber at Fort Wise to make substantial log buildings, which will be comfortable and permanent. There is no timber at either of

---

[9] A.G.O., Letters Received, 1860, 345 W.

these posts that will make shingles or flooring and without these essential articles, it is impossible to make good buildings.

Will you please lay this letter before the Secretary of War.

Very respectfully   Your obedt. Servant:

E. V. SUMNER
Col 1 Cavy   Comdg

COLONEL S. COOPER,   Adjutant General   U.S.A.
Washington City   D.C.   [cont'd]

P.S.   As the building materials, tools &c &c were bought, and a part of them shipped, for Forts Larned and Wise, before it was known that the War Department intended to quarter the troops in Mexican huts — I would respectfully suggest whether it will not now be better to let these things go forward, except perhaps the shingles and flooring, if it is decided that these shall not be furnished.

E. V. SUMNER
Col   1 Cav.

[On outside cover of letter.]
Rec'd. AGO, Aug. 22, 1860.
Read to Sec. War Aug 23/60 E.D.L.

---

7. SUMNER TO SEDGWICK[10]

HEAD QUARTERS,   DEPARTMENT OF THE WEST
Saint Louis, Mo.   Aug. 21, 1860

SEDGWICK, MAJOR JOHN,
1st Cavalry   Comdg. Kiowa Expedn
Ford Larned, Pawnee Fork, K.T.

MAJOR: The Department Commander directs me

---

10 Headquarters, Department of the West, Letters Sent, 1860, p. 239.

to inform you that in compliance with General Orders No. 8, Current Series, from the Head Quarters of the Army, all the necessary tools and material for Fort Wise were purchased, and a portion of the articles shipped, when an order was received from the Qr. Mr. Genl. saying that the shingles, flooring and all the other heavy articles would be stopped, and only such articles sent as are necessary to erect Mexican huts, as that is the style of building decided on for that Fort. Subsequently a letter was received, saying, that only fifteen thousand dollars ($15,000) can be expended in building the two posts, Forts Wise and Larned, this to include purchases, transportation, and all other expenses. Such tools and other articles as the Qr. Mr. Genl. may direct will be forwarded as soon as possible.

The Colonel wishes me further to say, that he is fully aware of the difficulty you will have in procuring the necessary amount of hay for your animals this winter, as the season is now far advanced, and owing to the drought this summer, grass suitable for hay must necessarily be scarce. He hopes, however, as full rations of corn will be sent, and as he has ordered a mill to be forwarded with which the corn can be cracked that you will be able to supply sufficient long forage to carry your animals through the winter.

The Colonel has forwarded your application, for a change in the mail route to the General-in-Chief, with a favorable endorsement.

Very respectfully, your obedient servant:

A. V. COLBURN

2d Lieut. & Adjt 1st Cavalry, A.A.A.G.

8. SEDGWICK PLANS CONSTRUCTION
OF FORT WISE [11]

FORT WISE, UPPER ARKANSAS,   September 12, 1860
MY DEAR SISTER:

I write this without knowing how or where it will
go; but the Indian Commissioner is soon expected
to hold a talk with the Indians, and the people that
come here generally wish to get back as soon as possible,
so that probably he will take it. I reached here on the
30th instant, having had a very pleasant march of two
hundred and thirty-five miles from Fort Larned, the
nearest post-office. I have assurance that we shall be
supplied with a weekly mail before long. We are
making preparations for building, and I hope by the
15th of November to have the huts ready to occupy;
but such buildings are rarely seen in the East – no
boards, shingles, flooring, or windows are to be used.
Thick stone walls, laid in mud, eighteen feet wide and
more than a mile long, with dirt roofs, are to be our
habitation this winter. The doors will be beef-hides
stretched on frames, windows the same, to be taken out
for light when the weather will permit. We know but
little about the climate, but it is said the winters are dry
and mild; but the proximity to the mountains and the
altitude would seem to indicate severe winters. Since
we have been here the weather has been delightful,
nights cool, days bright and warm, no frosts as yet. We
have one lady in camp who has braved everything to
come out with her husband. They have their tents close
by me, and I see them every hour of the day. She does
not seem to mind the hardship at all, has all the comforts
about her that she would have at home, except the
house. As she is the only woman here, it is not likely

---

[11] Sedgwick *Correspondence,* pp. 21-23.

that I shall get married this winter. Our stores are on the road from Leavenworth. There will be over three hundred wagons, carrying six thousand pounds each, at an expense of eight cents per pound for hauling, so that you can estimate something of the expense of keeping five hundred men for one year more than four hundred miles beyond all civilization. It will be impossible for me to come home this winter, or even to tell you when I can come.

Good-bye.   J.S.

---

9. SEDGWICK'S LETTER OF SEPTEMBER 19 [12]

CAMP WISE,   BIG TIMBERS,   September 19, 1860

MY DEAR SISTER: Judge Greenwood, Indian Commissioner,[13] leaves today for the States and will take our mail; but when we shall have an opportunity to send another is very doubtful. He says, however, when he reaches Washington he will certainly secure us a weekly one. This consummation is most devoutly to be hoped for, as we have some seven hundred persons here; most of them can write, and many have some friends.

I cannot see now how I can come home in the spring; yet something may turn up to take this command from me; in that event, I shall come. We have three hundred and fifty men at work on our quarters, and hope to be in them by the 1st of November – such as they are. They will be stone walls, laid and plastered with mud, with mud roofs, and no floors or doors, but windows made of canvas. Not a board of any description is to be had.

With love to all, I am your affectionate brother,

J.S.

---

[12] *Ibid.,* pp. 20-21.

[13] See Commissioner Greenwood's report below, in section E.

10.   SEDGWICK'S LETTER OF SEPTEMBER 25 [14]

FORT WISE, BIG TIMBERS
September 25, 1860

MY DEAR SISTER: A small train will leave here to-morrow for the States, and it may be the last opportunity we shall have for a long time to forward a mail, unless, as we hope, the mail to New Mexico is directed to come this way.[15] It seems very hard to be deprived of hearing what is going on in the States, but, like many other things, is bearable when you get used to it. We are all hard at work building our quarters for the winter, and hope to have them finished by the 1st of November. I have reserved two rooms for myself, in the event that the weather should become too tedious to live in a tent. Up to this time we have had delightful weather, cool nights and bright, warm days, only one frost, but that makes but little difference, as there is nothing for it to kill. As you approach the mountains it becomes colder, until you reach a point where you have ice almost every night in the year.

There is a mail, with an ox-train, that I hoped would reach here to-day, that I might hear from you before closing this; but if it should not arrive till to-morrow, I can send an express to take such mail matter as necessary to send. I have not received a Litchfield paper for several weeks – months it seems. Has it run out? Did I ask you to send me the semi-weeekly *New York Times?* If I did not, please ask one of your New York correspondents to subscribe for it, and direct: "Fort Wise, Big Timbers." Perhaps I may get it, but

---

14 Sedgwick *Correspondence,* pp. 23-24.

15 The mail to and from New Mexico took the regular Santa Fe Trail, along the Cimarron cutoff, rather than along the Mountain Branch (which would have brought it by Fort Wise and Bent's Fort).

the postmasters in this country can read, and take other people's papers. I get many papers from Denver City, but they are rather ancient when they reach this place. I hope there never was a viler set of men in the world than is congregated about these mines; no man's life is safe, and certainly not if he has fifty dollars to tempt one with. They have established a vigilance committee, and it may get rid of some of the scoundrels, but it would depopulate the country to kill them all. Half the murders that are committed on the plains, and laid to the Indians, are committed by white men. I am convinced of this. With all love,

Your affectionate brother, J.S.

---

11. SEDGWICK'S REPORT ON BUILDING OF FORT WISE [16]

HEAD QUARTERS, FORT WISE, K.T.
October 22d, 1860

CAPTAIN, I have the honor to present the following statement of the commencement and progress of the work necessary for the establishment of this Post, and of the condition of the command serving here:

On the 1st day of September the first steps were taken,— the locality for the Post selected,[17] timber

---

[16] A.G.O., Letters Received, 1860, s 382.

Regarding the building of Fort Wise, Robert M. Peck wrote on Dec. 5, 1907, from Whittier, California, to George W. Martin of Topeka, Kansas: "I was one of the soldiers of Major John Sedgwick's command – 4 Co's 1st Cav.– who built the original post Fort Wise at Bent's old Fort. This fort of Bent's stood on a high rocky bluff that hung over the river. The government through Sedgwick bought Bent out for $12,000, using Bent's old fort for a commissary store. Bent then moved up the river and established a new trading post opposite the mouth of the Picketwire or Las Animas river, which we called Bent's New Fort or ranch. The name of Fort Wise was changed to Fort Lyon in the fall of 1861. . . . I was stationed at the first Fort Lyon over a year."

[17] This was in the flat bottomland about one mile west of Bent's New Fort.

marked and stone-quarries chosen,– it having been
found from long drought impracticable to use, as was
at first intended, sod in the construction of quarters,
etc. The command, up to this time, has been constantly
and actively employed, not a man, excepting those
employed in the Hospital and Commissary Department, having been mustered on extra duty. Up to this
day, the following work has been accomplished ;– Four
ample and comfortable stables, with stone walls, and
good roofs of timber and hay,– two sets of company
quarters, whilst three more sets will be ready for occupation by the end of this week. The stone corral for
Quartermaster's animals, similar to the Cavalry stables
will be completed in four or five days, as will also a
proper guard-house, of the same material as that used
in the quarters. A Hospital is in process of construction,
which will accommodate comfortably at least twenty-
six patients, and the ground has been broken today for
the quarters of "H" Company, 10th Infantry, which
arrived at this Post two days since. The officer commanding confidently expects to put the company under
shelter by the 20th of November. A stone bake-house,
with oven of the same material, is nearly completed,
which will be ample for the supply of the Post. The
windows, etc, for the above mentioned buildings have
not yet arrived, but are expected daily. They can be set
after the quarters are occupied. The tools used until
within the last week, have been of the simplest description,– and even now the supply is neither sufficient nor
of the proper kind. We have had no stone-hammers,–
old axes, hatchets, etc., being used instead. Wood and
old camp kettles have furnished us trowels, and old
wagon-tires crow-bars. . .

I would respectfully call your attention to the fact that there are two companies of the 10th Regiment of Infantry serving at this Post, and that there is no Infantry officer with either. Both Captains are absent on leave, one first Lieutenant on detached service, the other on leave; one second Lieutenant on detached service, and one on leave, waiting acceptance of his resignation. It has been necessary to detail two officers of Cavalry – Lieuts. R. Ransom and J. E. B. Stuart to command these companies, thereby depriving their own companies of their services. Lieutenant Deshler,[18] 10th Infantry, proceeds by the first opportunity, via Saint Louis, to West Point. He is exceedingly anxious to remain with his company, and it would be for the decided good of the service could the order carrying him to West Point be suspended.

The sick report averages twenty-three or four. Many of the cases are the resultants of accidents in the handling of heavy timbers and stone, which, whilst they are not serious in their effects, yet deprive, for the time, the companies of those meeting them, of the benefit of their services. The symptoms of scurvy in the command show no abatement, and it is much to be feared that in the event of receiving no fresh vegetables, the consequences will be serious. The men are especially prone to the disease from the fact that they have been able to procure no vegetables since May 15.

Small parties of emigrants are, and have been constantly on the road between this Post, Denver City, and Fort Larned, since our arrival here, and, as yet, no

[18] James Deshler of Alabama, graduated from West Point in 1854. He became a 1st Lt. in the 10th Infantry in 1858. He fought for the Confederacy and was killed at the Battle of Chickamauga, 1863.– Heitman, p. 369.

depredations have been committed by Indians, nor has it been reported that any *hostile* have been seen.

I am, sir,   Very Respectfully,   Your obt. servt.

JOHN SEDGWICK

Major 1st Cavalry   Comdy Fort Wise

TO THE ASST ADJ. GENERAL

Head Quarters, Dept. West   Saint Louis, Mo.

---

12.   SEDGWICK WRITES HIS SISTER [19]

FORT WISE, BIG TIMBERS

October 22, 1860

MY DEAR SISTER: I do not know when I shall have another opportunity of answering your letter. When I last wrote there was a fair prospect of our being indulged with a weekly mail this winter; but this is a disappointment. They have granted us one hundred dollars a year to carry the mail two hundred and forty miles, once a week, and no one can carry it for less than that amount a trip. I shall try and send for it two or three times in the course of the winter to ascertain who the President is, although it is a matter of indifference to us.[20] We have few favours to ask, and none are granted. Our buildings are going up rapidly; the soldiers' quarters will be finished this week, and the officers' will be but a short job. I shall probably live in a tent all winter, unless the weather should become too severe; so far we have had no cold weather, and not a drop of rain, but we cannot expect this long. I am glad that you have had so much company, and I hope that

---

[19] Sedgwick *Correspondence,* p. 25.

[20] It is strange to find this apparent indifference to the results of the important election of 1860 — especially in view of the consequent Civil War.

you have entertained them in such a way as will induce them to visit you again.

Write as often as you can; your letters will come sooner or later. Believe me, as ever,   Your affectionate brother,   JOHN SEDGWICK

---

13. FORT WISE BECOMES A DOUBLE RATION POST [21]

FORT WISE, BIG TIMBERS
November 8th, 1860

TO THE ASSISTANT ADJUTANT GENERAL,
Head Quarters, Dept. West,

SIR,   I have the honor to ask that Fort Wise be made a double ration post, from the date of commencing work, August 28th, 1860.

I am, Sir,   Very Respectfully   Your obt. Servt.

JOHN SEDGWICK
Major 1 Cavalry   Comdg Post

[On outside document.]

HD. QRS. DEPT. WEST   FORT SCOTT, K.T.   Dec. 5, 1860
    Approved and respectfully forwarded,
            WM. S. HARNEY,   Brig. General, Comdg
    Respectfully submitted to the Genl in chief
                            H. L. SCOTT

WASHINGTON   Dec. 17, 1860
    Approved by the General in chief and respectfully for-warded to the Adjutant General
            L. THOMAS,   Asst. Adj. Genl.
    Respectfully submitted to the Secretary of War and recom-mended for favorable action.

DEC. 18, 1860   S. COOPER, Adjutant General
    Approved   WAR DEPARTMENT, Dec. 21, 1860.
                    J. B. FLOYD, Secy of War

---

[21] A.G.O., Letters Received, 1860, s 240 and s 412.

14. CONDITIONS AT THE FORT [22]

FORT WISE, BIG TIMBERS
November 17, 1860

MY DEAR SISTER: We have to-day been astonished by the receipt of another mail, and with the prospect of still another in about two weeks' time. I was disappointed in not receiving any letter from you. I am afraid that my complaining of our wanting mail facilities will discourage you from writing. When spring opens I hope, as emigration sets in, we shall have a mail at least weekly. We have had a delightful fall, dry, warm, and pleasant. To-day there is a drizzling rain, the first that we have had since reaching the post, over two months since. This is the character of all falls in this vicinity, although north and east of us they have had severe snowstorms and much cold weather. Our soldiers' quarters, and all the buildings except officers' quarters, are so far completed that they can be occupied, and two weeks more would enable us to finish all. This has relieved me very much, for I anticipated many difficulties which we have overcome, and am now at ease in regard to the comfort of the men for the winter. The last mail brought a complimentary letter from the Secretary of War, extolling our energy and perseverance. I had particularly written to Washington "that if Providence had not favoured us more than the Department there would have been intense suffering here this winter."

The hostile Indians sent in a runner some time since, asking to come in and have a talk. I granted it, and last Sunday six or eight of the chiefs came in, suing for peace. I sent their talk to Washington, recommending

---

22 Sedgwick *Correspondence*, pp. 26-27.

that terms be granted them;[23] what the result will be cannot be known for several weeks. I do not know what excitement can be got up now that the Prince is gone and the election over. The subject of politics loses all its savour before getting out here. It is never mentioned except when the papers come in, and then a short topic. All concede Lincoln's election, and think any change will improve upon the present one.

We have several daily papers within two hundred miles of us which get much later news than we do. I see them occasionally. With much love to Philo's family.

I am your affectionate brother,   JOHN SEDGWICK

---

15. SEDGWICK'S LETTER OF NOVEMBER 30 [24]

FORT WISE, BIG TIMBERS
November 30, 1860

MY DEAR SISTER: A mail will leave here in the morning, in which I will start this note, but there are some doubts whether it will succeed in getting through; the snow is very deep, and it is very cold, and for nearly two hundred miles there is not a stick of wood. We have to-day heard, by way of Denver, the result of the election. It seems to have been all on one side. The news was brought by a messenger, and I suppose cannot be accurately relied on. He says Douglas has not carried a State.[25] I can scarcely conceive this to be true. Hurrah for Lincoln! I say. It is not likely that our next mail will bring us the result, as our latest dates are up to October 19. I shall send to Fort Larned in a few days

---

[23] See B. D. Williams' letter of Dec. 12, below, doc. 17.

[24] Sedgwick *Correspondence,* pp. 28-29.

[25] Although Douglas' popular vote was 1,291,574, he received but 12 electoral votes.

for a mail, where I expect to hear more than is agreeable. I am still living in a tent, which is rather cold at night, and the weather is such that we can do but little work on our quarters. A few pleasant days would enable us to finish them.

It has been a long time since I have heard from you. I do not recollect the last date, but it was in August or early in September. I hope the next mail will bring two or three letters. I have never mentioned the subject of our seat in the church. I wish you to keep the one our father and mother always occupied. It is for yourself and Philo's family, whenever they choose to take it. Also the seat in the Hollow Church. This I would pay for as a matter of charity.

Write often, and believe me, as ever,

Your affectionate brother,   JOHN SEDGWICK

---

16. LETTER OF DECEMBER 10 [26]

FORT WISE, December 10, 1860

MY DEAR SISTER: Our winter of discontent has not as yet been made glorious by a mail, although the sun has favoured us almost daily for the last four months.

A messenger starts to-day for Denver City, and I will direct this to him, trusting that it may reach you in the course of the winter. Does it not seem strange that you can send and receive answers to letters from Europe sooner than from this post, even under the most favourable circumstances? I have nothing important to write. The only event we look forward for is for fair weather to help us finish our quarters. So far we have little to complain of, and two weeks more will enable us to shelter ourselves from the uncertainty of the

[26] Sedgwick *Correspondence,* pp. 29-30.

storms that sometimes do occur here. Yesterday a snow-storm came up that foreboded a violent one, but this morning the sun came out, bright and pleasant, and the snow, although in considerable quantity, is fast disappearing, and by to-morrow we can resume our work. The hunters are all out after deer and antelope, and with any luck will get enough to last a month at least.

If we receive no mail, we escape the excitement and turmoil of the election, that seems to have disturbed everything in the States, if it has not broken you to pieces. We have heard of Mr. Lincoln's election and the probable difficulty he will experience, if not direct opposition, to his inauguration. It seems lamentable that this Union that we have boasted of and glorified so much should be broken up, but I hope our next news will be more satisfactory. How a disruption will affect me I cannot foresee; probably would result in my leaving the service at once.[27] I do not feel quite ready to do this, but when I am ready I want to, in looking back, if I have any cause of regret, have no one to blame but myself.

Believe me, as ever,   Your affectionate brother,

JOHN SEDGWICK

---

17. DELEGATE WILLIAMS
WANTS TREATY WITH INDIANS [28]

HOUSE REPS   WASHINGTON D C
Dec 12th 1860

SIR   Col A. G. Boon agent for the Sheyane Arappahoe Kiwa & Camanch Indians is now in this city ingaged in preparing a treaty to be Signed by the two

---

[27] He is to serve the Union in the war and be killed in battle.

[28] A.G.O., Letters Received, 1860, 486W. B. D. Williams was elected by the people of the Pike's Peak gold region to represent them in Congress.

first mentioned tribes and will leave for Bents Fort or Wise [Fort] in a few days –

I am well assured that the Col Boon will be able to conclude a Treaty with the two latter Tribes, with whom the government is now at war. they having signified their desir to conclude a peace to Maj Sedgwick,[29] who is now at Fort Wise. I most respectfully call your attention, to the fact of Col Boon presents, who will go direct from this place to Fort Wise.

Instructions to Maj Sedgwick together with Col Boons presents and assistance, we think would accomplish this Treaty and open up the Arkansas rout for imigration to the Gold region in the spring.

I hope you will confer with the Coms of Indian Affairs on this subject at your earliest convenience,

Yours Respectfully   B. D. WILLIAMS

Delegate "Pikes Peak"

HON JOHN B. FLOYD   Sect War,
Washington D. C

[Notation on cover of letter]

Major Sedgwick is the commanding officer of Fort Wise & is in every respect well qualified to assist in making the treaty referred to.

AGO Dec. 14, 1860   S. COOPER   Asst. Adj. Gen

---

[29] Sedgwick mentions this in his letter of Nov. 17. Some effort was made toward a treaty. Gov. William Gilpin in his Report of June 19, 1861, to the Commissioner of Indian Affairs says:

"The Comanche and Kiowa Indians are within this Territory, and the same agency [as the Arapahoes and Cheyennes]. They are in a delicate position. The preparations for a treaty with them were matured and presents sent for that purpose. Subsequently, war was declared against them by your predecessor, the presents withheld, and the tribes turned loose. They are greatly humbled and perpetually beg for peace. Allow me to advise a treaty with them as soon as possible, and that instructions to that effect be sent here." *Annual Report of the Commissioner of Indian Affairs, 1861,* p. 99.

In his Report of Oct. 8, 1861, Gilpin writes: "Agent Boone is at Fort Wise, on the Arkansas. At the last extremity, to prevent the menaced outbreak of the Kiowa and Comanche tribes, he has made with them the preliminaries of a treaty (marked A) and distributed the remnant of supplies on hand for them." *Ibid.,* p. 103.

18. SEDGWICK IS FOR THE UNION [30]

FORT WISE, January 16, 1861

MY DEAR SISTER: Last week I sent you a letter via Denver City, but it is very uncertain whether you ever receive it. The mails here are very insecure, and then the chance of sending a letter two hundred miles to be mailed is still more unsafe.

Colonel Sumner has gone on leave for several months, which leaves me the only field officer with the regiment, and this may detain me here, and even prevent my getting a leave of absence. But great and terrible events seem to have transpired since you wrote. I trust they are greatly exaggerated, and that a remedy will be found to forge the links of the Union stronger than ever. All other evils compared with disunion are light, cemented as the Union is with so much blood and treasure. I shall wait a few days to receive a mail; if it does not come, shall send to Pawnee for it. I received one hundred and fifty papers in the last mail — some of them two months old. I sent you the slippers; a squaw brought them in just as the train was starting, and the clerk directed them.

Yours affectionately,   J.S.

---

[30] Sedgwick *Correspondence,* pp. 31-32.

E: THE FORT WISE TREATY

INTRODUCTION

Relations of the Arapahoes and Cheyennes with the whites prior to 1857, the Sumner campaign of that year, and dealings with these Indians in 1858 and '59 have been presented earlier in this volume.

The discovery of gold on the Arapaho-Cheyenne land in the summer of 1858 and the heavy emigration that ensued, greatly altered relations with these Indians. The Pike's Peak gold rush of 1859 was one of the major emigration movements of the West. Some 100,-000 persons set out for the land of gold in the spring of 1859, and although many turned back, thousands continued to the mountains. They opened mines, developed farms, and founded cities. They laid the foundations of the state of Colorado.[1]

As the numbers of whites multiplied, the Indian alarm increased. We have noted above, in Part II, the recommendations and the efforts for a peace treaty that were made by Indian Agents R. C. Miller, William Bent, and T. S. Twiss. Congress, by Act of June 19, 1860, appropriated $35,000 "for the purchase and transportation of provisions and presents, and to meet expenses necessary in holding a council with the Arapahoe and Chienne Indians south of the Platte, east of the Rocky Mountains, and north of the Arkansas River." [2]

---

[1] LeRoy R. Hafen, *Colorado and its People,* 2 vols. (New York, Lewis Historical Publishing Co., 1948), 139-98.

[2] *United States Statutes at Large,* XII, p. 59.

The effort of Commissioner of Indian Affairs A. B. Greenwood is related in document I, below. Inasmuch as his attempt was not entirely successful, Agent A. G. Boone [3] met with the Indians early the next year and negotiated the Fort Wise Treaty. These actions and the treaty document are presented below.

Although this treaty was not a final settlement of the Indian problem in this area, it was a notable effort, and it closed one phase of the Indian problem of the West.

---

1. COMMISSIONER GREENWOOD'S EFFORT FOR A TREATY, 1860 [4]

DEPARTMENT OF THE INTERIOR
OFFICE INDIAN AFFAIRS
October 25, 1860

SIR: In compliance with your instructions, under date of August 11, 1860, issued with a view to carry out the act of Congress, passed at its last session, appropriating thirty-five thousand dollars to enable the Secretary of the Interior to hold a council with the Cheyenne and Arrapahoe Indians, on the Upper Arkansas, I left this city on the 15th of the same month; passed St. Louis, where I purchased a portion of my outfit, and which I completed at Kansas City. I left Kansas City, on the 22d of the same month, for Bent's Fort, on the upper Arkansas, at which point I had instructed Agent Bent to inform the two tribes I desired to meet them. I arrived there on the 8th of September, a distance of nearly six hundred miles from Kansas

---

3 Albert G. Boone was a grandson of famous Daniel Boone of Kentucky. He had gone to the Rocky Mountains as a young man and became a notable frontiersman. He later settled in Colorado, and the town of Boone on the Arkansas River is named for him.

4 *Annual Report of the Commissioner of Indian Affairs, 1860*, pp. 228-30.

City. On the route I passed through the country claimed by the Kiowa Indians, who are known to be hostile, and whom, as well as the Comanches, the Secretary of War has ordered the army in the West to chastise, as the only means of compelling them to respect their engagements with the United States, and to stay their murderous hand. I did not avail myself of the orders of the War Department upon commanders of military posts for an escort, if desired by me, either going or returning. Citizens of the United States in advance of me as I went out, and also on my return, were brutally murdered and scalped upon the road. It is a fact also worthy of remark that the murders were committed almost within range of the guns of Fort Larned. The Indian mode of warfare, however, is such that it is almost impossible to detect them in their designs. They cautiously approach the Santa Fe road, commit the most atrocious deeds, and flee to the plains. On my arrival at Bent's Fort, now Fort Wise, instead of finding the Cheyennes and the Arrapahoes at the point, as expected, I only found the principal portion of the Arrapahoes and a few lodges of Cheyennes. Through the exertions of Captain Potts, who had been sent out with dispatches to Agent Bent, messengers had been sent to the Cheyenne camp, (supposed to be two hundred and fifty miles distant,) with the request that they repair at once to the fort. No intelligence having been received as to the success of the messenger, others were procured and started, in order to secure their presence; and a few days before my departure, White Antelope, Black Kettle,[5] and four or five sub-chiefs, came in without their bands, and informed me that they could not reach the fort short of twenty days. I imme-

---

[5] Southern Cheyennes.

diately convened the chiefs of the Arrapahoes, the chiefs of the Cheyennes then present, and informed them as to the object of my visit, and gave them to understand that their Great Father had heard with delight of their peaceful disposition, although they were almost in the midst of the hostile tribes. They expressed great pleasure on learning that their Great Father had heard of their good conduct, and requested me to say in return that they intended, in every respect, to conform to the wishes of the government. I then presented to them a diagram of the country assigned them, by their treaty of 1851, as their hunting grounds,[6] which they seemed to understand perfectly, and were enabled, without difficulty, to give each initial point. In fact, they exhibited a degree of intelligence seldom to be found among tribes, where no effort has heretofore been made to civilize them. I stated to them that it was the intention of their Great Father to reduce the area of their present reservation, and that they should settle down, and betake themselves to agriculture, and eventually abandon the chase as a means of support. They informed me that such was their wish, and that they had been aware for some time that they would be compelled to do so; that game was growing scarce every year, and that they had also noticed the approach of the whites, and felt that they must soon, in a great measure, conform to their habits. I pointed out to them a country that I regarded as fertile, upon which I desired them to settle. The chiefs of both tribes that

---

[6] This land of the combined Arapahoe and Cheyenne tribes was bounded by a line which ran from the forks of the Platte River, up the North Platte to its source, thence along the continental divide to the source of the Arkansas, down this stream to the crossing of the Santa Fe road (near Dodge City), and thence northwesterly to the place of beginning.– Fort Laramie Treaty of 1851, in C. J. Kappler, *Indian Affairs, Laws and Treaties,* *op. cit.,* II, pp. 594-96.

were present readily consented to the propositions I
made to them; but the chiefs of the Cheyennes present
requested that, in order that there should be no trouble
amongst themselves in future, that they should have the
opportunity of consulting their co-chiefs and braves
before executing any agreement; but when they had
submitted my propositions to their bands, if they refused to give their assent, that they, as the principal
chiefs, would enter into such agreement, and settle
down, and allow the remaining portion of their tribe to
locate where they saw proper, but expressed the opinion
that the absent chiefs would not hesitate to enter into
the agreement, as indicated to them. It should be remarked that a portion of the Cheyenne and Arrapahoe
bands reside north of the fort, upon the Platte River,
and belong to Agent Twiss's agency, and receive their
annuities from him;[7] and while the tribes there present
seemed anxious to induce their people to settle with
them upon the Arkansas, they did not regard their
assent to the proposed arrangement as important. The
only land fit for cultivation within the reservation I
proposed to settle them upon was upon the Arkansas
River, and on the north side; the south side below the
junction of the Purgatory River being regarded as
Comanche hunting grounds. The Comanches have never
lived on or claimed the country west of Purgatory
River. So it was my purpose to settle the Cheyennes
and Arrapahoes on both sides of the Arkansas above
the Purgatory, as far up as the vicinity of a stream called
Huerfano, and south to the northern line of New
Mexico, and on that line east to the Purgatory, and to

---

[7] These Northern Arapahoes and Northern Cheyennes did not come in to
confer with Greenwood; nor did they treat with Agent Boone in Feb., 1861.
Therefore they were not signatories to the Fort Wise Treaty, nor the one
that replaced it – the Little Arkansas Treaty of Oct. 14, 1865.

include a dry creek north of the Arkansas called Sand Creek, upon which there is some arable land. The country designated as the future homes of these tribes is much larger than their wants require; but the good lands included will not be more than sufficient to give each soul forty acres, with water, and a fair proportion of timber, which is exceeding scarce. The tribes are supposed to number 3,500 souls. In the vicinity of Fort Wise a country twenty-five miles in length is now held and claimed as a military reserve. This extent of country, so much larger than has been regarded usually as necessary for military purposes, contains more timber than any portion of that country visited by me, and might with propriety be reduced, at least one-half of its present extent, and still have sufficient timber for firewood and other ordinary demands. Stone is so abundant in the vicinity of the fort that but little timber is required for building purposes. It has not fallen to my lot to visit any Indians who seemed more disposed to yield to the wishes of the government than the Cheyennes and Arrapahoes. Notwithstanding they are fully aware of the rich mines discovered in their country, they are disposed to yield up their claims without any reluctance. They certainly deserve the fostering hand of the government, and should be liberally encouraged in their contemplated new sphere of life. The council closed with the understanding that when an agent should be appointed in the place of Agent Bent, who had tendered his resignation, that I should place in his hands an agreement in accordance with the understanding had, and that they would execute it without hesitation.*

---

* As an agent has been appointed, it is proposed, with your approbation, after he shall have been legally qualified, to give him the necessary instructions to consummate the agreement. [Greenwood's note.]

I purchased some goods and provisions to be given to those Indians attending the council. I issued a portion of them to the Arrapahoes, who had in good faith remained upon the ground at my request, and who were in great want. A few presents were given to the few Cheyennes present. The residue of the goods I placed in charge of a special agent and the military for safe-keeping, until such time as the agreement made should be finally consummated. I left Fort Wise on the 20th of September, and reached Kansas City on the 8th of October, having been detained two days on the Neosho river in council with the Kansas Indians, for the purpose of procuring their assent to an amendment to their late treaty made by the Senate, which was obtained in due form. Notwithstanding the many evil influences which surround the Kansas Indians, they seemed inclined to adopt the policy of the department, which looks to their ultimate civilization. It is proper that I should remark, in conclusion, that although I purchased a large quantity of goods and provisions, as contemplated by the appropriation, the purchase of outfit, and pay of assistants, and transportation of the goods and provisions, a considerable portion of the appropriation remains unexpended.

Very respectfully, your obedient servant,

A. B. GREENWOOD, Commissioner

HON. J. THOMPSON   Secretary of the Interior

---

2. THE FORT WISE TREATY WITH THE ARAPAHOES AND CHEYENNES, FEBRUARY 18, 1861 [8]

Articles of agreement and convention made and concluded at Fort Wise, in the Territory of Kansas, on the eighteenth day of February, in the year of our Lord

[8] Kappler, *Indian Affairs*, etc., *op. cit.*

one thousand eight hundred and sixty-one, by and between Albert G. Boone and F. B. Culver, commissioners on the part of the United States, and the following named chiefs and delegates, representing the confederated tribes of Arapahoe and Cheyenne Indians of the Upper Arkansas River, viz: Little Raven, Storm, Shave-Head, and Big-Mouth, (on the part of the Arapahoes), and Black Kettle, White Antelope, Lean Bear, Little Wolf, and Left Hand, or Namos (on the part of the Cheyennes), they being thereto duly authorized by said confederated tribes of Indians

ARTICLE I. The said chiefs and delegates of said Arapahoe and Cheyenne tribes of Indians do hereby cede and relinquish to the United States all lands now owned, possessed, or claimed by them, wherever situated, except a tract to be reserved for the use of said tribes located within the following described boundaries, to wit: Beginning at the mouth of the Sandy Fork of the Arkansas River and extending westwardly along the said river to the mouth of Purgatory River; thence along up the west bank of the Purgatory River to the northern boundary of the Territory of New Mexico;[9] thence west along said boundary to a point where a line drawn due south from a point on the Arkansas River, five miles east of the mouth of the Huerfano River, would intersect said northern boundary of New Mexico; thence due north from that point on said boundary of the Sandy Fork to the place of the beginning.[10]

---

[9] The northern boundary of New Mexico (east of the continental divide) was then along the 38th parallel of north latitude. Ten days after the date of the Treaty – on Feb. 28, when Colorado Territory was created by Act of Congress – the boundary line was changed to the 37th parallel.

[10] The wording is ambiguous.

The Arapahoe and Cheyennes, being desirous of promoting settled habits of industry and enterprise among themselves, by abolishing the tenure in common by which they now hold their lands, and by assigning limited quantities thereof in severalty to the individual members of the respective tribes, to be cultivated and improved for their individual use and benefit, it is hereby agreed and stipulated that the tract of country contained within the boundary above described shall be set apart and retained by them for the purposes aforesaid.

According to the understanding among themselves, it is hereby agreed between the United States and the said tribes that the said reservation shall be surveyed and divided by a line to be run due north from a point on the northern boundary of New Mexico, fifteen miles west of Purgatory River, and extending to the Sandy Fork of the Arkansas River, which said line shall establish the eastern boundary of that portion of the reservation, to be hereafter occupied by the Cheyennes, and the western boundary of portion of said reservation to be hereafter occupied by the Arapahoes.

ARTICLE 2. Out of the lands so set apart and retained there shall be assigned to each member of said tribes, without distinction of age or sex, a tract of forty acres, to include in every case, as far as practicable, a reasonable portion of timber and water; one hundred and sixty acres of said retained lands shall also be set apart and appropriated to the use and occupancy of the agent, for the time being, of said tribes; and one hundred and sixty acres shall also be reserved out of each division of the retained tract for the establishment and support of schools for the education of the youth of the tribe. The location of the tracts, the assignment of which is provided for in this article, shall be made in as regular and compact a manner as possible, and so as to admit of a distinct and well-defined exterior boundary, embracing the whole of them, and any intermediate portions or parcels of land or water not included in or made part of the tracts assigned in severalty. All such intermediate parcels of land and water shall be owned in common by the tribe occupying that portion of the reservation within the limits of which said parcels of land and water may be included; but in case of increase in the tribe, or other causes rendering it necessary or expedient, the said intermediate parcels of land shall be subject to distribution and assignment in such manner as the Secretary of the Interior may prescribe and direct. The whole of the lands, assigned and unassigned, embraced within the exterior boundary herein designated, shall constitute and be known as the Reservation of the Arapahoes and Cheyennes of the Upper Arkansas; and all laws which have been or may be passed by the Congress of the United States regulating trade and intercourse with Indian tribes, shall have full force and effect over the same, and no white person, except as shall be in the employment of the United States, shall be allowed to reside or go upon any portion of said reservation without the written permission of the superintendent of the central superintendency, or of the agent of the tribes.

ARTICLE 3.   The division and assignment in severalty among the Arapahoes and Cheyennes of the land hereinbefore reserved for that purpose, shall be made under the direction of the Secretary of the Interior, and his decision of all questions arising thereupon shall be final and conclusive. Certificates shall be issued by

the Commissioner of Indian Affairs for the tracts
assigned in severalty, specifying the names of the individuals to whom they have been assigned respectively,
and that the said tracts are set apart for the exclusive
use and benefit of the assignees and their heirs. And
said tracts shall not be alienated in fee, leased, or
otherwise disposed of, except to the United States, or
to members of the respective bands of Arapahoes and
Cheyennes, and under such rules and regulations as
may be prescribed by the Secretary of the Interior.
And said tracts shall be exempt from taxation, levy,
sale, or forfeiture, until otherwise provided by Congress. Prior to the issue of the certificates aforesaid, the
Secretary of the Interior shall make such rules and
regulations as he may deem necessary or expedient
respecting the disposition of any of said tracts, in the
case of the death of the person or persons to whom they
may be assigned, so that the same shall be secured to
the families of such deceased persons; and should any
of the Indians to whom tracts shall be assigned, abandon
them, the said Secretary may take such action in relation to the proper disposition thereof as, in his judgment, may be necessary and proper.

ARTICLE 4th. In consideration of the foregoing
cession, relinquishment, and agreements, and for the
purpose of establishing the Arapahoes and Cheyennes
comfortably upon the lands to be assigned to them in
severalty, by building them houses, and by furnishing
them with agricultural implements, stock animals, and
other necessary aid and facilities for commencing
agricultural pursuits under favorable circumstances,
the United States do hereby agree and stipulate as
follows, to wit:

1st. To protect the said Arapahoes and Cheyennes

in the quiet and peaceful possession of the said tract of land so reserved for their future home, and also their persons and property thereon, during good behavior on their part.

2d. To pay to them, or expend for their benefit the sum of thirty thousand dollars per annum for fifteen years; that is to say, fifteen thousand dollars per anum for each tribe for that number of years, commencing with the year in which they shall remove to and settle and reside upon their said reservation; making four hundred and fifty thousand dollars in annuities in the period of fifteen years, of which sum the Secretary of the Interior shall, from time to time, determine what proportion shall be expended for their benefit, and for what object such expenditure shall be made, due regard being had, in making such determination, to the best interests of said Indians. He shall likewise exercise the power to make such provision out of said sums as he may deem to be necessary and proper for the support and comfort of the aged or infirm and helpless orphans of the said Indians. Their annuities may, at the discretion of the President of the United States, be discontinued entirely, should said Indians fail to make reasonable and satisfactory efforts to advance and improve their conditions; in which case such other provision shall be made for them as the President and Congress may judge to be suitable and proper.

3d. It is hereby agreed that the expenses to be incurred in the purchase of agricultural implements, stock animals, etc., referred to in this article, as also the cost and expenses of breaking up and fencing land, building houses, store-houses, and other needful buildings, or in making such other improvements as may be necessary for their comfort and welfare, shall be defrayed out of the aforesaid sum of four hundred and fifty thousand dollars, to be paid to or expended for the benefit of the Arapahoes and Cheyennes as annuities.

ARTICLE 5th.   To provide the said Indians with a mill suitable for sawing timber and grinding grain, one or more mechanic shops, with necessary tools for the same, and dwelling-houses for an interpreter, miller, engineer for the mill, (if one be necessary), farmers, and the mechanics that may be employed for their benefit, the United States agree to expend therefor a sum not exceeding five thousand dollars per annum for five years; and it is agreed that all articles of goods and provisions, stock, implements, lumber, machinery, &c., referred to in this treaty, shall be transported to the respective tribes of Arapahoes and Cheyennes, at the cost and expense of the United States.

ARTICLE 6th.   The Arapahoes and Cheyennes of the Upper Arkansas, parties to this Agreement, are anxious that all the members of their tribe shall participate in the advantages herein provided for respecting their improvements and civilization, and, to that end, to induce all that are now separated to rejoin and reunite with them. It is therefore agreed that, as soon as practicable, the Commissioner of Indian Affairs shall cause the necessary proceedings to be adopted to have them notified of this agreement and its advantages; and to induce them to come in and unite with their brethren; and to enable them to do so, and to sustain themselves for a reasonable time thereafter, such assistance shall be provided for them, at the expense of the tribe as may be actually necessary for that purpose:[11] *Provided,*

---

[11] The Northern bands of the Arapahoes and Cheyennes did not comply, nor agree to the treaty. In 1868 some of their representatives for the first time agreed to a treaty replacing the Fort Laramie Treaty of 1851.

however, That those who did not rejoin and permanently reunite themselves with the tribe within one year from the date of the ratification of this treaty, shall not be entitled to the benefit of any of its stipulations.

ARTICLE 7th. Should any further aid from time to time be necessary to enable the Arapahoes and Cheyennes of the Upper Arkansas to sustain themselves successfully in agricultural or other industrial pursuits, such additional means as may be required therefor shall be taken from the moneys due and belonging to them under the provisions of former treaties or articles of agreement and convention, and so much of said moneys as may be required to furnish them further aid as aforesaid shall be applied in such manner, under the direction of the Secretary of the Interior, as he shall consider best calculated to improve and promote their welfare. And, in order to render unnecessary any further treaty engagements or arrangements hereafter with the United States, it is hereby agreed and stipulated that the President, with the assent of Congress, shall have full power to modify or change any of the provisions of former treaties with the Arapahoes and Cheyennes of the Upper Arkansas, in such manner and to whatever extent he may judge to be necessary and expedient for their best interests.

ARTICLE 8th. All the expenses connected with and incident to the making of this agreement and carrying out its provisions shall be defrayed by the United States, except as otherwise herein provided.

ARTICLE 9th. It is agreed that all roads and highways, laid out by authority of law, shall have right of way through the lands within the reservation hereinbefore specified, on the same terms as are provided by law when roads and highways are made through lands of citizens of the United States.

ARTICLE 10th. It is also agreed by the United States that the annuities now paid to the Arapahoes and Cheyennes, under existing treaties or articles of agreement and convention, shall be continued to them until the stipulations of said treaties or articles of agreement and convention relating to such annuities shall be fulfilled.

ARTICLE 11th. [Stricken out].[12]

ARTICLE 12th. This instrument shall be obligatory on the contracting parties whenever the same shall be ratified by the President and the Senate of the United States.

In testimony whereof, the said Commissioner [s] as aforesaid, and the said Chiefs and Delegates of the Arapahoes and Cheyennes of the Upper Arkansas, have hereunto set their hands and seals, at the place and on the day and year hereinbefore written.

A. G. BOONE
United States Indian Agent and Commissioner
F. B. CULVER
Commissioner and Special Agent

On the part of the Arapahoes:	On the part of the Cheyennes:
Ho-ha-ca-che, his x mark, or Little Raven	Mo-ta-va-to, his x mark, Black Kettle

---

[12] This Article, stricken out by the United States Senate, read: "In consideration of the kind treatment of the Arapahoes and Cheyennes by the citizens of Denver City and the adjacent towns, they respectfully request that the proprietors of said city and adjacent towns be permitted by the United States government to enter a sufficient quantity of land to include said city and towns at the minimum price of one dollar and twenty-five cents per acre."

Ac-ker-ba-the, his x mark, or Storm

Che-ne-na-e-te, his x mark, Shave-Head

Ma-na-sa-te, his x mark, Big Mouth

Vo-ki-vokamast, his x mark, White Antelope.

Avo-na-co, his x mark, Lean Bear

O-ne-a-ha-ket, his x mark, Little Wolf

Na-ko-hais-tah, his x mark, Tall Bear

A-am-a-na-co, his x mark, Left Hand, or Namos

John S. Smith,[13] United States interpreter.

Robert Bent,[14] United States interpreter

Witness to the signatures:

JOHN SEDGWICK,   major of Cavalry.

R. RANSOM, JR.,[15]   lieutenant of Cavalry.

J. E. B. STUART,   first lieutenant First Cavalry.

JOHN WHITE,   clerk to the Indian signatures.

P.S.– And it is further understood, before signing the above treaty, that it was the particular request and wish of the Chiefs and Councillors in general convention, in consideration of Robert Bent being one of their half-breed tribe, that he should have, as a gift from the

---

13 John Simpson Smith, born in Kentucky, went to the Rocky Mountains as a trapper and trader when a young man. He became a notable Mountain Man. Being a trader with the Indians at the site of Denver in 1858, he became one of the organizers of the Denver Town Company. Later he went with his Indian wife to the Oklahoma Territory, where he spent his last years. See his identification as the original of Killbuck in G. F. Ruxton's famous novel. See L. R. Hafen (ed.), *Life in the Far West by George Frederick Ruxton* (Norman, Univ. of Okla. Press, 1951), 240-44.

14 This was the son of William W. Bent and his Cheyenne wife.

15 Robert Ransom, of North Carolina, graduated from the Military Academy in 1850. In the Confederate army he became a major general. He died Jan. 14, 1892.– Heitman, p. 816.

nation, six hundred and forty acres of land, covering the valley and what is called the Sulphur Spring, lying on the north side of the Arkansas River and about five miles below the Pawnee Hills, and they wish the general government to recognize and confirm the same; and that Jack Smith, son of John S. Smith, who is also a half-breed of said nation, shall have six hundred and forty acres of land, lying seven miles above Bent's Old Fort, on the north side of the Arkansas River, including the valley and point of rock, and respectfully recommend the general government to confirm and recognize the same.

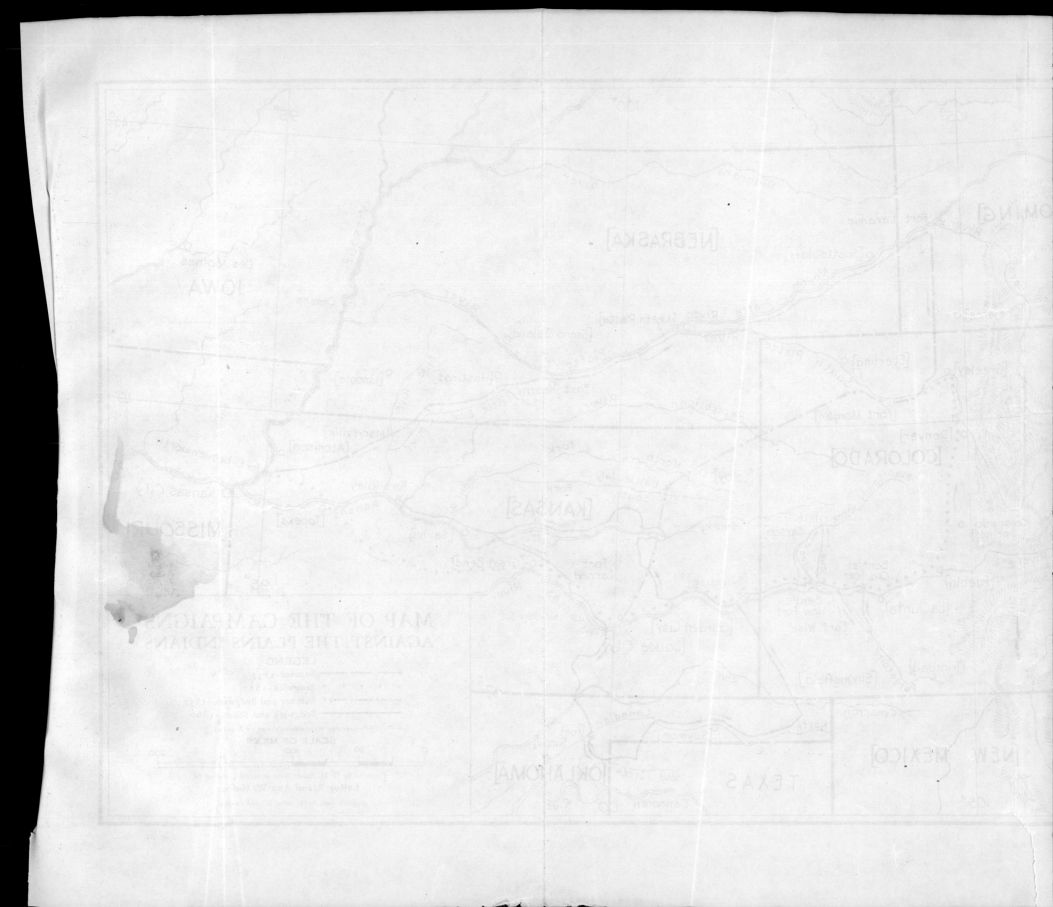

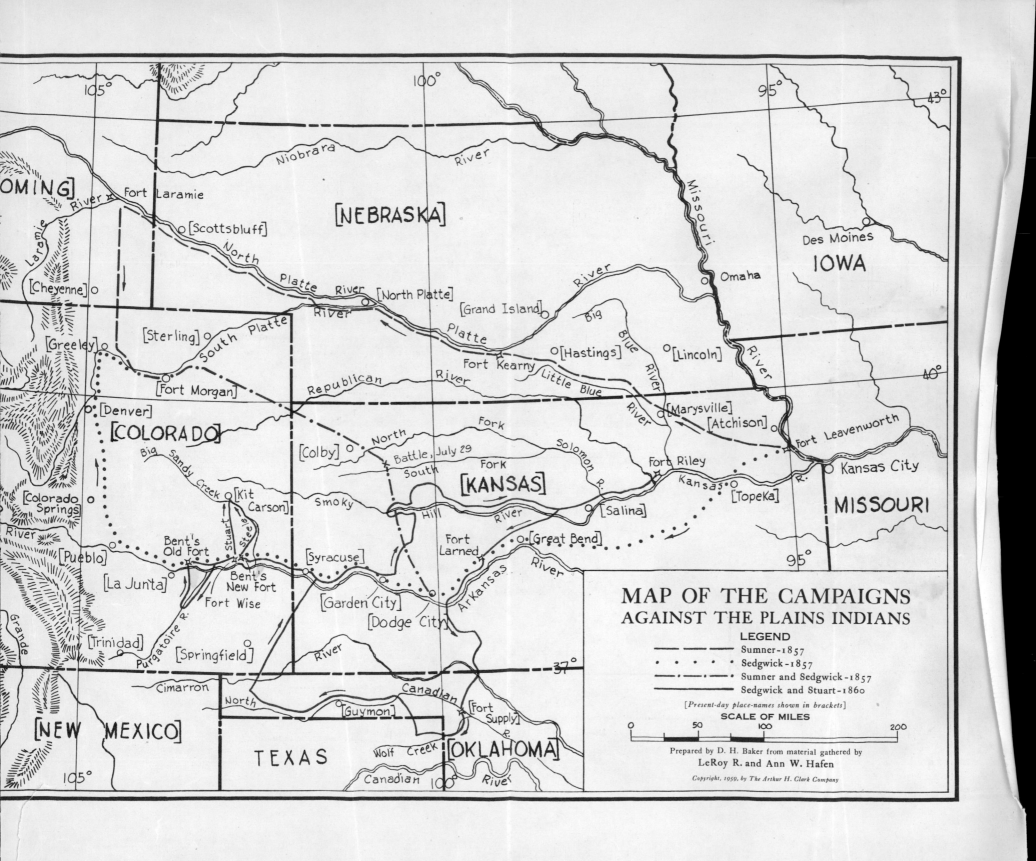

MAP OF THE CAMPAIGNS
AGAINST THE PLAINS INDIANS

LEGEND

———————————— Sumner - 1857
· · · · · · · · Sedgwick - 1857
—·—·—·—·— Sumner and Sedgwick - 1857
———————————— Sedgwick and Stuart - 1860

[Present-day place-names shown in brackets]

SCALE OF MILES

0   50   100   200

Prepared by D. H. Baker from material gathered by
LeRoy R. and Ann W. Hafen

Copyright, 1959, by The Arthur H. Clark Company

Index

Index

This brief index is for use until the comprehensive analytical index of the Series (volume XV) is available.